THEY
HAD THEIR HOUR

By Marquis James

Author of

The Raven: A Biography of Sam Houston
Andrew Jackson, The Border Captain

PUBLISHERS
THE BOBBS-MERRILL COMPANY
INDIANAPOLIS

Printed in the United States of America

PRINTED AND BOUND BY
BRAUNWORTH & CO., INC.
BOOK MANUFACTURERS
BROOKLYN, NEW YORK

CONTENTS

THEY HAD THEIR HOUR

THE REMARKABLE VOYAGE
OF
CAPTAIN THOMAS JONES, PIRATE

I

THE REMARKABLE VOYAGE OF
CAPTAIN THOMAS JONES, PIRATE

I

"Sail ho!"

"Sail O!" The lookout's shout from aloft rolled below in repetition from prow to stern of the *Lion*. There was life on deck at once as sailors sprang into the rigging and canvas was shaken out. The *Lion* wore around smoothly, hardly interrupting the uniformity of the ripples that flecked the surface of the Indian Ocean, and the steersman laid a course toward the welcome object glimmering in the haze where sea and sky seemed to meet.

Somewhat similar activity might have been observed on board the distant vessel, which crowded on sail and ran for it. But the *Lion,* of London registry, was the smarter craft and her master uncommonly experienced in a sea chase. Captain Thomas Jones diminished the distance between the vessels until, from his poop, he recognized the ship in flight as a native junk displaying the ensign of the Great Mogul.

The pirate ship overhauled the lumbering junk and the rifling of her seemed a matter of little time, until five other sail hove into view. This was disconcerting to the preoccupied Captain Jones. When the strange sail were identified as a fleet of the East India Company, with its distasteful flair for law and order, Jones knew the jig was up so far as taking a prize was concerned. Escape was his definite interest now. He put about—to fight or get away as best he could, with odds against him five to one. Had the odds been even, the *Lion's* master, competent seaman though he was, would have had his hands full to outwit the famous Martin Pring, admiral of the Indiamen.

[11]

Pring boomed down in his enormous flagship, the *Royall James*, headed off the *Lion* and set her on fire with a broadside. The *Lion* was burned and many of her crew perished, but Captain Jones was taken off a prisoner.

These were events of September, 1617. So important did Martin Pring consider his capture that he detached one of his ships, the *Bull,* to carry Jones home. The *Bull* docked at London on New Year's Day, 1618, with Jones in irons and with a letter from Sir Thomas Roe, the English ambassador to the Great Mogul of India, giving particulars of the case. The junk rescued by the adventitious appearance of Martin Pring belonged to the Mogul's mother, which added to the gravity of Jones's offense. The communication of Sir Thomas Roe pointed out that "these seas begin to be full of rovers," and that some of them should be made an example of. But, all this notwithstanding, there was a feature in connection with the case which even so zealous a foe of piracy as the ambassador could not omit to mention. Captain Jones had sailed on his free-booting cruise under the patronage of "Sir Robert Rich and one Philip Barnadol."

2

This created a distinction between Thomas Jones and common pirates. Sir Robert Rich, heir to the powerful earldom of Warwick, was one of the best-known young noblemen in the kingdom. He had been brought up in the shadow of the throne, and, although lately he had shown little taste for court life, his influence was still boundless. This prestige doubtless explains why Thomas Jones's career did not end then and there at Execution Dock, on the gallows which had discontinued the activities of so many of the Captain's profession. Sir Robert even went so far as to protest to the King against the loss of his ships—for another vessel as well as the *Lion* had been taken by Admiral Pring. King James made short work of this nervy remonstrance, and the ambassador to India was told to rest easy, as Rich "was so humbled ... that you shall hear no more of him."

The royal reassurance served its purpose of an apology to the Great Mogul and then found its way into the archives to keep dusty company with a clutter of similar parchments whose brief work on earth was done. Jones was set at liberty, free to resume the practise of his calling and service to his titled master. But it had been a narrow squeak for the Captain and so for a while he lay low. This seems to have been the same procedure followed by Sir Robert Rich in supporting his humility.

Two years went by before Thomas Jones sought to reestablish his position in the world of affairs. The attempt received immediate recognition from the law. In January, 1620, the Captain was arrested on complaint of the East India Company, charged with inducing seamen to desert the employ of that company and enter the service of the King of Denmark's rival East India concern. But Robert Rich was a man who stood by his friends of high and low degree—especially when they could be of use to him. It so happened that, at this moment, he had need of the talents of Captain Jones. Sir Robert had spent his years of good behavior quietly but not indolently. To be sure he had had leisure for thought, but his meditations were not those of a scholar in retirement. Sir Robert was a schemer and now the fruits of his reflections were ready for plucking.

It was always the sea and enterprises that had to do with the sea which appealed to him most strongly. As a lad he had been brought up at the court of Elizabeth, under whom piracy, though called by softer names, enjoyed the support of the Virgin Queen herself. Those were the days of Hawkins and of Drake, and the legends of them stimulated the imagination of the young peer. Sir Robert was sixteen years old when Elizabeth died and James I ascended the throne. This sovereign was a mediocre Scotchman, temperate in most things, including the virtues; but a desire for an alliance with Spain led him to take measures for the suppression of piracy. In this manner it fell out that an honored profession, once sponsored by royalty, declined, for, with Spanish treasure ships exempt, the perquisites of English pirates were scarcely attractive enough to make the calling worth while.

The lively young lord was irritated by the repudiation of one of the favored policies of Queen Bess. Who, indeed, was this slippery Scot that assumed to tell Englishmen how to conduct their affairs? Thus it was young Sir Robert began to withdraw from the life of the court and so open the breach which set him in opposition to the throne for the best part of an eventful life that was full of ups and downs.

For a time Sir Robert himself followed the sea. Off the coast of Brazil he narrowly escaped capture by a Spanish man-of-war. "At all times of the fight," says a contemporary account of this adventure, "he was as active and open to danger as any man there." He could "as nimbly climb to top and yard as any common mariner on the ship," and swear with the best of them. Such accomplishments and a knowledge of life at sea were useful to Sir Robert when, conscientiously preserving a tradition of Elizabeth's glamourous era, he became a protector of pirates and a sharer of their booty. But they could in no wise help him with King James. The capture of Captain Thomas Jones in the Indian Ocean was only one of a train of distressing incidents which so interfered with his buccaneering program that Sir Robert concluded to turn his more serious attentions to the colonization of Virginia, an activity in which he already had dabbled. Further, Sir Robert was now the Earl of Warwick—a great name in England.

3

The Earl of Warwick got his old skipper out of jail on the promise of honorable employment. A month later Captain Jones sailed in command of the *Falcon,* of one hundred and fifty tons, for Virginia with thirty-six emigrants, and fifty-two cattle and four mares for the settlers at Jamestown. His mate was John Clarke.

With an interest in vast grants in the New World, it was important to Warwick that he plant colonies in Virginia, as all the strip of Atlantic coast from Carolina to Maine was known. Already engaged in the business of colonization were two concerns, popularly called the First and the Second Virginia Companies. The First Company had rights to the southern part, extending up as far as Hudson's River. North of that was the domain of the Second Company. Warwick had taken up this new adventure with enthusiasm. He owned stock in both companies.

The First Virginia Company had the better land to offer, which seemed to place it in a favored position for attracting settlers. The Second Virginia Company, with its territory following the rugged line of the New England coast, must put forth greater efforts if it ever were to be populated. An early English traveler already had reported this region "a cold, barren, mountainous, rocky Desart . . . not habitable by our nation." But, fortunately for the stockholders of the Second Company, Sir Ferdinando Gorges, an energetic man, had taken hold of its affairs. Gorges was not discouraged after two colonies, which he had attempted on the "rocky Desart," had been starved out. In addition to his financial interest, Gorges really had faith in this northern land.

While Captain Jones was sailing the *Falcon* across the Atlantic to southern Virginia, Gorges was turning over in his mind a plan for a grand reorganization of his colonization project in the north, which was to send the late pirate and jail-bird on his second trip to America and give him a place in history. Gorges began his new undertaking by rechristening his company. The idea was to efface the memory of past failures by dropping the name Virginia. He selected New England possibly because the King's son, Prince Charles, had suggested it; and a little flattery for a prince could do no harm. Then he must have some personages of rank for officers and stockholders—names to impress prospective colonists. Particularly he wanted Warwick. By a lucky circumstance he got him. The Earl owned only a small share in Gorges's organization, his larger interests being with the rival southern company. Just as Sir Ferdinando was preparing to boom his newly named company, Warwick quarreled with his colleagues in the Virginia concern. Gorges did not lose a moment in enlisting the support of the dissenting stockholder for the New England scheme.

[15]

The next step was to plant a colony—one that would succeed. The logical mind of Gorges decided that something had been wrong with the personnel of his previous experiments. The personnel therefore would be changed—no more broken-down gentlemen and convicts. A different type of pioneer must go out to New England—a better class with a background of sturdiness and honesty. Already the appraising glance of Sir Ferdinando had fallen upon a group whose qualifications quite satisfied him.

4

In the town of Leyden, Holland, dwelt a party of English religious refugees, mistakenly known to history as Puritans. They were not Puritans but Separatists, or Brownists, as they were sometimes called after one of their early leaders. The Puritans were another group, much less outspoken than the Separatists, and therefore had not found it necessary to leave England in order to worship in peace. The emigrating Separatists gave themselves still a third name—Pilgrims, meaning travelers.

The Pilgrims had been living discontentedly in Holland for seven years. Denied admission to the Dutch guilds and trades unions, it was difficult for their artizans to make a living. The Dutch youths and maidens, who were not very strict about keeping the Sabbath, set a bad example for the young Pilgrims. Already Pilgrim boys were beginning to run off to sea or to join the Dutch Army. The country was absorbing them and the Pilgrims, desiring to preserve their language and English identity as well as their religious beliefs, began to look about for a new haven.

The leaders discussed several possible places to go. South America was reluctantly discarded, after which Dutch officials were approached for a concession in New Amsterdam. At this juncture Thomas Weston, a London merchant, arrived in Leyden. Weston knew the Pilgrim leaders. He spoke sympathetically of their desire to establish themselves in the New World, but advised them "not to medle with ye Dutch" or "too much depend on ye Virginia Company." The Pilgrims were impressed by Weston's interest and his hints about "sundrie Honble Lords" who were obtaining "a large grante from the king for the more northerly parts" of Virginia, "to be called New England." He advised the trusting Pilgrims to seek their new home in this quarter. So convincing were his persuasions that shortly thereafter this ambassador of Sir Ferdinando was able to take his departure for England where he reported to the "Honble Lords" the success of his errand.

It was a good start, too good perhaps, because Gorges and associates seem to have relaxed their vigilance. The next thing they learned was the disconcerting news that representatives of their competitor, the southern company, had gained the confidence of the Pilgrims and induced them to accept a patent to settle not in New England but in Virginia, apparently on what is now the New Jersey coast. The agreement had been signed, the Pilgrims had purchased in Holland a small vessel called the *Speedwell,* and hired a crew for a year to carry them to the New World. Deft and daring means would be necessary to recapture these desirable colonists for New England. Sir Ferdinando and his partners did not hesitate to employ these means.

The Pilgrims needed a second and larger vessel to transport their company across the ocean. Again the sympathetic Mr. Weston appeared on the scene. The Pilgrims appealed to him to engage this shipping for them. Before a suitable ship was found, however, a mate presented himself and was hired. Who recommended him we do not know, but the case suggests the influence once more of Mr. Weston. The mate was John Clarke, who had just returned from Virginia in Warwick's cattle ship, the *Falcon,* Thomas Jones, master.

Next Mr. Weston recommended a ship. Tied up at a London dock he had found a three-master of one hundred and eighty tons burden—larger than the average merchantman of the time. Her name was the *Mayflower,* a common name for English craft of that period. In 1620 there were more than twenty *Mayflowers* of English registry on the ocean. The name meant so little to the Pilgrims that they came to speak of her simply as "the ship," or "the larger ship," to distinguish her from the *Speedwell*.

The *Mayflower* was chartered and a candidate for captain appeared forthwith in the person of Thomas Jones. A factor in his favor was his previous association with John Clarke on a voyage to Virginia. So Captain Jones was employed, and with his old mate began to gather a crew from the Thames water-front. It was a godless, blasphemous lot, but the one uninteresting voyage which stood between Jones and a career of piracy had not given him much opportunity for cultivating a numerous acquaintance among church-going mariners.

Thus far the adroitness and audacity of Ferdinando Gorges had succeeded perfectly, with Thomas Jones again in the service of the noble Earl of Warwick.

On July 25, 1620, the *Mayflower* cast off at London, dropped down the Thames with the tide and ran around to Southampton. She carried about seventy passengers from England who were to join their Leyden brethren in this pilgrimage to Virginia. The little *Speedwell* arrived from Holland with about fifty persons. The union of the two contingents immediately brought on disputes over the permanent assignment of quarters. Rank was to have been a factor in the allocation of berths, but it proved difficult to dislodge passengers who had first come aboard and appropriated the most desirable quarters. Not until August fifth were the two vessels ready to leave Southampton, and meanwhile the Pilgrims were obliged to sell some of their butter to pay port charges.

For five days they beat down the English Channel and then the *Speedwell* signaled she had sprung a leak. The two ships put into Dartmouth to repair it. Resuming their voyage they caught a wind which carried them to sea briskly, but again the *Speedwell* reported a leak and the two ships turned back to Plymouth.

Apparently the Pilgrims never once suspected the origin of these leaks. According to confessions made later, the crew of the *Speedwell* had taken this ingenious means of obtaining release from a bargain of which they already had sickened. The ship's company had signed to remain for a year with the Pilgrims in their new home, but after short acquaintance with their inexperienced employers, these seamen did not care to risk such a rash adventure. And it is possible that they did not act altogether as a result of their own observations. Captain Jones may have seen to it that the word reached Captain Reynolds of the *Speedwell* that, regardless of how the passengers' patent read, the vessels were bound for that "barren, rocky Desart," the New England coast.

In any event the put-up jobs of the leaks succeeded so well that the Pilgrims determined to abandon the *Speedwell*. As many of her passengers as cared to continue the voyage were crowded aboard the *Mayflower*. Several were discouraged by their foretaste of sea travel and, unloading their belongings, went home instead. Several of the original *Mayflower* passengers also gave up the idea of trying the pioneer life in Virginia. When he heard of these defections, Sir Ferdinando Gorges could not have been altogether displeased, for it was best to find out the faint hearts in advance.

5

On the sixth of September, 1620, Captain Jones of the *Mayflower,* now in complete command of the voyage, sailed with a passenger list which has been of more interest to posterity than any other in modern history. It comprised one hundred and two persons, but these were not all Pilgrims in the religious sense. There were ten servants working for wages, four hired seamen, a professional soldier, a cooper and four little London orphans— three brothers and a sister—who were put aboard at the last moment, bound out to labor without wages until they should be twenty-one years old.

The professional soldier was Myles Standish, who is reported, though on inconclusive evidence, to have been a Roman Catholic. He was taken along to manage the Pilgrims' defense against the Indians.

The cooper was a boy of twenty named John Alden. He was hired at Southampton to conform to the English law governing the export of barrels and kegs. A ship taking these articles from England was required to bring back an equal number. The *Mayflower* had a number of barrels in her hold, including several which were filled with beer. Unless this beer were all drunk up on the voyage the only way to bring an equal number of empties back would be to make them. Alden was engaged to fabricate barrels in Virginia for the *Mayflower* to carry home. By the terms of his contract he could return with his barrels if he cared to.

The passengers had held an election, choosing John Carver to be their "governor." Deacon Carver was the oldest member of the party, and probably the most well-to-do. He was sixty and traveled in style for a Pilgrim. His wife had her personal maid. The Deacon also had a sort of secretary, John Howland, in addition to a "servant man," "servant boy" and Jasper More, one of the four bound children.

Elder William Brewster, another of the leaders, was fifty-four. He was a printer and publisher. He was accompanied by his wife, two sons and the other two indentured More brothers. A friend of Brewster was young Edward Winslow, twenty-four, a printer, who brought a wife, two men servants and Ellen More, the orphan girl. The other leaders won their spurs later.

The youth of the Pilgrim Fathers is notable. To start with there were only two over fifty and seven over forty. The deaths of the first year left the band largely in the hands of William Bradford, thirty-one, who became governor when Carver died, Edward Winslow, twenty-five, Captain Standish, thirty-six, and John Alden, twenty-one. Twenty-six of the *Mayflower's* passengers were married men, eighteen of whom had their wives along. There were eighteen single men and but one single woman— Mrs. Carver's maid; ten girls and twenty-nine youths and boys.

The first two weeks of the voyage were blessed with favorable winds and pleasant weather, but it probably did not seem very pleasant for the passengers except by comparison with the trials which came later. There was the usual seasickness. Captain Jones's sailors swore horribly, and, seeing how it shocked the Pilgrims, probably put a finer edge on their profanity than usual. Never in their seagoing lives had master, mates or crew laid eyes on such voyagers as these, who came out on deck and prayed and sang psalms every morning. In those days no passenger amounted to much in a seaman's eyes, and this lot was beyond all fathoming. One foul-mouthed fellow in particular took them for fair game. His especial delight was to poke ribald taunts at the sea-sick and tell them what satisfaction it would give him to heave their carcasses overboard. But his carcass went overboard first. A mysterious illness carried him off, and the Pilgrims were sure it was the vengeance of God.

But all this notwithstanding, the first fortnight was compara-tively enjoyable. The weather permitted the Pilgrims to gather on the spar deck and sun themselves in the bracing salt air. The waist was cluttered up with rope, baggage and other traps. It was overrun by objectionable sailors, but it afforded escape from the clammy regions below. Possibly Captain Standish improved the opportunity to teach the young men something of the use of firearms. In any event there were religious services—prayers, songs and sermons of hours' duration, during which even the children sat with clasped hands and countenances as immovable as statues. Only, perhaps, the four little urchins from the London orphanage were inclined to fidget.

This is the picture upon which Captain Jones, standing by the rail of the poop deck, must have gazed many times—sometimes with an amused fascination, but generally with contempt. Such people. And these he was to set down in the dead of winter to shift for themselves on the frozen New England coast. To live by fish-ing and hunting. And not one of them had ever felled a tree, caught a fish or fired a gun. Surely it takes all kinds to make a world. Captain Jones may well have regarded this voyage as a doubtful episode in an otherwise professionally ethical career.

About the first of October the *Mayflower* ran into a gale which brought an end to the pleasant hours on deck. The Pilgrims were driven below and the hatches battened. The *Mayflower* was a "wet ship," as sailors say. She was heavily laden and low in the water. The seas broke over the spar deck and dripped down on the passengers below.

The storm kept up. Day after weary day the ship pitched and there was nothing for the poor Pilgrims to do but lie in their foul wet bunks and bear it while the water dripped and dripped. One hundred and two persons, all miserable and most of them seasick, performing all the offices of life for days on end in a tilting space twenty-two by sixty feet, and so low that the tall men lurched about with a perpetual stoop to keep from whacking their skulls against the beams overhead. There was little or no cooking for those who retained their appetites. They lived on hard bread, Holland cheese, salt codfish, smoked herring, ham and the like. There were a few such delicacies as prunes and raisins. This diet was washed down with beer, which was the common drink in place of water. The Pilgrims had no tea or coffee. Their warming beverages were brandy and Holland gin, which they called "strong waters."

The storm increased in violence, the leaks grew worse and the main beam buckled. Even the hardened crew became alarmed, and a delegation went aft to request Captain Jones to turn back toward England. The Captain replied that they were half seas over, as far from one shore as another, and there would be no wages unless the voyage were completed. An iron jack-screw owned by one of the passengers was used to bolster the main beam, and the Captain said that by calking the upper works and not overpressing the ship with sail everything would be all right.

For days the *Mayflower* drifted under bare poles. John Howland, the retainer of Governor Carver, ventured on deck for a breath of air. A roll of the ship pitched him overboard, but as he fell he managed to catch the topsail halyards, which also trailed overboard. He went under the water but held on to the halyards, and a sailor took a boat hook and dragged him on board again.

Late in October after nearly a month of dirty weather, the gales subsided. The hatches were opened and the Pilgrims clambered on deck to dry their clothes. About this time a son was born to Stephen Hopkins's wife, and William Button, the servant of Dr. Samuel Fuller, the Pilgrims' physician, died. The baby was named Oceanus, and Button was sewed in a sack and buried at sea.

Land was sighted at daybreak on November ninth. But the exhilaration of a landfall was dampened by the announcement that this was not Virginia, but the bluffs of Truro, near the far end of Cape Cod.

6

The time had come for Captain Jones to play his hand. Calling a conference of the leading passengers, he announced that the storm had blown him off his course. Yet this misfortune, the Captain continued, had its compensations, New England being a very good place to settle. The Pilgrims insisted on going south, however, and, after warning them that a voyage down the coast this late in the season would be dangerous, Jones changed his course. The Captain's words were prophetic. A half-day's sailing brought the ship to the foaming shoals of Monomoy, south of the Cape.

These shoals were marked on English maritime charts of the period, and surely so capable a seaman as Thomas Jones could have avoided them had he desired to do so. Instead he plunged the *Mayflower* full into the roaring surf, and passengers were warned there would be great danger unless the ship put about immediately. The stout-hearted Pilgrim leaders argued the point, and in the end Jones flatly resorted to his authority as master and refused to continue the voyage down the coast. The Pilgrims acquiesced to a landing in New England. After all, with sixty-six days at sea behind them, the sight of solid ground made their arguments rather difficult to sustain. Thus Thomas Jones had performed his mission.

Two days later the *Mayflower* dropped anchor in Cape Cod Harbor at the tip end of the Cape. A number of passengers went ashore—the men to prospect for a place for a settlement, the women to do family washing. Captain Jones insisted upon a speedy selection of the settlement site. He wanted to get back to England. After several days of indecision, the Captain offered to lead a party of Pilgrims on a trip to find a location. There was a big snow on the day they left, and Susanna White, the wife of a young wool-carder, gave birth to a baby girl whom they named Peregrine.

The Captain's expedition came to nothing. There were more days of indecision and some bickering among the colonists. Jones was losing what little patience he had. He wanted these peculiar people off his ship—a desire not lessened by the fact that the Peck's Bad Boy of the party, Francis Billington by name, accidentally shot off his father's musket between decks while standing beside an open barrel of powder.

A third exploring party went out and was gone for a week. The searchers returned footsore and nearly frozen, with a story of hair-raising adventures. It had been so cold that the salt spray froze on their oars. The wreck of their boat in a storm had been averted only by the presence of mind of a sailor. There was an "encounter" with Indians, which, though bloodless, left a vivid impression with the Pilgrims. The Indians were more curious than hostile. They shot a few harmless arrows from within easy musket range, but escaped injury themselves because the Pilgrims' marksmanship was so poor. But the explorers had found a place to settle. It was in a snug little harbor called "Plimouth" by Captain John Smith, the founder of Virginia, who had visited that coast some years before.

There was bad news, however, to break to William Bradford, one of the leaders of the returning party. His young wife was dead and buried. She had fallen overboard and drowned. Three of the little More orphans were in tears over the death of their brother Jasper. And many on board the *Mayflower* were ill.

On Saturday December 16, 1620, late in the day, the *Mayflower* entered Plymouth Harbor, her voyage ended, one hundred and fifty-five days from London, one hundred and thirty-four days from Southhampton, one hundred and three days from Plymouth, England, her last port of call in a civilized land. She anchored half a mile from shore. The next day was Sunday and the Pilgrims never worked on Sunday, but Monday morning boatloads of men went aland, and Sir Ferdinando Gorges's scheme to plant a colony in New England was an accomplished fact.

But had the knight been on the spot he might have felt somewhat dubious about the outcome.

7

Except for two or three hired specialists like Myles Standish, not one of the colonists had any training in the work required of pioneers. They had found "spices" on Cape Cod. They shot an "eagle" and were afraid of "lions." They swallowed a sailor's tall tale about the money to be made in whale oil, and when a whale was actually sighted from the *Mayflower,* two Pilgrims tried to shoot it, one bursting his gun with an overcharge. They did not bring with them a horse or a cow, a cart or a plow, though luckily they had axes and garden tools. Their fishhooks and nets were too large for cod. But to fight the Indians they had brought along several pieces of artillery. Barring that first whimsical "encounter," however, the Indians never troubled them, except for an occasional drink of gin or beer, but actually kept the colonists from getting hungrier than they might have by showing them how to raise corn. History discloses few such parallels in fact of the fable of the babes in the wood.

Snows and blows held up work on shore for several days, but on Christmas they were landing tools and chopping trees to build the "common house." The Pilgrims did not observe Christmas because they found no mention of it in the Bible. Here was one more difference between Captain Jones and his passengers. The Captain was a faithful observer of the holiday because he enjoyed it. All sailors looked forward to the coming of Christmas at sea and the time-honored issue of grog it brought to the forecastle. But the Captain, with such a neat maritime adventure behind him, was so touched by the Yule spirit that he permitted his largess to pass beyond the barriers of the forecastle. There must be joy all around him and so he broke out a keg of the *Mayflower's* beer and treated the Pilgrims, who had begun to drink water in order to conserve their own supply of beer.

The Pilgrims showed their gratitude for this and a few other considerate acts of the Captain. Near their settlement was a crooked little stream which they named Jones River. An island in the harbor became Clarke Island, for the mate. But the irrepressible Francis Billington was the first of the colonists to write his name on the landscape. He climbed a tree and looking inland announced the discovery of a "sea." Investigation revealed a lake of fresh water which is Billington Sea to-day. Plymouth Rock was an afterthought. Boats plying to and from the ship sometimes landed at this boulder, if the tide was right, but generally the boats were simply run up on the sandy beach.

On the ninth of January, 1621, the walls of the common house were up—rough logs chinked with mud. A few days later a thatch roof was on. A "street" of nineteen private dwellings was started. This labor progressed under the supervision of Francis Eaton, the one carpenter of the party, and John Alden, who had no time to think of barrel staves now. Logs were cut, shaped and dragged by hand a distance of an eighth of a mile by cold, hungry and sick men and boys unskilled in woodcraft and unaccustomed to hardship. There had been only forty-four men in the party to start with, and now several of these were dead and more were dying.

8

The sickness increased. Six died in December, eight in January, seventeen in February and thirteen in March. The malady never has been diagnosed for certain, but, considering their diet, it may have been scurvy. There was no help or sympathy from Captain Jones, who seems to have grown hard again. William Bradford, who with Myles Standish alone escaped illness, tells of one poor fellow who, burning with fever, begged a seaman for "but a small can of beare." To which the tar replied that he would not part with a can of beer to help his dying father.

While the epidemic was at its height it spread to the crew. The Pilgrims went into the pest-ridden forecastle and nursed the stricken seamen. This was more than the case-hardened boatswain could stand. He had "cursed and scoffed" the Pilgrims with the rest. Now he came forward and apologized.

Ten of thirty seamen died. At the end of March the Pilgrims had lost half of their original number. Only four of fourteen wives and one of nine servants survived. Nineteen out of forty-six men came through. Ten of eleven girls and fifteen out of twenty-one boys were spared. Of the four little More orphans only Richard was living now to finish his long term of servitude.

There was plenty to do besides nurse the sick and bury the dead. The nineteen homes were built. The cannon were dragged ashore and posted on a hill. There were nervous alarms of Indian attacks, at which all who were able sprang to arms and jumped into their armor. The fact that these scares were baseless did not relieve the ever-present sense of peril. At times there were not more than six or eight who could keep to their feet and carry on. But never a whimper that has been recorded, never a word of complaint or a sigh for the pleasant lands left behind. Faith made them superior to such imperfections of the spirit.

By April, the plague having passed, Captain Jones was ready to leave. There is a pleasing tradition that he offered to carry back to England any who cared to go. In any event none went. Young John Alden remained by choice—to marry Priscilla Mullins, the catch of the colony, and win a place in romantic literature. On the fourth of April the farewell visits were exchanged between the ship's officers and the people on shore. The last brave letters home were sealed and taken on board. On the fifth the little colony climbed the hill where the cannon were and watched the *Mayflower* sail with the morning tide.

In thirty-one days Captain Jones was in the Thames—a record passage, but a round voyage of two hundred and ninety-six days.

After the remarkable voyage of Captain Thomas Jones, the Pilgrims' *Mayflower* fades from history, her identity confused with the twenty-odd other English *Mayflowers* then on the ocean. There are various *Mayflower* stories, but, like some *Mayflower* heirlooms, they are questionable.

Captain Jones went back to piracy, but never on an attractive scale. In 1622 and '23 he coasted the western Atlantic in the little *Discovery* of sixty tons. Dropping anchor in Plymouth Harbor, he found the Pilgrims in need of supplies and sold them some at exorbitant prices. He swindled Indians out of their furs—and so passed from view for a while.

On the twenty-fifth day of July, 1625, a leaking Spanish frigate lumbered into Jamestown. Captain Thomas Jones, late of the *Discovery,* reeled ashore with a case of tropical fever and a weird tale to tell the Virginia officials. His story was that, while in the service of the Dutch, he and one Captain Powell had captured this frigate in the Caribbean. Powell had turned the prize over to Jones to be repaired. The authorities were sure there was more to the narrative, but Jones was a sick man and in no danger of running away before they could ask him some questions. Jones did not run away and neither did he add anything to his story. Before the officials were ready for the interview, the Captain's fever rose and he died.

ON THE KING'S ERRAND

II

ON THE KING'S ERRAND

1

MORE than one Knickerbocker beau bit his nails in dismay when the banns were published and William Kidd led Sarah Oort to the marriage altar, by that means eliminating from the lists the richest widow in the Colony. She was a mother and, on good authority, still "a lovely and accomplished woman." The estimate seems reasonably correct for, in all, Sarah had four husbands of whom Captain Kidd was number three.

This is not to imply that Sarah Oort was lacking in discrimination. She had married none but wealthy spouses, and on accepting Captain Kidd, maintained the tradition by allying herself with social position as well as another comfortable fortune. "William Kidd, Gent," he appears in the official recording of the marriage, which took place on the sixteenth day of May, 1691—a time when the word gentleman was not thrown about promiscuously. Captain Kidd was an intimate friend of the royal governor, Mr. Sloughter, and most of the other notables worth knowing in the brisk little provincial capital of New York, with its public bowling green and six or seven streets of tidy Dutch brick houses. A list of his acquaintances in England was more impressive still. It extended to the steps of the throne; English acquaintances—this was what counted in the way of colonial prestige.

William Kidd was a sea captain and his calling gave him unusual opportunities for keeping in touch with persons and events in various parts of the world, and there were few parts of the world that he did not know. He had been well educated for a

Scotch country boy, and very well educated for a sea captain. Also, unlike the usual run of his profession, he was sober, saving and genteel, and, what is just as remarkable, he was a respecter of the law.

Several times Captain Kidd had been publicly commended by British colonial authorities in different quarters of the globe for policing the seas of pirates and shady maritime characters. Perhaps he would have been commended oftener if British colonial authorities had less frequently made partners of the pirates. Captain Kidd also had served His British Majesty as a naval officer—His British Majesty being, at this juncture, a Dutch prince and soldier who looked as if he belonged in a Franz Hals painting surrounded by his countrymen, drinking beer in a cellar. He is known to history as William III.

William Kidd had invested his pay and his share of prizes and awards in New York real estate. While he was courting Sarah Oort, the Legislature voted him one hundred and fifty pounds for expelling pirates from the local waters. When he married Sarah he seemed financially provided for for the residue of his days. So at thirty-seven the thrifty Scotch Captain retired from the sea to devote his time to the management of his property, and that which he had acquired by marriage.

The Kidds lived in a three-story brick house at the corner of Pearl and Hanover Streets. The Turkey carpet on the parlor floor was the first Oriental rug in New York. The élite of the Colony attended the social gatherings at Captain Kidd's, walked on the Turkey carpet and admired the other rare articles that he had brought home from his voyages. During the summers the family retired to a country estate called Saw Kill Farm, after the stream which ran through it, at what is now about East Seventy-Fourth Street. In the country the Captain looked after his stock and his crops. In town he collected his rents. It was the pleasant life of a gentleman of the landed class.

His wife bore him one and possibly two children; the records are vague. The Captain was a kind father and, worthy of notice, a kind stepfather. There seems to have been no difference in his eyes between his own children and those of his wife. He told them stories of his more exhilarating days, when he commanded a ship of the Royal Navy and was mentioned for conspicuous gallantry and seamanship in the attacks on Marie Galante and St. Martin in King William's War.

2

Occasionally the Captain spiced the tranquillity of his retirement with a voyage. He was in London in the winter of 1696, four and a half years after his marriage. There he met a fellow New Yorker, Mr. Robert Livingston, founder of the celebrated American family of that time. Mr. Livingston lived at Albany, the jumping-off place of civilization. His estate comprised what is now almost two counties, but the rapidity with which this gentleman had amassed a fortune was not attributed entirely to the prosperity of his plantations. His best-paying interests were said to lie closer to salt water, and concerning them there was a good deal of gossip. A curious maritime tradition pervades this family. A Livingston was associated with Robert Fulton in the invention of the steamboat. Another sat in Andrew Jackson's Cabinet, but before that he had achieved renown in other fields, notably as legal adviser to Jean Laffite of Barataria Bay.

Robert Livingston was delighted to see Captain Kidd. He had a scheme for making money which he had mentioned to several influential friends in England, and they had listened with interest. Livingston was a native of Scotland and it seemed to him that Kidd, a fellow-countryman, was just the dependable, honest seaman that he and his friends needed to realize the scheme. Captain Kidd, too, listened with interest, but he declined the proposal. He said that he did not need the money. It would be a long voyage and a perilous one. The Captain had done enough of that sort of thing in his time and had liked it, but with a family to bring up his days of adventure were behind him.

But Livingston was insistent. He wanted Kidd and no other man. Besides, he explained that he was not speaking for himself solely. He was the agent of his friends who likewise desired that William Kidd should accept this commission, and he named them. There was the Earl of Bellomont who shortly would be Governor of an American colony. There was also Edward Russel, First Lord of the Admiralty; and the Duke of Shrewsbury, His Majesty's Secretary of State; Lord John Somers, Keeper of the Seal and the King's private legal adviser; the Earl of Romney, the handsomest man in England, Master General of Ordnance and one of the King's personal cronies. And—in sacred confidence—there was the King himself. These were the gentlemen who solicited the services of Captain Kidd for a special expedition to capture pirates.

In the whole kingdom it would have been hard to find a more formidable list of names with which to overwhelm the demurrers of a simple sea captain. The rank and position of these men were high enough, but they were actually more powerful than these indicated. They were among the king-makers who seven years before had brought William across the Channel to frighten revelry-loving James II from the throne.

It would have been a simple thing to reject the invitation of the aspiring Livingston, but the King and his associates were a different matter. When these gentlemen solicited it was a command. For once Captain Kidd probably regretted his distinguished English acquaintances.

3

The bargain was made. Bellomont drew up the papers, the King himself signing the commission for "our trusty and well beloved Capt. Robert [a slip of the quill] Kidd, commander of the *Adventure Galley* ... to take into custody ... Capt. Thomas Too [Tew], John Ireland, Capt. Thomas Wake and Capt. Wm. Maze, as all such Pirates, Freebooters and Sea-Rovers ... which you shall meet upon the Seas ... and all such Merchandizes,

Money, Goods and Wares as shall be found on board or with them." The pirates were to be brought home for trial. So much for maintaining the dignity of the law and the security of English shipping; but His Majesty did not specify what his well-beloved Captain was to do with the merchandizes, money and so forth.

This point was covered in other articles, in which the King's name did not appear. "Serve God in the best Manner you can," wrote my Lord of Bellomont, in Kidd's supplementary instructions, and "sail directly to Boston, in New England, there to deliver unto me the whole of what Prizes, Treasure, & Merchandize you shall have taken." Most certainly Bellomont, who had been promised the governorship of New York, would be on hand to receive everything and supervise the division of the cargoes in which he was to share. One-fourth of the booty would go to Kidd's crew. This was the only wage the seamen would receive. The remaining three-fourths would be divided among Bellomont, Somers, Romney, Russel, Shrewsbury, Livingston and Kidd—the larger shares going to Livingston and Kidd.

This is the way the written agreement read, except for a secret clause stipulating that to the King would go a tenth part of all shares. If the booty should total one hundred thousand pounds, Kidd was to receive as a bonus the ship that he sailed in. If the venture were unsuccessful Bellomont was to be refunded what he had contributed to the initial outlay. The others took their chances.

To minimize the likelihood of failure Captain Kidd was provided with a second commission authorizing him to seize any ship, whether pirate or not, which flew the flag or sailed under the protection of France.

Six thousand pounds were expended to buy the new ship *Adventure Galley* and fit her out. Kidd was obliged to put in some of his own money for this. The *Adventure Galley* was of two hundred and eighty-seven tons burden, a fairly large ship, and she carried thirty guns.

The documents signed and sealed, William Kidd had begun

to scare up a crew, when Robert Livingston reappeared to add some private instructions which it would have been untactful to put on paper, even in secret clauses. He told Kidd not to vex his mind with thoughts of failure, even though pirates and French vessels should prove none too plentiful. Rather than let a handsome prize slip through his hands, the Captain was not to scruple over legal niceties, but should "act without regard to my Commission."

In other words Kidd was not to return empty-handed. He was expected to capture pirate ships and French ships, but if neither was available, he was to return with *something*. The gentlemen who had solicited his services must be recompensed for their investment. This was Kidd's own understanding of the conversation with Livingston and there is no reason for disbelieving that it was to be interpreted otherwise. The official morality of the time condoned such things. It was a common practise for privateers to sail after pirates and come back with *something,* cross the palms of a few officials and go their way.

With a short-handed crew the *Adventure Galley* left London in April, 1696. On the voyage to New York Kidd captured a little French fishing vessel and brought it into port, a lawful prize. Then he started filling up the ship's company for the grand cruise.

Finding it impossible to enlist a sufficient number of responsible seamen on a no-prize no-pay arrangement to which he was bound by instructions, Kidd wound up by taking any men he could get, and when the bars were let down there were plenty of applicants. "Many flockt to him from all parts," wrote Benjamin Fletcher, who was acting as Governor of New York pending the arrival of Kidd's partner, the Earl of Bellomont, "men of desperate fortune and necessitous, in the expectation of getting vast treasure." The Governor feared that Kidd would have trouble with such a crew. "It is generally believed here that they will hav money *pr fas and nefas,* that if he misse of the design intended 'twill not be in Kidds power to govern such men under no pay."

This situation could not have greatly disturbed Governor Fletcher whose broad views of crime on the high seas were making him a rich man. A lively sympathy with the objects of the Captain's cruise was practically precluded by the fact that Thomas Tew, of Newport, Rhode Island, one of the men Kidd was commissioned to capture, was the Governor's warm friend. He dined at the executive mansion and, with the merest show of secrecy, regularly landed his stolen cargoes at New York and shared them with Fletcher and other officials. But this was merely the way of the times, and made for the success of mutually interested parties. The notorious Blackbeard—Captain Edward Teach— who operated farther south, had three governors on his pension list at one time, and the Governor of South Carolina, not entirely because of curiosity, was present when Blackbeard married his fifteenth wife.

William Kidd showed no eagerness to leave New York. He remained there all summer, and not until the sixth of September, 1696, did he say farewell to his wife and children and sail away in the *Adventure Galley,* with a crew of one hundred and fifty-four—as finished a collection of cutthroats as ever tramped a deck.

4

Reaching the Madeira Islands the Captain found an English brigantine which had lost its mast and sails. He fitted it out with stick and canvas, and in return for this courtesy, the master sent a few barrels of flour and some sugar aboard the *Adventure Galley,* which then stood for the Cape of Good Hope. Presently a sail was sighted and the *Galley* gave chase, in three days over-hauling what proved to be a Portuguese trader from Brazil. Kidd demanded the trader's papers, and finding them in regular order, the two captains exchanged compliments and presents, according to sea custom, and went their ways. Next Kidd met up with four British war-ships. This time the *Adventure Galley* was obliged to exhibit her papers, after which Kidd was entertained aboard one of the men-of-war. He returned to his ship "much disguised with drink" from toasting the King's health.

Rounding the Cape the *Adventure Galley* stood for Tullear, on the island of Madagascar, off the east coast of Africa, dropping anchor January 29, 1697, one hundred and forty-seven days from New York.

The crew was restless. It was not interested in long voyages or the amenities of life at sea which, thus far, had so agreeably engaged the Captain. The men wanted money and reckoned that already there had been too many delays. Kidd left Tullear for a near-by port to careen his ship and prepare for action. En route he overtook two East Indiamen, but their papers were regular, and he did not molest them. The ship was beached and cleaned. During this operation fifty of the crew died, which would seem to back up the Captain's opinion that his surgeon, Doctor Bradinham, was an "idler."

His ship ready for sea again, Kidd's quest of pirate gold was resumed in earnest. He beat up the east coast of Africa, into the Red Sea, across the Indian Ocean and along the coasts of India and of Hindustan. He stopped several ships, but none of them being lawful prey, they were allowed to go their way.

So the months dragged by. The crew could see no sense to the scruples of their skipper. They wanted action. They got it in a fight with two Portuguese war-ships, in which fifteen of their number were wounded before the *Adventure Galley* crippled her assailants and drove them off. But there was no profit in this venture, and the temper of the crew grew more surly. The ring-leaders plotted to seize the ship and turn pirate on their own account. But Kidd had dealt with hard customers before and he kept his men in hand, hoping for a prize which would quiet their spirits. Finally a small vessel was overhauled, and, although it showed the English colors and carried English papers, it was boarded and rifled.

This was an act of piracy, but whether Kidd was responsible or whether the men took matters into their own hands is a question. Later the men said they had acted in obedience to orders.

The Captain said the men mutinied and the robbing of the Englishman was their own doing.

The booty obtained was trifling—"some rice, raisons and old cloaths and some money." These slender rewards merely sharpened the appetites of the crew. There were more adventures—ships stopped, searched, papers anxiously scanned only to be found in order. The scarcity of evil-doers was depressing. Fifteen weary months passed and no prize money for the penniless, growling crew. Kidd's situation became critical, as Governor Fletcher, in his wisdom, had foretold. The ship was leaking, provisions were low, the men treacherous, and the Captain's life itself was in danger. But these considerations, perhaps, were unimportant beside the realization that his voyage had been a financial failure. The noble gentlemen who had sent William Kidd to sea on the King's errand expected gold and not excuses.

5

Then luck turned. In the month of November, 1697, the *Adventure Galley* fell in with the well-stocked Indian trader *Rouparelle,* which was sailing under a French pass of safe-conduct and therefore seized. And on the first of February following, Captain Kidd made the haul that seemed to redeem the voyage.

The *Galley* was nosing about in the Indian Ocean under French colors when a sail of enormous spread was cried. Kidd ran up to her. Seeing the fleur-de-lis, the big ship made no effort to get away, but announced herself as the *Quedah Merchant* from Surat, property of the Great Mogul. Kidd invited her master to come on board and submit his papers. When the *Quedah Merchant's* skipper stepped on the deck of the *Adventure Galley,* the English flag was hoisted.

The visitor had brought along a French gunner as interpreter. He acquitted himself with the savoir-faire which has helped to make a reputation for his race.

"You are all English? Which is the Captain?" he asked.

William Kidd presented himself.

"Here is a good prize," said the Frenchman, placing in the Captain's hands the French passport of the *Quedah Merchant*.

The gunner told the truth. It was a fabulous prize—the Mogul's treasure ship. Kidd scanned the invoice: ingots of gold and bars of silver; bags of gold dust; chests of coin; boxes of diamonds, rubies, emeralds; bales of silk and damask. The value can never be told, but an inventory of the left-overs which Captain Kidd managed later to land in America, according to Lord Bellomont's instructions, assumes the sweeping dimensions of a maharajah's dream.

The captured treasures stowed, Captain Kidd turned his helm and stood for New York, but that was twelve thousand miles away and the *Adventure Galley* could not make it. She was leaking so badly that the eight-man shifts at the pumps were changed every two hours. Her hull was bound round with cable for fear the bottom would drop out. With his two prizes, the *Rouparelle* and the *Quedah Merchant,* in company, Kidd put in at St. Mary's, Madagascar, to refit.

The three vessels entered the roads of St. Mary's on April 1, 1698. At anchor in the harbor was the frigate *Mocca,* Captain Robert Culliford. The *Mocca* was a pirate ship and Culliford a pirate captain. Had Kidd encountered this mariner a little earlier the result might have been different, but with this belated meeting fortune seems to have turned her back completely on the *Adventure Galley's* captain.

Ninety-seven of Kidd's men rebelled. This was nearly all he had. They stole the *Rouparelle,* ransacked and sunk her. Then, joined by some of Culliford's followers, they raided the disabled *Galley* and the *Quedah Merchant* in which Kidd had proposed to sail for home. Kidd managed to hold the ships but the mutineers carried off nearly everything portable, including all the treasure they could find and the cannon. Next they marched inland and looted a planter's residence at which Kidd had stored some of the treasure.

When things quieted down Kidd had twenty men at his back and two vessels, one picked clean and the other falling to pieces.

It is set down as a black mark against Kidd that he went on board the *Mocca* and accepted the hospitality of a few drinks of grog from Culliford. Kidd denied this, but, after all, it does not seem such an imprudent gesture, if he really did fraternize with the pirate captain. Culliford had two hundred men and a seaworthy vessel. Under the circumstances, it would seem wiser for Kidd to be friendly than quarrelsome.

On the fifteenth of June, Culliford sailed away, leaving Kidd utterly stranded. He now had only thirteen men. The *Adventure Galley* was permitted to rot, but it took five months in that out-of-the-way port to get the *Quedah Merchant* in shape for the homeward voyage.

6

This delay was an evil thing for William Kidd. Unsettling rumors had begun to sift back to civilization. They seem to have started with a Jewish jeweler named Benjamin Franks whom Kidd had carried as a passenger from New York to India. When the crew first began to grow restive, Franks was ill in his cabin and knew nothing that went on except what the seamen told him. Franks got their version of the robbing of the little English ship, which, except that the name rather dignifies such petty thievery, was an act of piracy. Franks left the *Adventure Galley* shortly thereafter and proceeded to Bombay where he found more than one interested party eager to have from him an affidavit embodying the yarns of Captain Kidd's unruly sailors.

But even if Franks with his affidavit had not started the gossip on the wing, something was bound to transpire and place in disrepute the voyage of the *Adventure Galley*. The chief factor that operated against William Kidd was time. Two years and several months were too long for him to have been gone. In England there had been changes. Most of his backers, grumbling at the delay and dubious after the first year about hearing further of their investment, were involved by then in other interests to promote their fortunes. They had merely kept pace with events, for since the reformers had begun to tamper with piracy, this institution did not maintain its once popular place in the public's esteem. Concessions were the part of expediency.

Another factor was the all-powerful British East India Company with influence sufficient to set itself against the noble gentlemen on whose shoulders had rested the throne of England. It maintained a practical monopoly of the carrying trade between England and India by the simple but thriving policy of playing pirate on its own account with outsiders who sailed in those waters. The coming of Kidd was an embarrassment to this program, so the East India Company looked upon him as a competitor to be reckoned with. But Kidd's influential backers made it necessary to proceed with caution.

The arrival of Mr. Franks in Bombay and his subsequent affidavit were most agreeable to the East India Company. But more than this was needed against Captain Kidd and, although the next morsel of evidence was quite unsatisfactory in character, the company altered the facts to suit its requirements. The occasion was the arrival in London of news of Kidd's seizure of the two ships under French passes. The British East India Company simply represented to the authorities that these vessels had *not* sailed under French passes—and here was Mr. Franks's affidavit to show that Captain Kidd had done this sort of thing before. No one had the impertinence to suggest that representatives of the Great British East India Company would lie. Nor was it generally known that the Company had a special interest in the welfare of these vessels, their French passes notwithstanding. This vast concern's maritime interests were not bounded by the narrow confines of British nationality. It sometimes used French passes, although naturally London was not supposed to know of it.

With strange timeliness these charges and the affidavit reached His Majesty King William III at a period when he had launched a grand crusade against buccaneers. The crusade was not succeeding, and the King was aggrieved to hear that a man sailing under his own commission should be, as it was represented, in part responsible for this. In December of 1698 English authorities the world over were directed to arrest "that obnoxious pirate Kidd."

This was a master-stroke for the East India Company, although a few days before the order was signed it seemed as if their scheme to get rid of Kidd might fall through. Some one reached the royal ear with the suggestion that one way to attain the end of the crusade would be to forgive the pirates. The King thought the suggestion had merit and so he advertised an offer of immunity to every pirate who would surrender and promise to lead a different life. But of all the sinners on all the seas, two were excluded by name from the benefits of this act of grace. They were William Kidd and "Long Ben" Avery, a sure-enough pirate who used to strut about Boston with his pockets full of unset diamonds.

7

Even had Captain Kidd been included in the royal forgiveness, he could not have taken advantage of the offer. Marooned in an unfrequented tropical port, he knew nothing of the coil that was tightening about him. When the news of his proscription reached Madagascar, Kidd was at sea again, having gathered up a skeleton crew to carry the remnants of treasure to Lord Bellomont waiting in the New World. This crew, too, was a hard lot, but Kidd was in no situation to be fastidious.

In April, 1699, Kidd arrived at Anguila, in the Leeward Islands, southeast of Cuba, still pursued by ill-fortune. His crew was in a state of revolt and there had been a fight on deck in which thirty were killed. The *Quedah Merchant* was leaking and provisions and water were low. Kidd appealed to the authorities for relief only to receive the astonishing information that he himself was a fugitive from justice—and to tell the truth, he certainly looked the part.

Twenty men deserted at Anguila and with not more than twenty-five hands, fore and aft, the big ship lumbered away to St. Thomas. For three days Kidd anchored out of range of the fortress guns and begged for succor, but no one cared to harbor or help "that obnoxious pirate Kidd." More men deserted. Not enough remained to sail the *Quedah Merchant* to Boston, had the vessel been sturdy enough for the voyage.

Kidd dodged about the West Indies like a toad under a harrow. Giving a British war-ship the slip, he purchased a sloop called the *St. Anthony* and loaded it with fifteen thousand pounds of treasure. Sailing north he left the *Quedah Merchant* concealed in a cove near the coast of Hispanola, now San Domingo, under guard of a trusted friend and what crew he could spare. The big ship had from thirty thousand to a hundred thousand pounds of treasure aboard, which the guards lost little time in appropriating when Kidd was out of sight.

Moving cautiously up the Atlantic coast, Kidd believed that the worst of his troubles were over. He put in at Lewes, Delaware, to buy food, and departed again leaving a trail of trouble for the provisioners with whom he had dealt. When his identity was known, they were thrown into jail for doing business with the "obnoxious" pirate. The Captain remained in ignorance of this, but, before reaching New York, he took the precaution to send ahead and engage a lawyer. In June, 1699, the *St. Anthony* slipped into Long Island Sound. Captain Kidd had not seen his wife and children for thirty-three months. Yet he dared not go ashore. Presently, James Emmot, the lawyer, secretly rowed out to the vessel and brought word of the Captain's family. Mr. Emmot was a distinguished member of the colonial bar and a vestryman of Trinity Church. After hearing Kidd's story, he promised to see the Royal Governor at once. He assured the Captain that when the Governor was informed of the true state of affairs, he would send to London a recommendation that would release William Kidd from all his difficulties.

8

The Governor of New York was now my Lord of Bellomont, the same noble gentleman who had drawn up Kidd's papers in England and with whom he had made a rendezvous at Boston for the delivery of all captured prizes and treasures to be divided among the sponsors of the venture. The Governor resided in Boston, Massachusetts being a part of the Colonial Government of New York.

Emmot arrived in Boston at ten o'clock at night and, going straight to the Governor's house, asked for an audience on important business. The Earl received his visitor civilly and listened with great attention to what he had to say. The specific accusation that had placed Captain Kidd outside the pale of the King's clemency related to the seizures of the *Rouparelle* and the *Quedah Merchant*. But fortunately, through all his vicissitudes, Kidd had preserved the French passports taken from these vessels, and which, under his commission, made them lawful prey. Mr. Emmot placed these papers in the Governor's hands. The ordinarily relaxed lines of the fat florid face of the Governor tightened with interest as his small unsteady eyes took in the momentous import of these documents. Finally he remarked that apparently they established Kidd's innocence and that he would at once write the Captain a letter to relieve his mind. Leaving the passports with Bellomont, Mr. Emmot departed from the Governor's residence at midnight in the belief that he had done a good day's work.

He had done a bad day's work. Though James Emmot was the leading admiralty lawyer of New York, Captain Kidd had made an unfortunate choice of counsel. Bellomont disliked him, particularly because the lawyer's masterly defense of several dubious maritime characters had deprived the Governor of rewards that might otherwise have been his as a proponent of the King's campaign against piracy. Not only this, but there was in Bellomont a certain incapacity that urged him to the zealous performance of duties that he thought might attain advancement in the King's service. As Emmot related the adventures of William Kidd, the mind of this Executive reached the conclusion that Emmot was not to be trusted and that justice had been outwitted long enough by this facile barrister. This is not an altogether curious turn of affairs, and one must seek the reason farther back than the midnight interview in Boston. Stronger men in the Kingdom than Bellomont had turned their backs on William Kidd.

All the more eagerly, therefore, Bellomont performed his promise, writing Kidd a letter brimming with the fairest assurances. "If your case be so clear as you (or Mr. Emmot for you) have said you may safely come hither and be equipped to go and fetch the other side and I make no manner of doubt but to obtain the King's pardon for you. . . . I assure you on my word of Honour I will perform nicely what I have promised."

This communication was not dispatched by ordinary means. As a special mark of its import, Bellomont gave it to Duncan Campbell, Postmaster of Boston and an old friend of Kidd, to deliver in person to the Captain.

9

William Kidd breathed more easily than he had breathed in three years. Campbell returned to Boston with a letter in which Kidd assured the Governor that he would be in Boston in a few days to state his own case. Accompanying this communication, Captain Kidd sent a few small jewels to Lady Bellomont—a simple courtesy conforming with an established practise among ship masters of the seventeenth century. There was a happy reunion at the house in Pearl Street, and William Kidd kept tailors and shirtmakers working by candlelight to provide him with a wardrobe for his trip to Boston.

Thither Kidd arrived, with his wife and children, on July 1, 1699. At once he waited on the Governor who received him with his full Council. Bellomont wrote to London a lengthy account of this interview, saying that he could see guilt stamped on Kidd's countenance the instant they met and that the Captain "did strangely trifle" with the Council. Moreover, the Governor represented Kidd's small gift to Lady Bellomont in the dark aspect of a bribe.

When Bellomont saw guilt on Kidd's countenance, he was more discerning than Duncan Campbell who invited the Captain and family to be guests at his home, and more discerning than the fashionable of Boston, including members of the Governor's Council, who met Kidd at entertainments at the Postmaster's house. Nor did the Council appear to be aware that Kidd had trifled with that honorable body. And Bellomont did not take the members of the body into his confidence concerning his convictions.

Kidd promised the Council to put an account of his voyage in writing, explaining that this was not a simple task to perform with accuracy because the log of the *Adventure Galley* had been destroyed by the mutineers. At nine in the morning of July sixth he appeared before the Council and said that his report would be ready that evening. A few minutes after he had departed, Bellomont astonished the Council with the news that he intended to arrest Captain Kidd. The warrant was issued that afternoon. A constable found Kidd taking a stroll in front of the Governor's home. The Captain ran to Bellomont for protection, only to learn the value of the Earl's fair phrases.

The Captain stood charged with piracy in the seizures of the *Rouparelle* and *Quedah Merchant*. The orderly means of removing the prisoner from the shadow of the accusation were two: pardon by the King, or acquittal by a jury. In the beginning Bellomont had promised to speak for a pardon. He had a right to change his mind in favor of a trial, which, under the law, must be held in America, and which, indeed, would have relieved the King of some measure of embarrassment since the charge itself was baseless as evidenced by the French passports. But since the winds of favor had changed, Bellomont became most active in conspiring to hasten the Captain to his doom, just as, once upon a time, he had been most assiduous in shouldering his way into the august circle of courtiers who made Kidd their confidential agent. Now he became so spirited in his desire to please that he broke the law, and, ordering Kidd on board a vessel, delivered him into the hands of his betrayers in England. The Governor fancied that perhaps this high-handed act required for the sake of appearances some word of formal justification, which he offered with perfect candor. "In this Country, if a pyrate were Convict, yet he cannot suffer Death."

10

There is much to indicate that the King's counselors in London were not particularly captivated by the energetic solicitude of the Governor of New York. Had Kidd been set free in distant America, they might have made some public gestures of dismay and then permitted the unpleasant incident to slip gracefully into the limbo. Actually there could not have been much anger behind the official frowns for, with Kidd on their door-step, no virtuous haste was made to try him for his widely proclaimed crimes.

More than a year the Captain lay in Newgate jail, and at length he had begun to hope for an intercession on the part of the influential gentlemen who had obliged him to abandon the life of a colonial squire to go in quest of stolen goods. Like Bellomont none of these noble dignitaries had fared so badly during the intervening years.

John Somers had been promoted to Lord Chancellor of the Realm.

Edward Russel was still First Lord of Admiralty, with a few other titles thrown in for good measure—Baron Shingey, Viscount Barfleur, Earl of Orford.

The Duke of Shrewsbury, His Majesty's Secretary of State, had taken leave of his duties to travel on the Continent. This nobleman had been an intimate of the courts of three English Kings, and, according to the back-stairs gossip of the palace, the bed-fellow of an English queen. Nevertheless, these triumphs failed to repair an injury that his illusions had suffered early in life as a result of a domestic contretemps in which his father was killed by his mother's lover. Bearing in mind the destruction of his own youthful ideals and with a son of his own to launch in the world, Shrewsbury decided to remove the boy from England pending the disposition of the case of William Kidd. "I would

[48]

rather," he said, "see my son bound to a hangman than a states-man."

As for the Earl of Romney, King William had been obliged to remove this favorite from the lucrative post of Master General of Ordnance, on the interesting ground that his morals were such as to invite public criticism. This statesman still enjoyed a strong personal influence with the throne, however, as well as a handsome pension. But the swarm of illegitimate children who besieged him for doles modified the serenity of his retirement.

Any one of these might have saved the man they had ruined, might have opened the doors of Newgate and sent William Kidd back to his family in Pearl Street, restored his good name and indemnified him for the money and time he had lost. Despite the complications entailed by Bellomont's bungling zeal, this could have been done. Not one of the noble gentlemen, however, had the courage to raise his hand, though Shrewsbury's conscience did prick him somewhat. Robert Livingston was loyal and had the grace to do what he could. It might have been better had he done nothing. The Colonial counted for little in such splendid company and, unfortunately, in the beginning, he had rubbed Bellomont's fur the wrong way and harmed Kidd rather than helped him.

The motivating cause for this general desertion of Captain Kidd was a necessity for appeasing the relentless East India Company. Its duplicity in the matter of the French passports would have been exposed with Kidd's vindication. And the East India Company could never permit such a slip. There was another matter, too, which required a scapegoat, and this had developed with the pattern of political affairs in England. John Somers, the Lord Chancellor, was in hot water with the House of Commons which relieved its feelings by accusing the Chancellor of anything that sounded sufficiently disparaging, truth being not the elementary consideration. Some one in the House discovered Somers's connection with the cruise of William Kidd and straightway raised the cry that the Chancellor was a partner of the "obnoxious pirate."

Two courses were open to Somers. He could have insisted on Kidd's innocence, or, at least, that he be given a fair chance to establish his innocence, and thus substantiated the irreprehensible nature of the partnership. Or he could have disarmed criticism by joining in the persecution of Kidd and proving his virtue by seeing that a rogue got his due. The second course was the easier for John Somers.

II

Such was the alignment of the principals when William Kidd was hailed to court. Once a trial had been agreed upon, the dilatory tactics of the twelve months past gave way to a program of action in which events marched with celerity and the terrible precision of things foreordained. The arrangements stand as a model of their kind. Nothing was left to chance.

Four judges presided. Four lawyers represented the prosecution. Kidd asked for a lawyer, but the petition was denied. In open court he requested the return of his papers which he had surrendered before his arrest in America. He was insolently asked what he wanted with them. Kidd said that the French passes would acquit him of the charge of piracy. Whereupon, for the first time, the prisoner was informed that he was not to be tried for piracy, but for murder, upon which the passes had no bearing. He was ordered to "hold up thy hand" and plead to the following:

"... Indictment for Murther ... William Kidd, late of London, Mariner, not having the Fear of God before his Eyes, but being mov'd and seduc'd by the Instigation of the Devil, the 30th day of October in the Ninth Year of the Reign of our Sovereign Lord William the Third . . . by Force and Arms & upon the High Seas ... in a certain ship call'd the *Adventure-Galley* ... feloniously, voluntarily and with malice afore-thought, then and there did . . . with a certain wooden Bucket, bound with Iron Hoops, of the value of Eight Pense ... strike ... William Moore ... a little above the Right Ear ... giving the said William Moore one mortal Bruise . . . of which the aforesaid William Moore . . . did die . . . against the Peace of our Sovereign Lord the King, his Crown and Dignity."

To which the astonished William Kidd pleaded not guilty.

Taking the witness stand the prisoner admitted to striking the said William Moore who was a mutinous gunner on the *Galley*. He might have added that he had also killed other mutineers during that unfortunate cruise—the sad part of it being that he had not killed enough of them. Kidd told a straightforward story in a seaman's concise but simple language. He said that the death of Moore was unintentional, but that he had been obliged to strike him in order to restore discipline among the crew. These facts were corroborated by three seamen of the *Adventure Galley* who followed the Captain to the stand.

The Crown witnesses were Joseph Palmer, a seaman, and Robert Bradinham, the ship's surgeon, who still might have borne some resentment for the Captain's criticism of him when fifty of the crew died. However, granting that he and the other witness told the truth, neither made out a case of murder against Kidd.

This was all there was to this brief trial, except for the instructions to the jury which was practically directed to bring in a verdict of guilty. After some hesitation, it did so, and William Kidd was sentenced to death.

As a condemned man, the Captain was now in a situation to assist at the relief of circumstances embarrassing one of the great Englishmen of his century, Lord Chancellor John Somers. The day after sentence was passed the court broke its word and ordered Kidd tried for piracy.

The same prejudiced judges, unscrupulous prosecutors and perjured witnesses faced a brow-beaten jury. With the rope already about his neck, Kidd made a cornered man's fight to clear his name. He told the story of the French passes and demanded his papers that he might exhibit them. He was promptly told that his papers could not be found. In his address to the jury one of the prosecutors, whose ignorance of the true story of the passes is open to question, admitted that if Kidd had produced the French passports he could not be convicted. But, exclaimed this servant of the Crown, where are those passes? He scoffed at the Captain's pretension that he had surrendered them trustingly to the authorities.

This trial, like its predecessor, was finished in less than a day. This time the jury returned its verdict punctually, finding the defendant guilty as charged in the indictment. For the second time within twenty-four hours, William Kidd was again sentenced to death.

The man who had reposed his trust in a prince's favor was permitted to address the court. The speech was brief.

"My Lairds," he said in the peculiar accent of the North, "it is a very hard sentence. I have been sworn against by perjured witnesses."

On May 23, 1701, William Kidd was conducted down the worn stone stairs at Execution Dock, and, according to the custom with pirates, hanged on a gallows between the marks of high and low tides. Then his body was covered with tar and encased by chains, and suspended from a gibbet farther down the river. There, as a warning to passing seamen, it swayed with the winds until crows had picked the bones bare.

There was some truth in the statement that Captain Kidd's papers, including the French passports of the *Rouparelle* and the *Quedah Merchant,* could not be found. They had been concealed so well by the statesmen who wished to preserve their reputations that the hiding-place in the Public Record Office in Chancery Lane was not discovered for two hundred years.

BENJAMIN FRANKLIN, ELECTRICIAN

III

BENJAMIN FRANKLIN, ELECTRICIAN

I

MARVELS that the lofty imaginations of the Greeks declined to assign to their gods, lest they render them ridiculous in the eyes of rational men, are ours at the closing of a switch, the touch of a button. What marked the departure from old ways to new?

In the main it was the discovery of the powers of electricity upon which Americans have become so dependent that were they to fail us our elaborate social order would be chaos.

Fifty years ago the withdrawal of steam would have unhinged our scheme of living. One hundred years ago the extinction of horses would have placed mankind at a similar disadvantage. Man leaned on the horse for thousands of years. He began to lean on electricity only seventy years ago. Yet, at any time in his history, he could have got along in a pinch without horses more easily than he could now without electric current. So much for a roughly comparative idea of what this new agency means to us. It has become the all-pervading force of our lives, and this in the incredibly short space of time since, within the recollection of our grandsires, electricity performed its first practical service when Morse perfected the telegraph.

It is a curious thing that, in this country where such a short while ago a civilization was being hewn with the broadax, we should be more dependent upon the good-will of electricity than any people on the globe. But more curious is the almost forgotten story that an American played in the discoveries which placed this revolutionary force at the disposal of human beings.

Before the War for Independence a British colonial, residing in Philadelphia and proud of his allegiance to his King across the ocean, had carried the science of electricity beyond anything attained in the laboratories of Europe. To-day about the only knowledge of Benjamin Franklin's services in the field of science that survives in the popular mind is a misty school-days memory of the kite experiment. Yet Printer Ben was the first man to turn a wheel by electricity, the power that revolves more wheels to-day than any other force.

2

In 1746, at the age of forty, Franklin revisited his birthplace in Boston which he had left twenty-three years before as a runaway apprentice. He was now a settled man, married, the proprietor of a prosperous newspaper and member of the Legislature of the Colony of Pennsylvania. In Boston he was entertained at the residence of a Doctor Spence, who had lately brought from Scotland one of those novel electric tubes that were the rage of European drawing-rooms and the puzzle of European scientists. It was new to the visitor, and any new thing appealed to Benjamin Franklin. To broaden the scope of his reading he had taught himself, not long since, the French, Spanish, Italian and Latin languages, at the same time keeping up his swimming. Franklin had few equals as a swimmer and published a manual of instruction in the art.

A few weeks after Franklin's return home a parcel of books arrived from England for the public library in Philadelphia, of which Franklin was a founder. Accompanying the books was an electrical tube, such as Franklin had seen in Boston, with directions for using. It was the gift of Peter Collinson, a London merchant with interests in America, and amateur scientist and friend of the Philadelphia editor. Franklin took possession of the tube long enough to have duplicates blown by a local glassmaker. With these he mastered the simple experiments given in the chart of instruction and invented others.

The electrical tube was regarded as an entertaining toy. It was simply a glass cylinder two and a half feet long and as big around as a man's wrist. Briskly rubbed with cloth or buckskin it generated electricity so that, if held in contact with certain objects, it would produce a spark, lighting candles or the rum on an omelette, or firing a pinch of gunpowder in a lady's hand. The droll Franklin loved company and jokes and his tricks brought nightly gatherings to his comfortable parlor. But as the editor's interest in the mysterious power deepened so much society became a burden, and he gave away a number of tubes in order that his acquaintances might amuse themselves elsewhere. With three friends—Ebenezer Kinnersley, a brilliant but poverty-ridden school-teacher out of employment, Thomas Hopkinson, a man of means and the first president of the American Philosophical Society, and Philip Sing, a member of the Society—he began a serious study of electricity.

Europe was similarly engaged, society entertaining itself while scientists guessed and probed. Electrical experimentation had received a great impetus two years before when three Germans at the University of Leyden contrived, somewhat accidentally, the Leyden jar, by which the ephemeral electrical force generated by rubbing tubes could be artificially stored for future use. This invention marked the greatest stride since the electric properties of amber had been observed and discussed by the Greeks three hundred years before the birth of Christ. The next great discoveries were those of Franklin and, as he was careful to record, his three collaborators. In seven years, or until public duties drove him from his little workroom with its home-made machines, Franklin became the foremost electrician of the world, and the colonial outpost of Philadelphia, on the rim of civilized life, was the source to which savants, working under the eyes and by means of the bounty of European monarchs, looked for inspiration and authority.

As rubbing tubes was tiresome, Sing made a machine on the order of a grindstone, which accomplished this by turning a crank. A similar contraption had been devised in Europe, but Franklin's group knew nothing of it. In their isolation they conducted many experiments and made several minor discoveries which already were known abroad. This isolation seemed to favor the Americans, however. They worked untrammeled by mistaken theories which might have checked the bold and original progress of their labor.

During the first year of his experiments, Franklin revolutionized the science by his discovery of the positive and negative states of electricity, which he called plus and minus. It had early been his theory that electricity is not created by friction, but only collected. Franklin held that "the electrical fire," as he called it, exists in all bodies as a common ingredient. A body acquiring more than its normal amount of electricity he designated as plus, or positively electrified. A body from which had been subtracted some of its normal share of electricity was minus, or negatively electrified.

In the normal state of things the electricity was in a condition of "equilibrium," and there was no movement to it. But when a plus, or over-electrified body, was brought in contact with a minus body, electricity would pass from the former to the latter, restoring equilibrium. Franklin established this by an experiment with three men, undoubtedly his co-workers Kinnersley, Hopkinson and Sing, whom he denominated in his minutes as A, B and C.

A stood on a pad of wax, which is a non-conductor, and rubbed a tube, thus collecting "the electrical fire from himself into the glass." His electrical contact with the outside world being cut off, there was no means by which his body could replenish the store of electricity drawn into the tube, so he became negatively electrified. B, also standing on wax, passed his knuckles near the tube held by A and drew off the electricity therein into his body, thus becoming plus or positively electrified. Then C, with merely a normal store of electricity in his system, held out his hand to A, the negatively electrified. A slight spark passed from C, the normal man, to A, the negative man. Then C approached B, the positively electrified, and *received* a slight spark. Then B, the positively electrified, approached A, the negatively electrified, and *gave* him a *large spark,* showing that the electrical current is something like water running down-hill. It passes from the most charged body to the one least charged; the greater the difference between bodies the greater the rush of current to restore equilibrium.

Two months later Franklin connected his plus and minus discovery with the phenomena of attraction and repulsion. Already he had made the important discovery that the Leyden jar was positively electrified on the inside and negatively electrified on the outside. Running two wires up vertically, one from the positive inside and the other from the negative outside of the jar, he suspended a cork by a silk thread between the wires. The cork played back and forth like a pendulum until it exhausted the electrical force of the jar by distributing it equally between the wires. This experiment marked the beginning of man's understanding of electrical current and brought to notice the principle of the electric motor.

Franklin detailed the results of these experiments in letters which Collinson read before the foremost scientific body of England, the Royal Society. The reading took place after Watson, the leader of English electricians, had performed a series of experiments and promulgated a definite theory concerning the character of electricity. Watson discovered that earth is a conductor and transmitted an electric shock four miles over wire by grounding the ends. His explanation, however, contained no mention of the vital negative and positive principle of Franklin, whose letters threw the British experimenter and his associates into confusion. Doctor Watson wrote a clever paper contending that his theory and Franklin's were the same. This led to a long dispute—in which Franklin, who cared nothing for personal credit, took no part—as to the actual originator of the negative and positive theory. There can be no doubt but that Franklin first enunciated it, and Watson's attempt in this instance to appropriate the discovery of another is happily overshadowed by his whole-hearted praise of Franklin in later years.

Franklin read every line he could get from abroad on the subject of his hobby. "Where does the charge in the Leyden jar lie?" was a question agitating every one. Professor Musschenbroeck, one of the inventors of the jar, said it lay in the water. Watson said it lay in the inner tin-foil coating of the container. Others had different theories, and reasons for them. Franklin said nothing until he knew the secret beyond dispute. All Franklin's experiments seem so easy and so obvious it is little wonder that sometimes they nettled the Europeans, who felt rather out of countenance because such things had not occurred to them before. Franklin simply took the jar apart in such a way that the charge could not escape and thus tracked it down. It was a neat operation, though not essentially intricate or difficult. It was found that the charge resided in the glass of the jar.

This led Franklin to substitute for a jar plates of ordinary window glass, their flat sides joined by armatures of lead. He called this a storage "battery." It did not work very well, so he went back to the jars, joining several of them to obtain a larger amount of current. The predecessor of the battery as we know it now was invented the year that Franklin died by Galvani, an Italian.

At intervals Franklin continued to entertain his friends with electrical tricks. Kinnersley made an effigy of George II—"God preserve him," the loyal Franklin would say while conducting a demonstration—so electrified that when attempting to remove the crown from the royal head one would receive a shock. Franklin wrought what seemed a feat of pure magic as he directed a current across the Schuylkill River by no other means than the water as a conductor. The earliest witnesses to the operation of Marconi's wireless could hardly have been more astonished. But strange to relate it occurred neither to Watson, who first sent a current any distance by wire, nor to Franklin who first sent one without a wire, to devise a code by which human intelligence might be transmitted.

Franklin closed his second winter of experiments with "a party of pleasure" on the bank of the Schuylkill near town. Going to the opposite side of the stream he sent a current across, lighting a pan of brandy. Then he electrocuted a turkey and roasted it on a spit made to revolve by electricity before an electrically kindled fire. When the bird was ready and the feast spread, the healths of brother electricians across the sea were drunk as a salvo of muskets was discharged by a storage battery. In the playthings of Franklin's fantastic picnic of 1748, one can discern the ancestors of several household commonplaces of to-day, as well as the electric chair.

4

The following summer Franklin prepared to devote the remainder of his life to science. Selling the greater part of his business enterprises, he retired from active management and prepared to live on the income of his past labors which came to three thousand pounds sterling a year, or three times the salary of the Royal Governor. The retired printer moved into a roomy suburban house at Second and Race Streets. His garden extended to the river in which he spent two hours a day regaining the proficiency of his youth at swimming and diving.

Outside the windows of his workroom Franklin ran a chain to keep back the curious. So many people would hang upon this barrier that Franklin finally attached a concealed wire to it, and after giving one or two audiences a stiff shock, this sort of trespass diminished.

Kinnersley was provided with a set of electrical equipment and sent on a tour of the provinces. It was very successful, carrying the lecturer to the West Indies, and, one hopes, improving the chronically sorry state of his finances. Franklin continued his experiments of the effect of electricity on the bodies of animals and men. Electrocuted fowl "eats uncommonly tender," he wrote.

Turkeys were hardest to kill, and, while preparing to kill one at a private demonstration, he felt the world suddenly and without sensation go blank.

"I then felt what I know not well to describe—a universal blow from head to foot, which seemed within as well as without [and] . . . a violent quick shaking of the body." But this was not the impact of the shock Franklin had given himself instead of the turkey; it was the force of the shock wearing off as he regained his senses. Franklin had sent the full discharge of two six-gallon Leyden jars into his body. A blinding flash and a crack like that of a pistol had terrified the spectators, but Franklin had heard or felt nothing. He declined to believe what had happened until he saw the jars had been discharged. Franklin said this blunder compared with that of the Irishman who sought to steal gunpowder by making a hole in the keg with a hot poker.

Later Franklin knocked down six men who submitted themselves to the test. Paralytics flocked to him for treatment, perhaps giving rise to the quackery in this line which persisted for a hundred and fifty years. But Franklin soon came to the conclusion that there was no benefit from electricity. If the patients felt a little better for the time being, he thought it was because of the exercise in getting to his house and their buoyed spirits in the expectation of relief. While preparing to treat a sick pilgrim, Franklin again almost killed himself by accidentally making a circuit that sent "an immense charge" through his own head. The inventor was thrown to the floor unconscious. When he came to he could not at first believe, despite his earlier experience, what had happened, but where the charge had entered was a bump on his head that did not go down for several days. In any event Franklin had established the painless aspect of death by electricity.

The observation of the effect of electricity on animate and inanimate objects led Franklin to reflect upon its similarity to the effect of lightning. The identity of lightning was a question that had engaged the mind of man from the dawn of history. Although the supernatural theory still had its adherents, scientific explanations had been advanced, the prevailing one being that it

[62]

was due to the detonation of a mixture of sulphurous and nitrous gases, producing an explosion not unlike that of gunpowder.

After a number of observations, Franklin wrote for his friend Collinson in London a luminous and epochal paper comparing electricity to lightning, and proposed a test by drawing lightning from the heavens by means of a metal point on a spire or tower and examining it. The want of an object tall enough prevented Franklin from trying it in Philadelphia, he said. Moreover, Franklin suggested the feasibility of drawing lightning to metal points on tall buildings and masts of ships and conducting it to earth or sea by means of a wire, thus preventing damage.

Collinson read the paper before the Royal Society and suggested that it be published in the *Transactions* of that body. The experiments were voted down in derision and publication declined.

Collinson then offered the paper, with others of Franklin's, to the celebrated *Gentleman's Magazine* of London. The publisher declined to risk the prestige of his periodical, but published a small edition of the papers as a pamphlet. The booklet attracted little notice in England until its translation had made a sensation in France. Editions in German, Italian and Latin followed and Franklin's theories became the talk of Christendom. The Abbé Nolet, the foremost electrician of France, and a member of the King's household, increased the demand for the book by an amusing attack in which he declared it to be the product of his jealous enemies. When he learned that there was in fact a man named Franklin, he published a volume of letters addressed to him disputing the Philadelphia experiments wherever they pointed to conclusions contrary to his own.

Franklin did not reply, but awaited with some impatience the completion of the steeple on Christ Church in Philadelphia so that he might put his theory concerning lightning to trial. A lottery was agreed upon to raise money to finish the spire, and Franklin, not usually an active parishioner, consented to be one of the "managers" of the drawing in order to hasten the work. Before anything was done, however, Louis XV commanded a trial of the Franklin theory in France. It was successful. From a tall building lightning was drawn from a cloud and found to be electricity. "Franklin's idea ceases to be a conjecture," said the report to the French Academy. "It has become a reality."

5

With the news of this triumph on its slow way to America, doubts as to the conclusiveness of a steeple test began to steal into the active mind of the ex-editor. He thought a kite flown into actual contact with a thunderbolt would be the better way of determining if lightning, indeed, were electricity. Fearing ridicule in event of failure and possibly death in event of success, he kept the project from every one except his son William, who was not the small boy shown in many illustrations, but a young man-about-town of twenty-two with an expensive taste in clothes.

Beneath a sky that portended a June thunder-storm, father and son fared forth carrying a kite covered with a silk handkerchief. From its top side projected a stiff piece of wire as a point to attract the lightning. By the time they reached the grass-grown common at Eighth and Race Streets, a tricky wind stirred the sultry air and rain began to fall in great drops. The wet kite reeled, but rose and, catching a fortuitous gust, sailed high into the air. The Franklins took shelter under a cow-shed at a corner of the green.

A mist blotted out nearly everything. The kite was invisible except by flashes of lightning. In the shed Franklin had a Leyden jar in which he hoped to store any current that should come down the wet hemp cord to which a common latch-key was attached. Beyond the key the portion of the cord which Franklin held in his hand was of silk, a non-conductor.

A low dark cloud moved over the common, enveloping the kite. The sky was alive with lightning and thunder was almost continuous. But for what seemed a long time nothing happened, and Franklin was beginning to fear that nothing would happen, when suddenly the fibers on the hemp cord bristled like the tail of an offended cat. To all appearances the cord was charged with electricity, but the way to find out would be to touch the key.

Franklin stretched forth his knuckles, so accustomed to electric shock, not knowing whether in the next moment he would be alive or dead. But in the cow-shed there was only a spark and a harmless little crack. From the feel of his hand, Franklin knew that it was electricity he had drawn from the clouds. He did not know, however, how lucky he had been when he touched the key. As soon as the news of his experiment reached Europe, kites were flown everywhere and Professor Richman of St. Petersburg was killed as he brought his hand in contact with a key.

The daring experiment focused the eyes of the world on Benjamin Franklin. Europeans linked his name to those of Galileo and Newton. The Royal Society of London elected him to membership and published his letters. Yale and Harvard Colleges conferred honorary degrees and the following year, in 1753, the Copley medal of the Royal Society was carried across the ocean by the newly arriving Royal Governor of Pennsylvania, Captain Denny.

The presentation took place at the Governor's mansion amid a flow of oratory and Madeira. The viceroy got tipsy and gravely confidential. Drawing Franklin aside he engaged him in a long conversation on politics and diplomacy. To the world of science that conversation may have been unfortunate. It marked the beginning of a new career for the retired publisher, then only forty-seven, entailing the abandonment of the researches by which, in seven happy years, Benjamin Franklin had brought the science of electricity out of the realm of academic philosophy and put it to work for mankind.

LISTEN, MY CHILDREN

IV

LISTEN, MY CHILDREN

I

When peppery young Appollos Rivoire emigrated from the Isle of Guernsey in the English Channel to Boston in the Colony of Massachusetts Bay, he changed his name to Revere, "so these dunderheads can pronounce it." This completed his Anglicization. Pure French blood coursed the veins of Appollos, but his loyalties were unswervingly British. In Boston he married Deborah Hichborn who proved a thrifty helpmate and contributed no little to his success as a gold- and silversmith. The nicely wrought pitchers and plates of Appollos adorned the sideboards of some of the best homes.

Revere died in 1754 leaving to his son Paul a profitable business. On occasions Paul had been a refractory youth, but the father went to his eternal rest unworried as to what the heir would do with his legacy. Appollos had brought up his son strictly. He had given him more schooling than fell to the lot of the average artizan's boy, but, when the youth was old enough, the father put him into a leather apron and established Paul at a bench in the shop to serve his apprenticeship. Revere, père, had been content, and proud too, with being a good craftsman, but his son developed supplementary ambitions. At school he had met the sons of the gentry. Far from calling them dunderheads, he cultivated their acquaintance. They crowned their academic years by joining the militia and so did Paul. In his classes young Revere had been brighter than most of the students and his superior endowments shone forth again when he took up soldiery in an amateur way.

As a lieutenant of artillery, he participated in a six-months campaign against the French, which was all work and no glory even after having dragged the guns through the wilderness to distant Lake Champlain in bootless quest of the enemy. Home again he led Sarah Orne to the altar and then settled down to his trade.

2

Paul diversified and expanded the business he had inherited. The mark of Revere on a piece of plate or a mug acquired a greater prestige. The grace and delicacy of his designs and the skill of their execution made Paul Revere the best craftsman in the growing, prosperous Colonies. That was not enough for the ambitious silversmith. He made himself the best-known craftsman. In a day when advertising was practically an unborn science, Paul Revere discovered its fundamental benefits. The material advantage went to his work—increased demands for his services and better prices for his silver pieces. This was quite satisfying to the scion of frugal French middle-class ancestry.

But Paul's persistence in keeping his name before the public brought even more desirable results. He made that name as well known in England as those of his fellow-townsmen, John Hancock and Samuel Adams. Notwithstanding his vanity on this particular point, Paul Revere was a worthy citizen, and his advertising did not promote inferior wares. He was never idle. His vitality and ambition urged him to endeavors to which his upper-class contemporaries in their social security were not impelled.

It was a fortunate day for him, and for the Colonies as well, when Paul Revere's diligence awakened his interest in copper-plate engraving. When he had mastered this art, he published a song-book with ninety-six pages of music engraved by himself. He illustrated other books, published several maps and a bird's-eye view of Boston. For the *Royal American Magazine* he executed portraits of Adams and Hancock. He made the seal of

Phillips Academy at Andover. After the war started, he found time amid a clamor of concerns to put on copper a likeness of General George Washington whom he had seen take charge of the troops under the elm at Cambridge.

But it was Paul Revere's engraved cartoons that spread his fame fastest and farthest. Circulating through the Colonies, they quickened resentment toward the measures of repression adopted by the English Government. From the early seventeen sixties he caricatured the principal events of the day with a growing bias against England. The evils of the Stamp Act were pertinently portrayed, and, eventually when that ordinance was repealed, there was a noisy celebration on Boston Common about an obelisk designed and profusely ornamented on each of the four sides with cartoons and patriotic verse by Revere. On one side the figure of an eagle was displayed, this being perhaps the earliest use of that bird as symbolic of the aspirations of the American people. After British troops arrived in Boston, merchants showed in their shop windows none-too-flattering representations of the Red Coats by Revere. When those troops fired on the citizens, March 5, 1770, Revere engraved his most famous illustration— that of the Boston Massacre.

These activities spread the renown of the house of Revere, and the indefatigable Paul continued to branch out. In the *Boston Gazette and County Journal* for July 30, 1770, he inserted a card whose rhetoric could leave no doubt in the reader's mind that Mr. Revere believed himself at the top of his new profession.

"ARTIFICIAL TEETH

"PAUL REVERE . . . would inform all who are so unfortunate as to lose their Teeth by accident or other-ways, that he still continues the Business of a Dentist, and flatters himself that . . . he can fix Teeth as well as any Surgeon-Dentist who ever came from London, he fixes them in such a Manner that they are not only an Ornament, but of real use in Speaking and Eating."

An early patient was Dr. Joseph Warren, the well-known physician. He went away perfectly satisfied with Paul Revere's dental work. Certainly it must have possessed the quality of sturdiness for later Doctor Warren fell at the Battle of Bunker Hill, was buried on the field, and, sometime afterward, when his remains were disinterred, his dentist was able to identify them by the repairs he had made in the Doctor's mouth.

3

As Paul Revere prospered, he acquired the external signs of prosperity. In 1770, he bought, with the aid of a mortgage it is true, a three-story frame house in exclusive North Square. He lived on the upper floors and used the lower for his display room and shop. Once he was arrested, fined and put under a peace bond of ten pounds for settling with his fists a grudge against Thomas Fosdick. But this blemish on an otherwise faultless private life did not disfigure his character in the eyes of the congregation of the New Brick Church where he was a pew-holder and a member of the Standing Committee.

In May of 1773 Sarah Revere died leaving Paul with seven children, the youngest, Hannah, being five months old—satisfactory evidence, certainly, that in his domestic life the unflagging Revere had maintained the zestful tempo that characterized his business and public concerns. In those days neither widow- nor widowerhood was a social state ordinarily borne for long. Paul's mother was still alive, but she was old and some one else was needed in the house to look after the children. Not many weeks elapsed before Paul was writing tender verses to Rachel Walker, making the rough drafts on the backs of his business accounts. He was not a handsome man, and so it must have been that Rachel liked his poems and cheerful disposition. At any rate, in September she was married to the short, thick-set dentist and goldsmith of North Square.

4

Revere stood high in the inner councils of the Sons of Liberty, a secret political society with chapters in nearly every town and hamlet from Boston to Philadelphia. So closely were the affairs of the Sons safeguarded that no full list of membership has come to light, but one knows that Doctor Warren, Samuel and John Adams, the Otises and James Bowdoin were leading lights of the Boston branch and that their influence was felt throughout New England.

The usual foregathering place of the Sons was the Green Dragon Tavern, though they sometimes met at Chase & Speakman's Distillery, or at the quarters of St. Andrews Lodge of the Masonic Order, of which Warren was Master and Revere and most of the other leaders were members. By a formula of passwords and countersigns, visiting Sons could identify themselves and attend. The meetings were occasions for good-fellowship. "We had punch, wine, pipes and tobacco, biscuit and cheese," wrote a diarist of an assemblage at Chase & Speakman's. "Chose a committee to make preparations for grand rejoicings upon the repeal of the stamp act."

But the joy of the Colonists over the abandonment of the stamp tax was not long lived. Other distasteful measures followed, including a levy on tea. The temper of the Bostonians was rising. A series of political clubs, or caucuses, more or less related to the Sons of Liberty, grew up. Revere belonged to the most famous of these, the North End Caucus, which met at the Salutation Tavern and at the Green Dragon. With three tea ships on the way to Boston, the North End Caucus decided upon a bold course. The ships arrived and the night of December 16, 1773, was fixed for the execution of the settled plan.

This was also the night of a regular meeting of St. Andrews Lodge, but the books of the order show that the meeting was postponed "on account of the few members in attendance."

Revere was among those who were absent, as usual busily occupied with more than one work. On this evening he was at Griffin's Wharf where, with fifty others dressed as Indians, he boarded the three ships and emptied the contents of their holds into Boston Harbor.

Nor was he present the next night at the postponed meeting.

He was on horseback well out upon the Post Road to New York, with letters from the Boston Sons to their comrades in New York and in Philadelphia asking support in their refusal to permit the landing of tea in the Colonies.

In eleven days Revere was back from his round-trip journey of six hundred and eighty miles, which would have been good riding for a younger man more habituated to the saddle than this Boston shopkeeper. There is an odd circumstance in connection with the hero of America's most famous horseback ride. For all his experiences in the saddle, Paul Revere's private accounts contain nothing to indicate that he owned a horse. On his longer journeys he rode many horses in relays, but they were always hired or loaned by supporters of the Colonial cause.

The excursion to Philadelphia had taken Revere away from his family at Christmas time, but on his return Boston rang bells in honor of the news he brought, which was that New York and Philadelphia would receive no tea.

George III responded to Boston's defiance with an Act intended as a boycott of the port of Boston. The Sons answered this with an open meeting at Faneuil Hall to which twelve neighboring towns sent representatives. Motions were adopted urging the "other colonies to come into joint resolution to stop importation from and exportation to Great Britain till this act is repealed." Messengers set out to spread the news, and to Paul Revere, whose last ride had added greatly to his renown in circles opposed to the Crown, was delegated the longest and most important journey. Back he galloped to New York and to Philadelphia.

On this mission Revere was more than a courier. He was a diplomat and advocate of the cause of the Colonies. In Philadelphia a public meeting was called to consider the intelligence he brought. A resolution pledging "firm allegiance to the cause of American Liberty" was adopted, recommending the convocation of a "general congress of all the Colonies." As a result the First Continental Congress convened at Philadelphia in September, 1774, thereby increasing the itinerant nature of Paul Revere's responsibilities. Within sixty days he made two additional trips between Boston and the Pennsylvania capital. In December he was in the saddle again, bound not for Philadelphia but for New Hampshire, on a journey second in importance to none in his career.

Dr. Joseph Warren had learned of a Crown order prohibiting the importation of gunpowder by the Colonists and of preparations to send a garrison to Fort William and Mary at Portsmouth where a quantity of arms and powder were stored. At the moment, however, these munitions were guarded by a British captain and only five men. Revere's mission was to induce neighboring Sons of Liberty to seize the war material before the captain should be reenforced.

On a lathered horse Paul presented himself at the farm, near Durham, of John Sullivan, a former militia major. Sullivan organized and led an expedition of three hundred men who surrounded the fort. They were fired upon from three four-pounders and small arms, these being the first shots of the American Revolution. No one was injured, however, and, before the defenders could reload, Sullivan rushed the place and overpowered them. Ninety-seven barrels of powder and considerable arms were taken away and hidden. Six months later they were used at Bunker Hill.

5

Thus events drifted surely toward open rebellion. Samuel Adams and John Hancock were obliged to flee Boston with a price on their heads. But Revere remained in the city, acting as chief of an espionage corps of about thirty young men—printers, clerks and mechanics for the most part—to observe the movements of British troops and of Tories. The corps maintained day and night watches, meeting at the Green Dragon where at each rendezvous each man placed his hand on a Bible and renewed his oath of fidelity and of secrecy. Though fugitives, Hancock and Adams were not far away. They spent the daylight hours at Concord, eighteen miles from Boston, where Hancock presided over the provincial Congress, or legislature. At night they slept at the residence of Reverend Jonas Clarke in Lexington, six miles from Concord. One of the duties of Revere, who reported directly to Doctor Warren, was the protection of Adams and Hancock, and of the Congress itself.

On Saturday night, April 15, 1775, Revere's men informed Warren that the grenadiers and the light infantry encamped on the Common had received confidential orders, which seemed to presage a troop movement, and that there was a stir aboard the troop-ships in the harbor. The next morning Doctor Warren asked Revere to ride to Lexington and put Hancock on his guard against a British foray upon Concord.

This journey, performed in daylight on a tranquil April Sunday, was quite as productive of useful results as the "midnight ride" which Revere made two nights later to the same destination. Apprised of the probable danger, Hancock had Congress order the removal of military supplies from Concord and authorized the raising of an artillery company. On his return to Boston on Sunday evening, Revere tarried at Charlestown to complete his plan to give Hancock the earliest intelligence of any movement of the British troops.

The British could approach Concord by two routes. One was by land, by heading south over the neck of the peninsula on which Boston stands and circling around north by way of Cambridge. But a shorter way would be to cross the harbor in boats directly to Cambridge.

In Charlestown Revere sought out a responsible Son of Liberty named Conant and put the case before him. If the British departed in the daytime their route could be observed from the Charlestown shore. If they started at night, Revere would arrange a signal in the tall spire of Christ Church in Boston—one lantern if by land and two if by water. Then Conant would send riders to forewarn Hancock at Lexington.

Revere then crossed over to Boston on the ferry and informed Robert Newman, sexton of Christ Church, about the signals. Unlike the New Brick Church, at which Revere worshiped,

Christ Church was attended by many Tories, but Newman was a loyal Son of Liberty whom Revere had known as a boy.

6

On Tuesday night, April eighteenth, at ten o'clock, Paul Revere was at home with his large family, lately increased by the birth of a son, when a messenger from Doctor Warren appeared at the door. At the Doctor's house Revere was told that the British were leaving by water, and that William Dawes had set out over the land route to notify Hancock. As a precaution against the possible capture of Dawes, Warren directed Revere to go by way of Charlestown.

But Revere did more than he was asked to do. Hurrying to Newman's home in Essex Street, he told the sexton to show his lanterns, which would start messengers to Lexington ahead of him and of Dawes. Then he returned to his house where he kept boots and a riding cloak always in readiness.

The Charlestown ferry made its last trip at nine o'clock, but Revere had also taken this into account in his preparations. He knew where a rowboat in the service of his espionage corps was secreted under a wharf. On the way to this spot he picked up two Sons of Liberty, one of them a waterman by trade, who suggested the advisability of muffling the oars. The moon and the tide were rising as the dory bearing the three men passed almost in the shadow of a British man-of-war. On board six bells, or eleven o'clock, had just been struck.

On the Charlestown shore Revere was met by Conant and Richard Devens, a friend of Doctor Warren. They had seen the lights in the steeple, and, according to instructions, had sent an express to warn Hancock, Adams, and the country generally. But this was not enough for Paul Revere. Warren had told him to go to Lexington, and Conant, knowing the character of his colleague, had a horse saddled and waiting in Deacon Larkin's stable. While it was being brought, Devens told of seeing a party of British officers that afternoon near Menotomy, now Arlington.

Revere said he would look out for them. He rode away slowly, feeling out the gait and disposition of his horse. He liked the animal, and, as he had a clear, pleasant moonlight night on which to travel, put his mount to a gallop as soon as he had cleared the last houses of Charlestown. But he had proceeded hardly more than a mile when beneath a roadside tree ahead he saw the figures of two mounted British officers. They saw Revere also. One dashed toward him while the other took off up the road to intercept the American in case he should elude the first officer.

Paul Revere knew the lay of the land and it flashed on him that his best chance for safety was in stratagem. Wheeling his horse to the left, he galloped into an unfenced field. One of the Britishers followed, and, being mounted on a fleet horse, attempted a detour to head off the American. But he was unfamiliar with the field and rode straight into a clay bog. While floundering there, the dismayed officer saw his quarry disappear from view. Less than a mile away, Revere gained the Medford Road, another route to Lexington. Passing through Medford he aroused the captain of the Minute Men and galloped on to Menotomy, shouting "The British are coming!" at nearly every house on the way.

Shortly after midnight he reached the hamlet of Lexington where the big, rambling Clarke house stood just off the village Green. Sergeant Monroe and eight members of the local Minute Men company were posted about it. This precaution had been taken by Captain Parker, their commander, upon receipt of news from Devens that British soldiers—two of whom Revere had just eluded—had been seen prowling the road from Boston. When Revere asked admittance, the sergeant said that the family had retired after requesting the militiamen not to make any noise.

"Noise!" panted the perspiring horseman. "You'll have enough noise before long! The regulars are coming out!"

An up-stairs window rattled open and Hancock's head appeared. He recognized the voice below.

"Come in, Revere," he called down.

Candles were lighted and at the courier's story the household was soon astir. In addition to Hancock and Adams, Mr. and Mrs. Clarke were entertaining Hancock's fiancée, the beautiful Dorothy Quincy.

Hancock ordered Sergeant Monroe to ring the church bell summoning the remainder of the Minute Men, and brought down-stairs a sword and a musket which he fell to cleaning, over the protest of Mr. Adams who held that his friend could better serve his country in the council-room than on the field. But Miss Quincy seems to have beamed approval of the warlike preparations of her suitor, and the point was undecided a half-hour later when William Dawes, the second messenger of Warren, rode up.

The two couriers departed for Concord, leaving Hancock and Adams still in debate. On the Green they were joined by a third horseman, young Dr. Samuel Prescott, who gave the Sons of Liberty password. He had been courting a girl and was on his way to his home in Concord.

The three rode together alarming the houses. They had covered half of the six miles to Concord when Dawes and Prescott stopped to arouse a family. Revere continued on the way, riding slowly so that his companions might overtake him. Suddenly, as if they had sprung from the ground, two British officers appeared ahead of him. He shouted to Dawes and Prescott, "Here are two of them, come up!"

But when Revere looked again he saw four British officers with drawn pistols. One of the Englishmen appeared to be in a stern frame of mind.

"God damn you stop, or you're a dead man!"

An unarmed wayfarer looking unexpectedly into muzzles of four pistols is apt to consider himself in a false position. Revere stopped.

Seeing what was up Dawes retreated, dropping his watch in the excitement, but Prescott came on at a furious gallop as if to charge the line of Englishmen who blocked the road. They drew their swords and Prescott checked his horse alongside Revere. Opposite them was a gap in the fence where the bars had been let down, and the two men instinctively put their horses through the opening into a meadow.

Prescott turned his mount to the left, leaped a high stone wall and vanished. He reached Concord, and it appears that Dawes did also. In any event when daylight came he went back and found his watch.

Revere raced toward a woods, intending to abandon his horse there and hide. Instead he rode into a trap, the bars of the fence having been deliberately removed as a lure. Prescott had saved himself by an unanticipated feat of daring. A party of British soldiers emerged from the woods and with drawn pistols ordered Revere to dismount. He obeyed.

An officer "who appeared much of a gentleman," as Paul later said, asked the rider from whence he had come.

"From Boston," said Revere.

The officer asked what time he had left.

"At eleven," said Revere.

The officer seemed surprised. "Sir, may I have your name?"

"My name is Revere."

"Paul Revere?"

"Yes."

8

The British party escorted their prisoner back along the road toward Lexington, a sergeant riding at his side with a cocked pistol. Idleness had no place in the nature of Paul Revere. He occupied himself now by giving an exaggerated account of the alarm he had spread and of the number of Colonists that were rising to oppose the British march. When the church spire at Lexington became visible in the moonlight, the party heard a small volley of musketry from that direction. The British had to do little questioning in order to draw from their captive an admission that this was the signal of assembly for the rebels. They waited to hear no more. Hastily dumping the prisoner in the road, the soldiers took his horse and galloped away.

Paul Revere stumbled through a graveyard and a pasture into Lexington where Captain Parker's Minute Men were gathering on the Green. To the Clarke house he went a second time that night. The scene had not changed. Hancock was still nursing his musket and Adams telling him to put it away. Revere's story seems to have decided the argument in favor of Adams's reasoning, for the two statesmen withdrew on foot to the Widow Jones's residence in Woburn two miles away. Revere accompanied them, and then with young Mr. Lowell, Hancock's clerk, retraced his steps to Lexington to see to the safety of a trunk filled with official papers at the tavern house. Asking the Minute Men for news of the British, Paul was assured that nothing had been seen of them and that they must be far away. Revere wished to assure himself, however, and, mounting to the highest window of the tavern, he peered southeastward. Through the graying dawn he made out the line of the road to Boston. At first glance its undulating surface seemed in motion. Straining his eyes to make out the cause of this phenomenon, he saw that the British were coming.

Revere shouted the news to Captain Parker who began to call out commands to his men standing in groups about the Green. Then Revere and Lowell dived back into the tavern to rescue the trunk containing the archives of the provincial Congress. When they tugged it out upon the Green, Paul noticed that Parker had arranged his men in a line across the Common facing the road from Boston. As the line parted to let the two men pass through with the trunk, Revere heard an officer say:

"Let the troops pass and don't molest them unless they begin first."

The bearers of the trunk had not taken many more steps when they heard a shot—from a pistol, as Revere thought. Then followed two discharges from muskets. The head of the British column was in view and there was smoke in front of it, but

Revere could not see the Minute Men because a house stood in his way. Consequently he did not know for certain which side had fired first.

Breathing heavily, he and Lowell put down the trunk to see what they could. The British advanced a few paces at a run, halted and aimed. A flash and a roll of smoke: the regulars had let go a volley.

The war of the American Revolution had begun and Paul Revere had just witnessed about half of the "battle" of Lexington. But there was work to be done and this industrious man could pause no longer at that early hour in the morning to watch the engagement whose battle-ground was to become a shrine.

"We made off with the trunk," he wrote, summarily concluding a recital of his experiences in a letter to a friend.

THOMAS JEFFERSON GOES SHOPPING

V

THOMAS JEFFERSON GOES SHOPPING

I

A TALL slender Virginian with a boyish face and red hair rode
into Philadelphia in the May sunshine. He had been seven days
in the saddle coming from his home in Charlottesville, which was
better than average traveling in 1776. It lacked but one day of
equaling his record for the route. Twice before he had covered
the road lately, going and coming to make a total of four trips.
As the crow flies Charlottesville is only two hundred and some
miles from Philadelphia, but the meanderings of the road added
another hundred miles over a highway which, in stretches, was
no more than a path through the mountains. Mr. Jefferson was
one of those spare fleshless men who save themselves and save their
horses. He was better than an ordinary horseman, but that was
the only outdoor exercise in which he excelled.

The traveler hastened because he was late. His mother had
died in Virginia; he himself had been taken down with ague;
and there was a tangle of personal accounts to attend to. The
latter were only half straightened out when he left, being too
conscientious to delay longer. But they were on his mind as he
rode. The improvement of Monticello was costing more than
he had calculated, and the war with England threatened his
personal income alarmingly. During the current year he needed
about five thousand dollars to make ends meet, and not half of
this amount was in sight.

At the end of his journey Mr. Jefferson put up his horse at a
boarding stable—perhaps the one convenient to His Majesty's

fine brick Court-House, which patriotic Philadelphians were having a hard time remembering to call by the new name of State-House. Nowadays no one ever thinks of it as anything else than Independence Hall. Jefferson himself moved into his old rooms in the home of Ben Randolph, a cabinet-maker. Before leaving the city the previous winter, Mr. Jefferson had designed a small writing desk which his cabinet-maker-landlord was commissioned to build. Randolph had finished the desk and with pride submitted it to his boarder for approval. Jefferson, too, was a carpenter and he went over the workmanship carefully before counting out the money in payment. He found no flaws, as one can see for himself if one chooses. The desk Mr. Jefferson acquired that day stands in the library of the Secretary of State at Washington.

Even so, the visitor's stay in Philadelphia started off disagreeably. He was behind with his work and his lodgings did not suit him. Philadelphia was a vast city of forty-two thousand people—the metropolis of the Colonies. It was twelve thousand larger than its nearest rival, New York, and much more imposing because of its greater wealth and smarter airs. But these splendors meant little to young Mr. Jefferson, a country lawyer, unaccustomed to city ways. Virginia was the largest and richest of the Colonies. Its population of seven hundred thousand placed Pennsylvania, with four hundred thousand, a distant second, but the largest city in Virginia was Richmond, with three thousand inhabitants. Williamsburg, the capital, had only fifteen hundred, and Mr. Jefferson's home-town of Charlottesville was not much more than a wide spot in the road. So the lawyer felt cramped and out-of-place in the midst of a bewildering beehive of human beings like Philadelphia. It was hot when he arrived and it became hotter. In a week the country gentleman from Virginia moved into the suburbs.

He chose new quarters in the residence of Mr. Graaf, a German bricklayer, whose thrifty wife took in lodgers. Their three-story brick house stood in a field, on the lot which is now at the southwest corner of Seventh and Market Streets. Mr. Jefferson engaged the second floor for thirty-five shillings, or about four dollars and thirty-seven cents a week. The apartment consisted of two large chambers, airy and comfortable, though a far call from what the young southerner was accustomed to at home. Doubtless few suspected this, however, because of Mr. Jefferson's habitual reserve concerning his personal affairs.

The bricklayer's good-looking lodger had one of the finest residences in America. He had only recently moved in, and was carrying on further enlargements and improvements. On the summit of a mountain called Monticello, overlooking Charlottesville and the country for miles around, the house was filled with clever contrivances designed by the owner—a pair of enormous self-closing doors, for instance, and concealed in the dining-room mantelpiece a contraption for noiselessly hoisting wine from the cellar. The grave young colored man who conducts visitors through Monticello to-day will demonstrate it for them and explain that posterity should remember Thomas Jefferson as the inventor of the dumb-waiter.

The elegance of Mr. Jefferson's mansion in Virginia was responsible for the modest tone of his surroundings in Philadelphia. The squire of Monticello had laid out so much on his new place that he was strapped for ready cash.

A few days after establishing himself at Graaf's, Mr. Jefferson noted in the little book in which he kept a minute record of his pocket expenses that he paid a shilling to see a monkey. Mr. Jefferson was an advanced thinker on many subjects, including the sciences, but nothing anticipating the Darwinian theory grew out of that visit to the Colonial capital. More closely allied to Mr. Jefferson's intentions was the mission of another caller whom Mrs. Graaf had received a day or so before the polite southerner had rapped on her door. We fancy this visitor rapped a bit more briskly than Mr. Jefferson and was rather more businesslike in his conversation. He had asked the lady of the house to exhibit the articles of lead she owned.

The likelihood is that Mrs. Graaf knew what her caller was about. Probably neither she nor her husband read the newspapers, but this news concerning lead was the sort that would get around regardless of the press. Philadelphia was fortifying. It did not wish to share the fate of Norfolk, in Virginia, or Falmouth, in Maine, which towns had been visited by the British fleet and set on fire. Jefferson had served on a committee of Congress to inspect Philadelphia's new defenses, which consisted of armed row-galleys, an invention of the handy Doctor Franklin, and log impediments to be sunk in the river as a barrier to frigates. A civilian body called the Committee of Safety was cooperating with the military in assembling metal for bullets. The Committee had published an order that inhabitants should sell their old lead for sixpence a pound. Clock weights were exempt, "the iron weights to replace them being not yet made." Three men were sent around to knock at every door in Philadelphia and make purchases, which were voluntary, of course, but—

". . . if any person should be so lost to all sense of the public good as to refuse, a list of their names is directed to be returned to the Committee."

We feel sure that Mrs. Graaf did not refuse, and probably did less concealing than was customary, for, like her quiet roomer, she was an ardent patriot. But Thomas Jefferson was giving up more than a few articles of lead. He was serving in the Continental Congress while his neglected affairs at home were getting into the mess which finally swept away nearly all he owned.

About sixty gentlemen in pigtails and silk stockings sat in a room in the State-House which they filled to the point of crowding. This was the Continental Congress, of which Lord Chatham has said that for "solidarity of reasoning, force and wisdom of conclusion" no body ever surpassed it. But the appreciative Englishman could have observed the actual sessions of the Congress for a long time before picking Thomas Jefferson as one who contributed anything especially to the remarkable qualities named. Jefferson was not even rated very highly by most of his colleagues. He had been in Congress for a year, but John Adams, of Massachusetts, had "never heard him utter three sentences together."

3

Mr. Jefferson's obscurity as a legislator was due to the fact that parliaments are seldom captivated by silent men. Jefferson had an abhorrence for public speaking which he never conquered. His age—Jefferson was thirty-three in 1776—also was against him. He was overshadowed by older and more vocal men in his own delegation. Yet a few were beginning to perceive that the member from Charlottesville was no ordinary man. Although helpless in debate, he was explicit and decisive on committees. The name of Thomas Jefferson began to show up more and more among the committee assignments. Often he would do most of a committee's work, while another member, who talked well, would present the report and receive most of the credit.

Out of Congress the repressed but increasingly useful Jefferson seemed a different man. He was gay and good company—fond of dining and dancing, a glass of good wine and a fast horse. He could sing and play a fiddle agreeably.

Mr. Jefferson had two violins. One of them cost five hundred dollars and the investment had proved worth while. It had helped him to persuade a comely, wealthy and much sought after young widow to become Mrs. Jefferson. So, except for his financial entanglements, the cares of the world rode rather lightly on the slender shoulders of this Virginia gentleman, who stood on the threshold of immortality—no one suspecting that fact less than himself.

On the seventh of June, when Mr. Jefferson had been in Philadelphia three weeks, Richard Henry Lee, of Virginia, rose in his powdered wig and introduced a resolution:

"Resolved, That these United Colonies are, and of right ought to be, free and independent States, that they are absolved from all allegiance to the British Crown, and that all political connection between them and the State of Great Britain is, and of right ought to be, totally dissolved."

The break with Great Britain long had been a topic in the air. The members of Congress had discussed it for months—in their lodgings, at the taverns where they took their meals, on their walks to and from the State-House where they met. Yet, not until now, had the subject been mentioned on the floor of the House. It had been excluded by tacit agreement because of the difference of opinion which still existed on the question of independence. But Mr. Lee was bound by instructions from the people of Virginia, and had no choice but to introduce his resolution. It caused a heated debate, and next day further consideration of the brief but momentous document was postponed for three weeks.

4

Leaving the State-House Mr. Jefferson strolled along Chestnut Street looking in the windows of the stores. It was a form of recreation—a very satisfactory form, because it also had its practical side. A Blue Ridge Virginian got in touch with America's greatest market so seldom that every trip to one of the cities, regardless of the principal errand, was also a shopping expedition. To-day Mr. Jefferson purchased for his house some new-fashioned window-shutter fasteners, a find which delighted the shopper and momentarily released his mind from more serious thoughts. The events of the past few days filled him with an acute dismay. He regretted the postponement of the Lee resolution and had voted against postponement. Then, besides, he had just drawn another committee assignment—no very important committee this time, as he thought, but it would be a responsibility nevertheless. Jefferson's committee work was piling up. He was on six such bodies already, and, though others might shirk committee work, Jefferson never did. He was up at five-thirty in the morning, putting in two hours at his writing desk before going to Smith's City Tavern for breakfast.

The new committee did not have any special name, but it was charged with writing a manifesto, or declaration, on the subject of independence—a sort of popular advertisement and recommendation of the Lee resolution. This resolution would not come up again for three weeks, and even then action on it might be further postponed. In that case the committee's labors would be of no immediate use. Jefferson had so much other work to do that, given his own way in the matter, he would have crossed this bridge when he came to it.

He was not given his own way, however. Of the five members of the committee two simply ignored the assignment. That left Franklin, John Adams and Jefferson. Of these Adams said that at present he could be of no assistance. Other matters engrossed his attention, and furthermore he already had made himself "obnoxious" by his constant clamor for independence. Therefore the Congress would be less critical if it were known in advance that Mr. Adams had had little to do with the present committee's work. As for Doctor Franklin, who was the most important man in Congress, no one expected him to give his time to details. Thus it was that the Virginia lawyer sat down, none too eagerly, to perform the committee's task.

Mr. Jefferson invariably read the newspapers. It was a habit that served him well in this instance. The current press informed him of the attitude of the public mind which he was to address on the subject of independence. An article in the *Virginia Gazette* of Williamsburg gave him some especially valuable material for his composition. He had only to polish up the wording. Columns of advertisements, like these, in the home paper also quickened the young statesman's receptive mind to the changing temper of the times:

"I intend to leave the Colony immediately.
"THOMAS STEEL."

"The Schooner Rebecca, John Harvey, Commander, now lying in Wycomico, near the Mouth of the Potowmack River, well fitted, will take Passengers to any part of Britain. . . . Each Passenger to pay twenty Guineas, and find his own Bedding."

"I intend for *England* immediately, to return in a few months.
"Anthony Roxburgh."

The Tories were pulling out, and, notwithstanding the note of optimism expressed by Mr. Roxburgh, the national spirit for independence was on the rise.

Such items interested Mr. Jefferson from a personal as well as from an official point of view. Among these departing loyalists were law clients, old friends and neighbors, and chums at college, even kinsmen, at whose homes Jefferson had spent many a pleasant sojourn in the enjoyment of old Virginia hospitality, and with whom Jefferson's differences of opinion, even now, were purely political. Yet he was preparing to draft the document which would separate him from these pleasant people for ever. When the trouble first started between the Colonies and the mother country, few thought independence would result. But matters had gone too far now.

"I purpose leaving the Colony soon. Those to whom I am indebted are desired to apply for payment.
"Robert Donald."

Most of the Tories were wealthy and could afford to pay their debts. The *Gazette* was watched closely for items such as these. Jefferson could use any money that was owing him. His law practise which had been bringing in three thousand dollars a year had been practically abandoned. Last year his plantations had yielded a profit of scarcely two thousand dollars and he was running behind. His "family," as he called it, consisted of one hundred and seventeen persons besides his wife and little daughter Martha. There were thirty-four whites and eighty-three slaves,

rare judgment and literary skill the essence and some of the form
of three already existing documents.

6

June continued to be a month crowded with small but significant
triumphs for the cause of independence. One warm day the *Evening Post* described a little scene which Jefferson could have witnessed from his window.

"Yesterday the grand question of INDEPENDENCY was proposed to the first, second, fourth and fifth battalions . . . consisting of about two thousand officers and men. Against it in the
first battalion, four officers and twenty-three privates; second battalion, two privates; fourth and fifth battalion unanimous for
independence. The lieutenant colonel of the third battalion refusing to put the question gave umbrage to the men. . . . Take
heed, Tories, you are at your last gasp!"

In the *Virginia Gazette* Jefferson read the Bill of Rights which
the Virginia Legislature had adopted on June twelfth. In the
Bill these lines occur:

"All men are by nature free and independent and have certain
inherent rights of which . . . they cannot by any compact deprive
or divest their posterity, namely, the enjoyment of life and liberty
. . . and pursuing and obtaining happiness and safety."

With a little help from Franklin, Jefferson turned this into one
of the world's most famous phrases:

"We hold these truths to be self-evident, that all men are created
equal, that they are endowed by their Creator with certain unalienable Rights, that among these are Life, Liberty and the pursuit
of Happiness."

Next Mr. Jefferson picked up a paper of his own composition, which he had written in his rooms in Philadelphia expecting to have it incorporated in the new Virginia constitution. He saw a chance to put this idle writing to immediate use and did so. He incorporated it almost bodily into his Declaration, where it appears as twenty-two of the twenty-eight enumerated reasons for separating from Great Britain.

The third document of which Jefferson availed himself was R. H. Lee's resolution, which he copied word for word.

Mr. Jefferson then rolled up the four sheets of paper he had covered with writing and took them to Franklin and Adams. Franklin was laid up with gout that week, so Jefferson saw him at his rather pretentious residence farther down on Chestnut Street. The wisdom of Franklin shines through in small matters as well as large, but bear in mind that the tentative literary composition of Thomas Jefferson was considered small potatoes indeed. The important thing was the Lee resolution.

Benjamin Franklin was seventy-two years old. He knew the world as a philosopher, a politician, a diplomat, a scientist, an editor. In this instance he was the editor. Adjusting his silver-rimmed spectacles, he took Mr. Jefferson's manuscript and went over it with a kindly master's critical faculty.

"When in the course of human events it becomes necessary for a people . . ." He read that far and paused. His pen struck out the weak "a" and made it read *"one* people."

" . . . causes which impel them to threaten separation." Old Ben's quill was busy again. Out went the equivocal "threaten" in favor of simple *"the."*

"We hold these truths to be sacred and undeniable . . .," wrote Mr. Jefferson. "We hold these truths to be *self-evident,"* revised Editor Franklin.

Franklin made eleven changes in Jefferson's manuscript—seldom more than a word or two in any one place—but each change bears the touch of genius.

On June twenty-eighth the Lee resolution came before Congress again and on July second it was passed. The United States of America was an accomplished fact.

On July third the Congress began consideration of four sheets of paper which a stammering young man with red hair had laid before the house.

7

The polite suggestions of Franklin and Adams gave way to the clamorous criticism of sixty men in pig-tails and silk stockings. They objected to this; they did not like that. Being unable to speak on his feet, Jefferson was powerless to defend his paper. That task was earnestly undertaken by Adams while Jefferson squirmed in his chair. Kind-hearted old Doctor Franklin came and sat beside him. "Now you see," said Franklin, "why I avoid drafting state papers." He related an ancedote of his days as a journeyman printer, which Jefferson could repeat and laugh at fifty years later. A friend of his, Franklin said, set up a shop displaying a handsome sign: "John Thompson, Hatter, Makes and Sells Hats for Ready Money." Below was a picture of a hat. Well, first one and then another offered suggestions as to how to improve the sign and pretty soon all John had left was his name and the figure of a hat.

The criticism of Congress was continued on July fourth. Mr. Jefferson was up at six o'clock, looking at his thermometer. It registered sixty-eight, the coolest it had been for several mornings. At nine o'clock Mr. Jefferson was in his place at the State-House. Speaker Hancock called the Congress to order, and the consideration line by line of Mr. Jefferson's paper was resumed.

As the morning wore on it grew warmer. The powdered wigs were hot and sweaty. John Adams was on his feet, the defender of the Declaration. Mr. Jefferson sat in silence, unconsciously practising his habit of the observation of small details which sometimes have important bearing on large things. He watched the flies swarm through the window from the livery-stable near by and assail the legs of the debaters. Handkerchiefs were used alternately to mop perspiring brows and flick the buzzing visitors from silk-stockinged shanks. Those flies, thought Mr. Jefferson, are on my side.

[97]

The climax came early in the afternoon. The Congress had talked itself out. The debate languished. A motion was put and seconded. State delegations voted under the unit rule. Every vote was aye. The Declaration of Independence had been adopted.

The corrected draft was hurried off to John Dunlap, a printer who worked until late that night fulfilling a rush order for printed copies. The next morning these imprints, or "broadsides," were started by pony express throughout the Colonies to be read to all troops and proclaimed in cities and towns.

8

All and all, Mr. Jefferson's handiwork had come off much better than John Thompson's sign. After a day and a half of picking and pecking, Congress left the document substantially as it found it—thanks largely to Adams—and several of the changes were unmistakable improvements. But Mr. Jefferson did not think so. Particularly he disliked the deletion of his reflection on King George for not suppressing the slave trade.

"He has waged a cruel war against human nature itself, violating the sacred rights of life and liberty in the persons of a distant people who never offended him, captivating and carrying them into slavery . . . This piratical warfare, the approbrium of *infidel* powers, is the warfare of the *Christian* king of Great Britain, determined to keep open a market where MEN are bought & Sold . . ."

This sounds more like the declamation of a Massachusetts abolitionist of a succeeding generation than the Colonial Virginia master of eighty-three slaves. It was stricken from the Declaration at the request of Georgia and of South Carolina, whose protests were supported by New England delegates, mindful of the interest of the hardy Yankee sea captains who made their livings in the slave-carrying trade.

But, as he had done at times before, Mr. Jefferson sunk his disappointment in a tour of the Chestnut Street shops. He bought a new thermometer for nine dollars and thirty-five cents, seven pairs of gloves for Mrs. Jefferson for three dollars and thirty-seven cents, and "gave in charity" thirty-one cents. The next day he replenished his stock of writing-paper at an outlay of thirty-one cents, and the day after that invested in a shilling's—twelve and a half cents—worth of beer. His rooms now fairly filled with the results of his shopping excursions, Jefferson began his preparations to leave Philadelphia.

While at work on the Declaration, he had decided to retire from Congress. Henceforth, he planned to live in Virginia where he hoped to serve his country and find some time to keep an eye on his personal concerns as well. Something had to be done about them, with particular reference to finances.

On July eighth beginning at noon the serenity of Philadelphia was disturbed by the ringing of bells. One of them was in the steeple of the State-House, prophetically inscribed, "To Proclaim Liberty. . . ." The din announced the first public reading of Thomas Jefferson's Declaration. The clamor of the bells continued into the night. Mr. Adams, seeking repose to refresh his mind for the problems of the morrow, complained that the noise kept him awake. Probably young Mr. Jefferson felt much the same way, but consoled himself with the reminder that shortly no more of this sort of thing could disturb his slumbers on his quiet Virginia mountaintop. A few weeks later, he packed away with his luggage the original draft of the Declaration and carried it off to Monticello.

9

For forty-seven years this manuscript, with the interlined changes in the hands of Benjamin Franklin and John Adams, lay untouched in Jefferson's private files before the country suddenly awoke to the fact that the Declaration of Independence was an imperishable state paper. A curious squabble between two publishers had reintroduced the document to the American people. With the surprised satisfaction which unanticipated recognition brings to authors, Thomas Jefferson received a nation's tardy acclaim of the forgotten paper he had composed in a bricklayer's house in Philadelphia. A lonely widower of more than eighty, living in the great manse of Monticello by tolerance of creditors, amid the mute companionship of books, fumbled with faded memories. Then he took a pen and revised the wording designed for his tombstone to include: "Author of the Declaration of American Independence."

THE WRONG ROAD

VI

THE WRONG ROAD

I

On the night of the nineteenth of September, 1780, Private John Paulding of the First Westchester County Regiment of Militia, a prisoner of war in the hands of the British army in New York City, escaped from the North Dutch Church, which had been turned into a military prison. Eluding the English sentries north of the city, he was again in Westchester County and reentered the American lines near Tarrytown.

The flight of Private Paulding did not greatly disturb His Majesty's forces. It had occurred at a moment when General Sir Henry Clinton was occupied by larger matters. Within a few days Sir Henry expected to have the war won for his sovereign. Indeed, he had already written to London about the terms of peace to be offered the Colonies. Sir Henry was not an illiberal foe, nor without foresight, and so suggested rather generous conditions.

While Private Paulding had been working his cautious way northward, another soldier of the Revolution also was saying farewell to New York. Major John André was the guest of Colonel Williams's mess that evening. Colonel Williams commanded the Eightieth Infantry of British Regulars. He was fortunate to have André at his table. None was insensible to the honor of being host to the adjutant-general of the British Army in America and right-hand man of Sir Henry Clinton. Major André was twenty-nine years old, brave, able, gay and handsome. He brought the gathering at Colonel Williams's to a close by mounting a chair and leading the singing of a resounding barracks ballad entitled, *How Stands the Glass Around?*

That was in the small hours. After a snatch of sleep John André set out on a bold adventure.

2

Sundown next day found André, as well as Private Paulding, safe within the American lines. The British officer was safe because he was on board the man-of-war *Vulture,* which was anchored off Teller's Point—now Croton Point—thirty miles up the river. But the *Vulture* dared not venture farther than the Point, beyond which the Hudson gradually narrows from a width of three miles to half a mile. Lofty cliffs look down from both sides of the stream. Those heights were fortified for miles and were vigilantly manned by more than one-fourth of Washington's army.

The loss of the Highlands of the Hudson would have opened a road for the British from the Atlantic Ocean to Canada. This would have cut the Colonies in two. The British held New York City with twelve thousand soldiery and a fleet. The sole remaining link for the passage of American troops between New England and the South was a ferry below West Point. So Washington was obliged to hold the Highlands at all hazard. To this task was allotted three thousand men. Their commander had been selected with care, Washington's choice finally falling upon Benedict Arnold.

The fortunes of the Continentals were low. Washington's army was reduced to eleven thousand four hundred men, half of whom were militia whose terms would expire in three months. Prospects for reenlistments were dark. Washington had just attempted a campaign for recruits to bring his force up to thirty-five thousand. It had failed sadly. His troops were ill clad, badly fed and rarely paid. Some had drawn no money for three years. The Treasury was empty and credit was poor. Congress was jealous of the army when it won and nagged when it did not win.

Washington based his immediate hopes on the French. Rochambeau and De Lafayette were encamped in Rhode Island with five thousand troops. While Private John Paulding and Major André, their fates soon to be curiously joined, were making their separate ways into the American lines along the Hudson, General Washington was a short distance away at Hartford, Connecticut, conferring with the French Generals about getting their men into action.

When Major André boarded the *Vulture,* his youthful head carried the details of a scheme by which he hoped to win the war practically single-handed. For fifteen months he had been at one end of the most interesting conspiracy ever laid on American soil, and now in fifteen minutes' time he expected to learn the result of these persistent efforts. Aboard the *Vulture* he was to receive a mysterious stranger, and his hopes were based on the anticipation that this caller would prove to be Major General Benedict Arnold.

3

Benedict Arnold was a singular man, possessed of many of the qualities of a capable military leader. He had done good work earlier in the war, though there has been a tendency on the part of historians and biographers to over-emphasize the brilliancy of this chapter of his career. Arnold was seldom happy in his relations with his fellow-officers and some of the reasons for this are not difficult to understand. He was a spendthrift with a short memory for personal loans. He was extremely vain and one could not always be sure that he was telling the truth. These defects of character were advertised by those who had been inconvenienced by them, and perhaps by others who were merely jealous of Arnold's abilities as a soldier.

But as Washington needed all the good men he could find he had rather taken Arnold's part, and decided on an attempt to salvage the good in him and put it to the service of the Colonial cause. To this end, when the British evacuated Philadelphia, Arnold was given the command there with a small force. Philadelphia was a soft and desirable berth, but Arnold was lately out of bed and his wounds still troubled him.

The smart society of Philadelphia appealed to the luxury-loving General and his health and spirits were restored quickly enough. As a matter of course he met Peggy Shippen, one of the belles of the city and daughter of a rich Tory. During the previous winter when the British were in Philadelphia living on the fat of the land and Washington a few miles away at Valley Forge, the Shippen mansion had been the scene of many splendid entertainments for His Majesty's officers. Now Benedict Arnold was received with equal honors and attentions.

The American Commander professed his love for Peggy at once, but success did not immediately prosper this courtship because Peggy's heart had been at least half won already by a young gentleman who was fighting on the other side. His name was John André.

Nevertheless, in a few months, the captivating Major General and beautiful Peggy Shippen were married. The bridegroom rented a large house and shortly owed eighteen thousand dollars. With tradesmen pressing for payment, his situation was uncomfortable. Perhaps Arnold appealed to his wealthy Tory father-in-law, but if he did it seems to have been without the result the embarrassed debtor sought. At any rate, all we know is that General Arnold undertook most extraordinary means of replenishing his purse. He wrote a letter to New York and signed it "John Moore."

Some time thereafter Washington ordered his commandant at Philadelphia to field duty again, assigning him to the vital post of West Point. This unexpected change suited "John Moore's" plans so well that Arnold was disturbed a little at first. Could Washington suspect anything? In any event a greater degree of caution could do no harm.

4

Accordingly, the next time Benedict Arnold shut himself in a room to write a letter to New York he signed it "Gustavus." This letter was addressed to Sir Henry Clinton and took up matters precisely where "John Moore" had left off. Indeed it was written in the same obviously disguised hand. The first of the "John Moore" letters had purported to be from an American general who was willing to turn his coat. As Clinton's adjutant it fell to the lot of Peggy Shippen's old suitor, John André, to respond to this communication. Thus the correspondence had developed, but in such guarded form that little progress was made. André signed his letters "John Anderson." He assumed the rôle of a merchant in New York. The letters were couched in the terms of mercantile transactions, and in the course of numerous exchanges a code was developed which baffles experts to this day. André and Clinton appear not to have been sure that "John Moore" and "Gustavus" was Arnold, and, if so, that Arnold really was sincere in his treasonable proposals. But when Arnold went to West Point, he had something tangible to offer to the British and the negotiations took on new life.

André had not forgotten Peggy Shippen who was a mother now. When dispatching code messages to "Gustavus," the chivalrous Major sometimes sent along ribbons and other pretty things for Mrs. Arnold's little boy. Finally the more serious aspects of the correspondence came to a head. Clinton resolved to discover if "Gustavus" were in truth Arnold and if he would hand over West Point, the key to the Highland forts, for a consideration. It was arranged that the author of the "Gustavus" letters should come aboard the *Vulture* and meet André there. "Gustavus" was to devise a legitimate military excuse for openly visiting the British war-ship under a flag of truce.

On the appointed date, André arrived aboard the *Vulture* about fifteen minutes early for the interview. But he waited for his visitor long beyond this quarter of an hour. No Arnold appeared that day or the next. André was disappointed, also suspicious. Either Arnold had cold feet or his proposed treason was a stratagem to entice André into the American lines. Luckily the Major was aboard a war-ship in the river, and could get back safely.

André had about made up his mind to return to New York

when, on the second night, at ten o'clock, a rowboat approached the *Vulture* under a flag of truce. Arnold was not in it, however. The passenger identified himself as Joshua Hett Smith, a wealthy American whom the British regarded as a rebel, though Joshua's brother was a well-known Tory. Smith asked to speak to André, and told him that General Arnold had found it impossible to come aboard, but was anxious to meet André—or "Anderson," as Smith called him—on shore.

This was not the bargain "Gustavus" had made. He was to meet André on the ship.

5

Before sending André up the Hudson, Sir Henry Clinton had given his adjutant explicit instructions on three points. He was not to remove his uniform. He was not to enter the American lines on shore. He was to receive nothing from Arnold in writing. The caution which prompted these directions is obvious. But André was a daring young man. Dazzling rewards seemed within his grasp. He was willing to risk everything—and did so. Despite the urgent remonstrances of the captain of the *Vulture* he climbed down into the boat with Smith and they were pulled toward the western shore.

Rightly enough André found Arnold waiting on the edge of a fir thicket below the village of Haverstraw. He led the Englishman into the tangle of trees, telling Smith to wait by the river bank. The civilian resented this exclusion. He wanted to be in on what was happening, or rather, what he fancied to be happening. Smith was the dupe and tool of Arnold, and had no suspicion of the real business that was afoot. But what the story Arnold had told him of that evening's work lacked in truth was made up by ingenious plausibility.

It was midnight and there was no moon. In the darkness of the fir thicket André could not see his hand before him. But he could hear Arnold's voice, and that voice had not spoken long before the young Englishman dismissed any qualms which the eerie circumstances of his adventure may have formed in his mind concerning his disobedience of orders in going ashore. The American outlined a project which must fairly have taken away André's breath. Arnold would surrender not only the supremely important Highland forts, but he would contrive the capture of George Washington by the British army!

The plot was to be carried out in such a way as to give the traitor a coat of whitewash for historical purposes. There was to be no open surrender. The British were to embark an expedition at New York, ostensibly for the Chesapeake. But the ships would head up the river instead, and attack. Arnold would have his troops distributed so as to render this "surprise" certain of success. The date was fixed for September twenty-seventh. This was only five days off. On September twenty-seventh Washington was due at West Point on his return from Hartford. Arnold would so arrange that, in the confusion of the action, the Commander-in-Chief and his staff should fall into British hands. Thus the last prop would be knocked from under the Colonial cause. Arnold, of course, would be "captured," too—taken fighting. As a "prisoner" he would reflect on his situation, decide that the Colonies were beaten, and sue for the King's mercy. This would be forthcoming, with additional rewards in the form of a brigadier-general's commission in the British Army and ten thousand pounds in gold.

Arnold gave André a series of documents describing the fortifications and the Americans' plans of defense. No one knows why André accepted these papers. The gist of them could easily have been committed to memory. The best guess seems to be that André wanted to make sure that Arnold was in his power. The documents were all in Arnold's handwriting and they established his treason.

The conspirators had so much to say to each other that the coming of dawn found them still talking. They adjourned to Joshua Hett Smith's house on a bluff four miles away to finish. En route they passed an American picket. Arnold gave the countersign and received a salute. André hurried by, thankful for the blue cape which reached to his boot tops and concealed his uniform. At Smith's they ate breakfast. Then, everything settled, André prepared to leave in the rowboat for the *Vulture,* and hasten to New York to apprise Sir Henry Clinton of the wonderful news.

Just then a cannon shot was heard. It was followed by another and another. The conspirators ran to a window. Smith's house commanded a view of the river for miles. The watchers saw the *Vulture* enveloped in smoke. She was under fire from the east bank of the river. André was frightened. Had Arnold deceived him? Arnold was thunder-struck. Had his treachery been discovered? The cannonade lasted for an hour, and the *Vulture* was driven down-stream, leaving André high and dry.

6

Arnold was soon able to relieve the tension in some degree. He convinced André that he had not been deceived. He boldly assumed that by no possible chance could the attack on the *Vulture* have been due to the discovery of his plot. And in this General Arnold was correct. An impetuous Canadian had caused all the trouble—little suspecting the full extent of it. History has slight acquaintance with his name, and the same thing is true of several other contributors to this drama. It was James Livingston, and he was the colonel of the Second Canadian Regiment, part of a tiny expeditionary force which friendly Canadians had sent to help the American cause.

The presence of the *Vulture* in American waters off Teller's Point, safely out of range of the Highland forts, had annoyed Colonel Livingston. He liked action. Two or three times he had asked Arnold to lend him a cannon, so he could drag it down the river and shoot up the *Vulture*. Naturally, Arnold evaded these requests. Finally, by his own devices, Livingston got an old brass four-pounder. He asked Colonel John Lamb, commanding the artillery, for some powder, but the old artillery-man demurred, saying it would be a waste of ammunition to fire at a ship with a four-pounder. But Livingston insisted and finally Lamb issued a small quantity of powder to humor his friend. Then Livingston borrowed a work-horse of William Teller, whose farm occupied Teller's Point, and dragged the gun out to the tip of this projection of land. He did this at night while Arnold and André were whispering in the fir thicket on the other side of the river. In the morning Colonel Livingston began shooting. The *Vulture* was taken by surprise and utterly unprepared for action. Livingston and his handful of men soon had the satisfaction of seeing the British war-ship retreat down the river.

Major André passed an anxious day at the Smith house despite Arnold's assurances that everything would work out all right. It was arranged for Mr. Smith to escort André overland to the British lines. Arnold provided the two with passes. Smith insisted that André exchange his uniform for civilian clothes. André protested that he had no other clothing. Smith went to a closet and brought out a suit of his own—a second-best ensemble which the fastidious André looked at with double disdain, but very reluctantly he put it on. Once out of uniform he knew he became a spy. Of course, he could have thrown away the papers Arnold had given him. Then, if he were taken, his captors might have a hard time proving very much. But André kept the papers. He believed them worth the risk.

At dusk that evening the pair set out on horseback. It was Friday, September 22, 1780. Ferrying to the east side of the river, they landed at Peekskill. The first man they met was Colonel Livingston, still in great spirits over his private fight with the *Vulture*. He knew Smith and invited him and his young friend to supper, but they hastily pleaded another engagement and headed south over a hilly back-country road. At eight-thirty they were challenged by a sentry and taken before an officer who held up a lantern and looked at their passses. The passes were recognized, and, as a special consideration to gentlemen traveling under the personal protection of General Arnold, the officer urged the pair to put up for the night. He said the road was unsafe to travel in the dark. André wanted to go on regardless of the road, but Smith refused and they remained for the night, occupying the same bed. André kept his boots on and did not sleep a wink. Moreover, he disturbed his companion's rest by pricking his bare skin with spurs.

Next morning they were on the road at dawn. Arnold's passes worked like charms, but near Yorktown Heights the horsemen rode squarely into Colonel Samuel Webb of the Third Connecticut Infantry. André said his hair stood on end. Webb knew André well. The acquaintance had been made when the American was a prisoner of war. But for some reason Webb failed to recognize the British officer and the two rode on. When within fifteen miles of the British lines, danger seemed past. There were no more American patrols out, except possibly a few militiamen, and "John Anderson" had General Arnold's personal pass. So Mr. Smith turned back and André continued on alone.

As Smith had some business of his own to attend to at Fishkill, he thought that while on the east bank he might as well go there before returning home. He reached Fishkill that evening and stayed overnight. The next day George Washington and his staff rode into the village, on their way from Hartford to West Point. Smith called to pay his respects and the Commander-in-Chief asked him to remain for dinner.

7

About nine o'clock in the morning André reached McKeel's Corners, now in the village of Pleasantville. He stopped at the gate of Staats Hammond's house, six or seven miles from the British outposts, and safety. Hammond was a sergeant in the First Westchester County Militia, and at home in bed with a wound. Looking from a window, he saw David and Sally, his children, get a drink of water for the good-looking stranger. With a small boy's impulse toward conversation, David remarked that there was an American patrol at Young's Tavern a mile down the road. André decided not to put his pass to another test unless necessary. He thanked the children, gave Sally sixpence and turned his horse, taking the roundabout road to White Plains which goes by way of Tarrytown.

As a matter of fact David's information was incorrect. The direct road to White Plains was unguarded, but the Tarrytown road was not. A patrol of seven young men of the First Westchester, under a sergeant, had been sent out to watch roads to New York. Primarily the patrol was looking for "cow boys," or marauders who drove off Westchester cattle and sold them to the British quartermasters. The patrol divided to watch two roads. John Paulding, in charge of two other privates, took up a position on the outskirts of Tarrytown. Paulding's companions were David Williams and Isaac Van Wart.

Although a home guard organization, the ranks of the First Westchester contained a number of experienced soldiers. Both Paulding and Williams had served in the Continental, or Regular, Army, Williams having been discharged with frozen feet after the Quebec campaign. Westchester militiamen made no pretense at wearing uniforms. They wore whatever they could find. This morning Paulding had on a long green coat, such as was issued to Hessian troops serving with the British—a castoff acquired while he was a prisoner of war in New York City. A neighbor woman in Tarrytown put up a lunch for the soldiers. Another neighbor loaned them a deck of playing cards, and the three men sat under a tree to pass their watch as comfortably as possible.

Presently John André galloped up, trying to read a map without slackening the pace of his horse. They halted him.

"Gentlemen, I hope you belong to our party," said André in answer to the challenge.

"What party is that?" asked Paulding guardedly.

"The lower party," said André, meaning the British who were down the river.

Paulding said they did. These words were a great relief to André, who thereupon committed the astonishing blunder which so mystifies historians.

"I am a British officer," he said. "I have been up the country on particular business."

Later André himself declared he could not explain his words and he did not claim—as often has been said—that Paulding's coat misled him. The explanation probably lay in André's anxiety and fatigue. Several small circumstances indicate that his nerves were on edge, for instance, his addressing three country yokels as "gentlemen."

It was unnecessary for Paulding to continue a deception which had served its end. He announced that he and his companions were American soldiers and that André was a prisoner.

André tried to correct his unfortunate slip by saying he, too, was an American, and had claimed otherwise only to establish the identity of his questioners. He displayed Arnold's pass to prove it. This document had never been questioned before. Sentry after sentry had passed it. But Paulding, an old soldier, was suspicious—without knowing exactly why, being by no means certain that he had found a questionable character. Later he said that, if André had shown the pass at first, they would have permitted him to proceed immediately.

Paulding ordered André to dismount and submit to search. The Arnold papers were found in the prisoner's shoes. They meant nothing to Williams or to Van Wart who could not read. The papers were handed to Paulding who was no scholar, and he pored over them for a long time.

"He's a spy!" he announced finally.

André became persuasive. He offered his horse, saddle, bridle and a hundred guineas for his freedom.

"We would not let you go for a thousand guineas," said Paulding, naming what he considered an impossible sum.

"Then I will give you ten thousand," said André. That was more money than the three poor farmers knew was in the world. André said two of them could hold him as a hostage while the other rode to New York for the money.

The services of Paulding, Williams and Van Wart were not for sale, however. They marched their prisoner twelve miles to the nearest American post and turned him over to Lieutenant Colonel John Jameson, commanding the Second Light Dragoons.

8

If John André had displayed poor judgment when confronted by the three militiamen, he made up for it in the presence of the Colonel. He assured Jameson that it was a great mistake to detain him, which fact could be established if the Colonel would communicate with General Arnold. The Colonel was half convinced and sent André, accompanied by Lieutenant Solomon Allen and a squad of Connecticut militia, for an interview with Arnold at West Point. But the Colonel mitigated this error of judgment by giving the papers that had been found on André to another messenger to deliver to General Washington, who was known to be somewhere on the road between Hartford and Arnold's headquarters.

Colonel Jameson's bungling actions are inexplicable, except to say that no suspicion of Arnold's disloyalty entered his mind. He gave Lieutenant Allen a letter to Arnold, detailing the story of the capture as related by Paulding. He described the papers found on André, saying he thought them "of a very dangerous tendency" for an unexplained civilian to be carrying around. He said that he had sent the originals to Washington. One might assume that perhaps Colonel Jameson was led into his blunder because he did not recognize that the treasonable papers were in Arnold's handwriting—his natural, and not his disguised hand. But Jameson knew Arnold's handwriting perfectly. His act was one of sheer stupidity.

The question now was, which of three things would happen first: André reach Arnold, Washington reach Arnold, or Washington receive the papers betraying Arnold's treachery before Arnold could take steps to intercept them?

This was the state of affairs on the afternoon of Saturday, September twenty-third. A little later Major Benjamin Tallmadge rode up to Colonel Jameson's headquarters. He had been on outpost duty and finding out what had happened was aghast at the Colonel's action. He suggested that the prisoner—who still called himself "Anderson"—should immediately be recalled and detained until Washington had had a chance to see the captured papers. Jameson refused to do this but at length he yielded to a compromise. A courier was dispatched with an order to Allen to bring André back, after which Allen was to proceed to Arnold's headquarters alone and deliver Jameson's letter to Arnold. Jameson insisted on the delivery of this letter.

The courier overtook Allen and André within a few miles of Arnold's headquarters, and the prisoner was turned back on the brink of safety.

9

The next day was Sunday, September twenty-fourth.

André was turned over to Tallmadge for safe-keeping. The moment Tallmadge laid eyes on the prisoner he was sure "Anderson" was no civilian—and his manners unmistakably were British. André was removed to South Salem, a remote village in the Westchester hills, where he was comfortably lodged, provided with a clean shirt and surrounded by a guard of twenty dragoons. André chatted pleasantly with a few of the American officers and then asked for a pen and paper. These were provided. The prisoner amused his guard for a while by making facetious sketches of himself and his captors. Then he wrote a letter, addressed to General Washington, and handed it to Major Tallmadge to read. It began:

"What I have said as yet concerning myself was in the justifiable attempt to be extricated, but I am too little accustomed to duplicity to have succeeded. . . . The person in your possession is Major John André, adjutant general to the British Army."

Tallmadge increased his guard and sent the letter on its way.

The next day was Monday, September twenty-fifth.

Dispatching a messenger in advance to apprise Arnold of his

coming, General Washington, his staff, and the Marquis de Lafayette crossed the river en route for West Point. The receipt of this message was an unpleasant surprise for General Arnold, who had not expected his chief until September twenty-seventh when he had arranged the "surprise" attack by the British and the capture of Washington. Arnold did the correct thing, however. He sent an orderly with a note expressing the hope that the Commander-in-Chief and his party would arrive by breakfast time. Washington responded that they would be there for breakfast.

But the Commander-in-Chief had hardly landed on the western bank when he decided to inspect some of the defenses of the locality. De Lafayette asked if this could not be postponed so as not to keep Mrs. Arnold waiting breakfast.

"Ah, Marquis," replied Washington. "You young men are all in love with Mrs. Arnold. Go and breakfast with her and tell her not to wait for me."

De Lafayette remained with Washington and, instead, Colonel Alexander Hamilton, Washington's Chief of Staff, rode on to inform Mrs. Arnold of the delay and ask her not to postpone her meal.

General Arnold, his wife and the General's staff were waiting breakfast when Hamilton arrived. They asked him to join them and the meal was served. Mrs. Arnold delighted the company with her usual vivacity, but her husband was preoccupied. Washington's early arrival had upset the plan he had given André. By what devices could he detain his chief for three days? That might be done, but then how was he to explain the lax state of his defenses which were prepared to make the British success swift and simple?

Presently a messenger entered. He came from Washington to say that the Commander-in-Chief had finished his inspection and was on his way to Arnold's house.

In a few moments another courier arrived. He was Lieutenant Allen from Colonel Jameson's headquarters. He delivered to Arnold the Colonel's letter.

Never once in his life did Arnold's amazing powers of self-command desert him. No muscle of his face moved as he read the overwhelming news of André's capture.

Folding the note, he placed it in his pocket and calmly concluded an anecdote which Allen's entrance had interrupted. Then he arose and begged to be excused, saying that a trivial emergency required his presence at the defenses, but that he would return as soon as he could and welcome the Commander-in-Chief. Asking to speak to Mrs. Arnold in private, he took her up-stairs and told her he was obliged to flee for his life on the instant, and that they might never meet again. Peggy Shippen fainted.

10

An hour later Washington arrived, and, being informed that General Arnold was at the defenses, the Commander-in-Chief went to find him. He did not find him, however. Leaving his wife insensible, Arnold had kissed his sleeping baby boy, leaped on a horse and ridden down an almost precipitous cliff to the river. There he had boarded a small army sailing scow and fled to the British war-ship *Vulture,* which had come back up the river in search of news of André.

In the middle of the afternoon Washington retraced his steps toward Arnold's headquarters, perplexed at his inability to discover the slightest trace of the General. Alexander Hamilton saw the Commander approaching and hurried to meet him. Colonel Hamilton's countenance was grave. During Washington's absence the courier from Jameson had arrived with the papers that had been found on André. This messenger had been trailing the Commander for twenty-four hours. Another runner had delivered the letter of the providentially detained André. As Washington's Chief of Staff and confidential adviser, Hamilton had opened both communications. Briefly Hamilton sketched the terrible story, including the flight of Arnold and the hysterical condition of his wife, which confirmed everything.

Washington was stunned. Turning to Lafayette he exclaimed: "Whom can we trust now?"

The next few hours reveal much of the essence of the man who won America's independence simply because he had a heart for any fortune. Already the Colonies' cause was reeling. Defeats, desertions, doubts—they had been multiplying fast of late—and, on top of all, the revelation that one of the ablest generals, commanding the most vital of defenses, had gone over to the enemy. None knew how deeply the conspiracy went—who was friend, who was foe in the West Point garrison. Washington's very life might have been in peril from desperate confederates of Arnold in the American lines. A British attack on a betrayed army was expected at any hour.

With devastating energy Washington summoned reenforcements. He transferred troops and commanders to break up any possible traitorous combinations within the ranks, and directed the hundred and one details of putting the Highlands of the Hudson in readiness to resist to the last gasp.

The attack never came, the chief reason being that Washington himself was in possession of the papers containing the British plan of assault which an American general had laid down. Washington could not guess this, however. All he knew was that the British fleet had prepared to sail on what appeared to be a business-like mission. Yet it did not leave New York Harbor. Nothing, simply nothing, happened. From their actions, the British seemed to have been too dazed by the discovery of their scheme and the capture of André to do anything. They needed a Washington.

André was tried as a spy. On the court-martial sat three noblemen who were major generals in the Continental army—De Lafayette of France, Baron von Steuben of Prussia and the American-born Lord Stirling. Washington had no wish to punish André alone; Arnold was the man he wanted. He permitted a young sergeant major from Virginia to risk his life in a rash and unsuccessful attempt to kidnap Arnold on the streets of New York and carry him into the American lines for trial.

The pleasant manners of André endeared him to his captors. At his trial the compunctions of a gentleman impelled the doomed man to try to shield Arnold at his own expense. Or was this a last, little service of chivalry to Peggy Shippen? There has always been a mystery as to the extent of Peggy Shippen's knowledge of this affair. For André himself there was no defense. The evidence against him was unanswerable. The laws of war recognized but one penalty. On the second day of October, 1780, nine days after his capture, Major John André shaved and dressed himself in his uniform with great care. He climbed upon an army baggage wagon, which answered the purpose of a scaffold, and died with perfect courage. His body rests in Westminster Abbey.

II

George Washington obtained medals, pensions and bonuses of land for Privates Paulding, Williams and Van Wart. The Commander-in-Chief himself bestowed the medals and invited the soldiers to dinner. This was an unprecedented honor. Washington was an aristocrat and an austere disciplinarian. During the terrible winter at Valley Forge, he had severely punished a captain for eating with his men.

Taking leave of his guests Washington gave each of them a brace of pistols as his personal presents. He said they would need them as they might expect "to be hunted like partridges." Something of that sort happened. A great outcry, in which many patriotic Americans mistakenly joined, went up against the three soldiers. On the floor of Congress they were called outlaws and thieves, and the implication that they surrendered André because he would not buy his liberty finds a place in several histories. But they outlived much of this malice and at a green old age each died in his bed.

DEGUELO

VII

DEGUELO

I

Most of the boys had been to a fandango the night before last and still felt tired and sleepy. Travis was hard put to get any work out of them. What need to work? Herrera was either a liar or a fool who believed everything he heard. Santa Anna with an army already across the Rio Grande? Preposterous! Let the excitable tenderfeet lose sleep over a tall tale such as that.

William Barret Travis was no tenderfoot in Texas. His soldiers might not take much stock in the story that Herrera had brought to Bexar, but the inhabitants seemed to view matters in a different light. These easy-going Spaniards bestirred themselves to activities difficult to assign to any light motive. An atmosphere of suppressed excitement hung over the sunlit stone and adobe town. There was a great hurrying to and fro along the narrow streets and through the white dust of the plazas. Big two-wheeled carts loaded with household goods made their way in long files over the roads that led into the country.

On the morning of February 23, 1836, Travis posted a sentinel in the tower of San Fernando Church to keep a lookout to the west and, at first sight of anything resembling Mexican troops, to ring the bell. With this precaution the Texan army of occupation very leisurely went about the business of putting the Álamo in a state of defense. The soldiers preferred to lounge about the cantinas and mix with their friendly enemies among the native population. They regretted the departure of so many comely señoritas. The town was dull enough as it was.

This boredom was relaxed, however, when shortly before noon on the twenty-third the population and garrison alike were startled by the furious clanging of the bell in the tower of the Church of San Fernando. An officer scrambled up the dark little stairway. What had the sentinel seen? He had seen Mexicans—cavalry on the heights of Alazan—their lances glittering through the mist of a fine rain. But where were they now? demanded the officer. Gone, said the sentinel—vanished at the first taps of the bell. The officer scanned the horizon. He saw nothing and the sentinel was accused of giving a false alarm. But Travis thought it prudent to investigate the soldier's story. Dr. John Sutherland and Scout John W. Smith had their horses saddled, and volunteered to reconnoiter.

That was the way of the soldiery of the Texas Revolution—time to prepare for a fight when the enemy was in sight. Texans made the poorest peace-time soldiers on earth and the best in battle, where their feats over and again seemed beyond belief. A good man was required to command them in battle or out. Buck Travis was a good man, but when there was no fighting to do he had his hands full. A few days before the incident of the sentinel in the tower, he had written a letter to Henry Smith, the Governor of Texas.

"If you had taken the trouble to answer my letter I should not now have been under the necessity of troubling you. My situation is truly awkward and delicate. Col. Neill left me in command, but wishing to give satisfaction to the volunteers here and not wishing to assume any command over them, I issued an order for the election of an officer to command them with the exception of one company of volunteers that had previously engaged to serve under me. Bowie was elected by two small companies, and since his election has been roaring drunk all the time, has assumed all command . . . turning everything topsy turvy. If I didn't feel my honor and that of my country compromitted, I would leave here instantly. . . . I hope you will order immediately some regular troops here as it is more important to occupy this post than I imagined when last I saw you. It is the Key to Texas. . . . Without a foothold here, the enemy can do nothing against us. . . . I do not solicit the command of this post, but as Col. Neill . . . is anxious for me to take command, I will do it. . . . The enemy is on the Rio Grande with 1000 strong, and is making every preparation to invade us. By the 15th of March I think Texas will be invaded and every preparation should be made to receive them."

2

Governor Smith's situation was quite as "awkward and delicate" as that of the quasi-commander at San Antonio de Béxar. Three months before, in November, 1835, the Mexican province of Texas, largely settled by Americans, had revolted against Santa Anna who had repudiated the liberal professions that had actuated the Mexican people a few years earlier to win their independence of Spain. Texas had not declared its independence, but merely its opposition to the dictatorship of Santa Anna. To administer its affairs in this crisis, Texas had elected Henry Smith as Governor. An advisory Council was created to consult with Governor Smith and Sam Houston was chosen as Commander-in-Chief of the Army.

Trouble had started immediately between the Governor and his Council, and between Houston and a clique of his officers. The Mexican Government's first attempt to bring Texas to time by force of arms had resulted in victory for the Texans and not a Mexican soldier remained north of the Rio Grande. But the Texas troops could not stand idleness. They wanted to keep on fighting even if they had to cross the Rio Grande to do it. Houston advised that they stay where they were and get ready to fight because the Mexicans would be back soon to give them their fill of fighting. This was the situation army officers who were jealous of Houston had been waiting for. They sneered at the Commander-in-Chief and stirred up the soldiers with oratory about carrying the war to the enemy. Governor Smith backed Houston but the Council backed the jingo officers. Smith fought the Council and was deposed from office. Houston remained loyal to Smith and was deprived of command of the army.

In the beginning Houston had planned to defend the town of San Antonio de Béxar, but when the invasionists lured away most of the garrison Houston ordered Neill, the commander at Béxar, to blow up the fortifications and leave. Neill failed to do this and was relieved by Lieutenant Colonel W. B. Travis, a red-haired Georgian of twenty-eight who had come out to Texas to practise law, but had made his reputation in the earlier skirmishes of the war. Houston paid a flying visit to the main body of his army, which under the influence of the extremists was marching toward Mexico. The officers were as unreasonable as ever, but Houston convinced enough of the soldiers of the foolhardy nature of the enterprise to break it up. In accomplishing this he also practically broke up the army and the result was greater confusion than ever in the face of what Houston knew to be an invasion of Texas by a powerful Mexican force. Already shorn of his power, there was nothing Houston could do to put the quarreling soldiery in a proper mood for cooperation. He had saved them from risking their foolish heads in the enemy's country and he had told them what the enemy was going to do to their country. Houston then disappeared among the Indian tribes of the frontier where he could really accomplish something. Mexican agents were at work among the Indians. Himself the trusted friend of the red men, Houston was not long in winning their friendship for the Texas cause, thus destroying the shrewdly conceived Mexican plan of an Indian attack on one front while they were attacking on the other.

Meantime what Houston had predicted came to pass. Santa Anna invaded Texas with seven thousand men, many of them veterans of the old war for Mexican independence, officered by experienced leaders, including soldiers of fortune of several nationalities. To oppose them Texas had about twelve hundred men in the field, scattered everywhere, poorly equipped, without discipline, under leaders who refused to support one another and with no man in the Government strong enough to enforce obedience. This was the posture of affairs in February, 1836.

At Béxar was a handful of men under Travis who was doing

his best to augment his force. Jim Bowie joined the garrison with a small following which, until the fighting started, rather increased Travis's difficulties than otherwise. James Bowie was not the man he had once been—the half-legendary figure whose tremendous exploits were a tradition from St. Louis to Mexico City. In the old days Bowie was a power in northern Mexico. He had married the daughter of a grandee and, turning his abilities to less spectacular pursuits, accumulated a fortune and his family lived like royalty. Just when his wild days seemed behind him, a plague swept Bowie's beautiful wife and their children into the grave and the lion-hearted Jim almost died of grief. Nothing mattered after that. Life became a quest for activity to turn his mind from his loss. Abandoning his property, he threw himself into the Texas struggle and supported Houston in the contest that had demoralized the Texas army. With little left but blind courage and a name at which enemies still trembled, Jim Bowie then decided to stand by the wreck. His enormous form was gaunt and worn, his blue eyes unnaturally bright from the fever of tuberculosis. Whipping up his flagging forces with whisky, Jim Bowie had plunged into Béxar, determined to sell his life dearly. He could not have come to a better place.

3

Some other recruits, dressed in fringed buckskins, rode into town and, in the drawl of a southern mountaineer, their spokesman said they wanted to fight. This was Davy Crockett with his twelve Tennesseans. Davy had been a Tennessee congressman from a backwoods district. With a good head and an amusing way about him, he had become something of a national figure. Unfortunately, he committed the error of opposing Andrew Jackson and this had lost him his seat in Congress. Texas was in the public eye and Davy had come on looking for excitement.

A few other volunteers straggled in, bringing Travis's command to the neighborhood of one hundred and forty-five men who, on February twenty-third, awaited the return of Scouts Sutherland

and Smith with an indifference born of a picturesque contempt for peril. They did not have long to wait. The two horsemen were seen returning at a dead run across the plain. Travis immediately gave orders to evacuate the Béxar and occupy the Álamo Mission beyond the eastern purlieus of the town. From the way his scouts were riding, Travis knew the Mexican army was coming. Travis now had one hundred and fifty men, having gathered up a few loyal native Mexicans in the town. His first—and last—impulse was to fight.

Sutherland and Smith found their comrades in a fever of preparation to defend the Álamo. The scouts said they had seen fifteen hundred troops drawn up in line of battle, with an officer riding up and down, flourishing a sword and exhorting his men with oratory. Doctor Sutherland had injured his knee during the reconnaissance and could not walk without assistance. But he could ride and, at three o'clock in the afternoon, he sped through the Álamo gate with a message to the "Citizens of Gonzales," a little town fifty miles to the eastward. "The enemy in large force is in sight. We want men and provisions. Send them to us. We . . . are determined to defend the Álamo to the last. Give us assistance."

The message had not been long on its way when the Mexican troops filed into Béxar. A picket on the Álamo wall announced the approach of a horseman under a flag of truce. Travis suspected the object of his visit. He sent Major Morris and Captain Marten to meet the flag. These officers received Santa Anna's demand of surrender "at discretion." They gave Travis's answer. It was a refusal—which Travis rendered the more emphatic by sending a cannon ball into the town when the Mexican emissary had withdrawn. Santa Anna replied by raising the red flag of No Quarter over the tower of San Fernando and opening on the Texans with a mortar battery. The seige of the Álamo had begun.

The following day Travis spared another of his precious men to carry to the outside world a message that has been called the most heroic in American history.

"Commandancy of the Alamo, Béxar, Feby 24th, 1836.

"To the People of Texas and All Americans in the World——

"Fellow Citizens and Compatriots: I am beseiged with a thousand or more of the Mexicans under Santa Anna. I have sustained a continual Bombardment and cannonade for 24 hours and have not lost a man. The enemy has demanded a surrender at discretion, other wise, the garrison are to be put to the sword, if the fort is taken. I have answered the demand with a cannon shot, and our flag still waves proudly from the wall. *I shall never surrender or retreat.* Then, I call on you in the name of Liberty, of patriotism and everything dear to the American character, to come to our aid with all dispatch. The enemy is receiving reinforcements daily and will no doubt increase to three or four thousand in four or five days. If this call is neglected, I am determined to sustain myself as long as possible and die like a soldier who never forgets what is due his honor and that of his country. VICTORY or DEATH.

"WILLIAM BARRET TRAVIS
"Lt. Col. Comdt."

"P. S. The Lord is on our side. When the enemy appeared in sight we had not three bushels of corn. We have since found in deserted houses 80 to 90 bushels and got into the walls 20 to 30 head of Beeves."

4

The Álamo, which means the cotton-wood tree, was a mission more than one hundred years old—a large and strong establishment with superior advantages of defense. Its size was an embarrassment, however. There was a stone church, partly unroofed in previous fighting, with walls four feet thick, and two stoutly walled enclosures adjoining. The smaller of these enclosures was the convent yard; the larger, more than two acres in extent, the general plaza of the mission. Built against the walls of these enclosures were several stone buildings—a convent, a hospital, barracks, a prison. The walls varied in height from five to twenty-two feet and to defend them Travis mounted eighteen guns. At intervals scaffolds were built for riflemen. The defensive arrange-

[129]

ments were intelligently supervised by an engineer named Jameson, but neither scientific skill nor valor could make up for the lack of men. To garrison works so extensive required a thousand troops.

Travis knew that everything depended on reenforcements, and they must come soon. Battalion after battalion of Mexican troops showed themselves on the prairie, and began to encircle the Álamo beyond the range of its guns. Batteries were pushed up and the bombardment grew heavier. Parties of Texans sallied from the walls to gather fire-wood and to harass the Mexican artillerymen with rifle-fire.

To whom was the beleaguered commander to appeal for aid? Travis knew something of the confusion existing in the Texan civil government, but this situation was more serious than he imagined. After taking away Governor Smith's authority, the Council members had fallen to quarreling among themselves. Unable to assemble a quorum of their own number, the Council thus deprived Texas of even the name of a government, and left the bewildered little bands, called the army, to shift for themselves.

Travis was shifting. The largest and best equipped body of troops in Texas was the four hundred and twenty men under James W. Fannin at Goliad, one hundred and fifty miles away. In the squabble that had disorganized Texas, Fannin had been a leader of the clique against Sam Houston, while Travis had supported Houston. Nevertheless, Travis appealed to Fannin. That officer received the letter on February twenty-fifth, the third day of the seige. Three days later he carefully packed his baggage wagons and began a leisurely march toward the Álamo.

Travis sent other messages elsewhere and Henry Smith, the deposed Governor, scattered a heart-rending call far and wide. But Smith was not the type of leader to rally men for a desperate throw. The response to Travis's heroic appeals likewise was a disappointment, a black disappointment, to the beseiged garrison. After seven days and seven nights of fighting not a man had come to join the defenders. But on the eighth day of battle, March first, at three o'clock in the morning, faithful Scout John W. Smith piloted through the enemy lines thirty-two settlers from Gonzales—practically all in the town who were able to bear arms. Twenty of them had left wives and children behind. The weary garrison received these recruits with a cheer. The outside world heard from at last! Hope was revived for Fannin, whose force would surely turn the tide of battle. The watch on the parapet strained his eyes at the southern prairie, but he saw only ever-increasing numbers of Mexicans methodically throwing up works behind which to maneuver with greater safety and precision.

The Gonzales men raised the strength of the Alamo defenders to about one hundred and eighty-three, not counting some twenty refugees from Béxar, mostly women and children and two or three negro slaves. So far the Texans had lost the services of only one man—Jim Bowie, who had fallen from a scaffold while helping to mount a gun. With a fight at hand Bowie and Travis had composed their differences. The main difficulty between these officers was that each had red hair. Jim Bowie crippled was still worth a half-dozen ordinary men and he hobbled about ready for the finish fight until a piercing "norther" brought on pneumonia. Half-delirious Jim was carried to a cot and nursed by a sister of his late wife who was among the refugees.

5

The Texans suffered greatly from fatigue and loss of sleep, practically the whole command being on duty constantly. The bombardment was continuous and two hundred shells had fallen within the enclosures. The Texans replied with artillery and rifle-fire from the walls, but their ammunition was low and they saved it for the general assault they knew must come. With the red flag of No Quarter snapping in the north wind, the Texans witnessed every hour new preparations for this attack. The Mexicans were advancing batteries on all sides of the Álamo. Sallying parties of Texans made these maneuvers expensive to the enemy, but Santa Anna had men to spare and he used them. The long hunting rifles of the Texans would no sooner clear out one parcel of gunners than another squad would appear to carry on the work.

During the tenth day of the seige, March third, the enemy bombardment increased in violence and a hostile battery was planted within pistol shot of the north wall. On that day Travis received his last news from the outside. It was brought by James Butler Bonham, a colonel in the Texas military establishment before dissension had demoralized it, and now serving as a volunteer scout under Lieutenant Colonel Travis. He had carried the Commandant's message to Fannin and, regardless of what Fannin intended to do, returned alone to stand with his comrades. Bonham's report of the mission to Fannin was a blow. While the whole truth of Fannin's behavior was never known to the Álamo's defenders, Bonham left Travis with little hope of aid from the source on which the garrison had built such high expectations. Fannin's half-hearted march toward the Álamo had ended within an hour after it began. One baggage wagon broke down and Fannin had returned to camp at Goliad, without so much as sending a messenger to warn Travis to try to escape.

Fannin could have got word to Travis in time to enable him to retreat. Whether Travis would have done this is a question. The chances are he would not for, even after Bonham arrived, the escape of the garrison was possible. There would have been a fight, but most of them could have got away. But Travis had said, "I shall never surrender or retreat," and he kept his word. The men who remained with him remained on those terms. A story that has been published many times relates that Travis called his men together and drew a line on the ground with his sword. Those wishing to stay were invited to step across the line. The tradition is that Jim Bowie had his cot carried over the line and every man, save one, followed him. The story, like much Álamo literature, is legend, not history.

In any event the fact stands that no man deserted the twenty-eight-year-old leader, although abundant opportunity presented. William Barret Travis lives in the history of the world for his thirteen-day defense of the Álamo. It is his sole claim to a renowned memory, and it is enough. The feat has few parallels in any annals. Bands of men have died, before and since, to show devotion to a cause or their loyalty to a leader they had long known and served, but this was not strictly the case of the Álamo. Texans were fighting Mexican tyranny—technically, that is. Actually most of them were fighting for the thrill of it, for fancied riches in the form of land, or because they were under the spell of professional adventurers who dominated a large part of the Texan stage. Travis, however, was no professional adventurer, which gentry, as a class, do not die needlessly for a cause. Neither had he any special claim on the loyalty of the men who followed him at the Álamo. Most of these men were unknown to him and he to them. His rank did not impress them, for Texans cared nothing for rank and proved it on every occasion. With them it was the man that counted—and Travis was the man.

6

Bonham came in at eleven o'clock in the morning. There was still a chance—a bare chance—of help from without. Three days before, March first, an attempt to reorganize the Texas civil government had been scheduled to be made at the town of Washington-on-the-Brazos, two hundred and twenty-five miles away. After talking to Bonham, Travis prepared appeals to the leaders at Washington, writing all afternoon amid a cannonade and constant interruptions by his lieutenants with more bad news: the ring of investing troops was drawing closer. The appeals of Travis embodied a temperate account of the action to date.

"The spirits of my men are still high," he wrote, "although they have had much to depress them. We have contended for ten days against an enemy whose number are variously estimated at from fifteen hundred to six thousand men. . . . A reinforcement of about one thousand men is now entering Bejar, from the west. . . .

"Col. Fannin is said to be on the march to this place with reinforcements, but I fear it is not true, as I have repeatedly sent to him for aid without receiving any. . . . I look to the colonies alone for aid; unless it arrives soon, I shall have to fight the enemy on his own terms. I will, however, do the best I can ... and although we may be sacrificed ... the victory will cost the enemy so dear, that it will be worse for him than defeat. I hope your honorable body will hasten on reinforcements. ... Our supply of ammunition is limited. ... The bearer of this will give your honorable body a statement more in detail, should he escape through the enemy's lines. God and Texas—Victory or Death."

When his official communications were finished, Travis wrote to a friend to "take care of my little boy."

Night came on. The Commandant handed his letters to Captain Albert Marten and wished him well. Marten stole through the gate into the shadows. The last of Travis's soldiers had left the Álamo.

The next day the Mexicans kept up a heavy fire of artillery, the Texans replying occasionally. The day after that, Saturday, March fifth, the bombardment eased off in the afternoon and by ten o'clock at night it had stopped altogether. Travis suspected a ruse and posted all his men, who loaded their rifles and their guns and began their twelfth night of vigil. Since the siege had begun there had been no reliefs. The entire command had been continuously on duty. Beef and cornbread had been served on the walls. This was the sole ration. There was no coffee, which would have helped to keep the men awake, and sleep was an enemy more dreaded than the Mexicans. For days men had been dozing in snatches at their guns during the thunder of bombardment. Now the roar had ceased. A silence almost tangible, a starlit southern night: the defenders of the Álamo leaned against their guns—and slept.

At two o'clock on Saturday afternoon, Santa Anna called his commanding officers to headquarters in Béxar. He distributed copies of a general order. "The time has come to strike a decisive blow upon the enemy occuping the Fortress of the Álamo. ... Tomorrow at 4 o'clock A.M., the columns of attack shall be stationed at musket shot distance from the first entrenchments, ready for the charge, which shall commence at a signal to be given with the bugle."

The attacking columns would be four in number—one to storm each side of the Álamo simultaneously. They would be composed of fourteen hundred infantry who had enjoyed three days' rest. "The first column will carry ten ladders, two crowbars and two axes; the second, ten ladders; the third, six ladders; and the fourth, two ladders. The men carrying the ladders will sling their guns on their shoulders, to be enabled to place the ladders wherever they may be required. The men will wear neither overcoats nor blankets, or anything that will impede the rapidity of their motions. The men will have the chin straps of their caps down. . . . The arms, principally the bayonets, should be in perfect order." Behind the attacking infantry and the infantry reserve, cavalry would prowl the country to see that no man in the Álamo escaped.

7

At four o'clock in the morning the moon had risen. A mild radiance softly outlined the irregular white walls of the fortress which betrayed not the slightest sign of life. Santa Anna's orders had been carried out exactly. Noiselessly, each column of assault had taken its places to encircle the Álamo. The signal bugle sounded and the Mexican band struck up the savage air of *Deguelo,* or *Cutthroat.* The troops gave a cheer for Santa Anna and advanced at a run.

Not until the charging assailants were within easy rifle range did a sound come from the walls of the Álamo. Then a flash, a roar and a pungent curtain of smoke. The Texans had let loose their guns loaded with grape-shot and scrap iron. They followed with a deadly fire of musketry. Gaps were torn in the attackers' ranks, but the impetus of the charge carried it on.

The Texans defending the north wall sent up an exultant shout. The column of attack in front of them had recoiled and was in full retreat. East, west and south Travis's men took heart and increased their fire. The east column faltered and fell back. The west fell back. The panic spread to the south column, which had reached the walls; it broke and fled. The moonlit plain was dotted with the vague shapes of the fallen. Among the slain was Colonel Francisco Duque, commander of the north column, wounded and then trampled to death trying to stem the rout of his men.

The first assault on the Álamo had failed.

The confused masses were reformed into battalions. Battalions were regrouped for attack, commanding officers riding up and down, heartening their men. The eastern sky was growing gray and the stars were fading when the four columns again sprang forward over the pallid plain and the corpses of the dead. Once more the dim advancing lines were staggered by a broadside from the walls. The north column recoiled, the west column retired, the east column was routed. Colonel José Vincente Minon's sturdy south column tottered, but came on and applied its scaling ladders to the walls. The retreating east column veered to the right and the west column to the left. These spontaneous movements had the effect of reenforcing the flanks of the north column which, though stopped, held its ground. Officers grasped the situation and drove this combined force against the north wall in the face of a furious fire. The wall was reached, but the assailants had no will left to try to scale it. They broke and fled. On the south side the fighting was hand to hand. The Mexicans climbed their ladders, but the Texans beat them back with clubbed rifles and bowie knives.

The second assault had failed.

The break of day looked upon preparations within and without the Álamo for a renewal of the struggle. Travis and his band were in hard case. Their guns were hot and ammunition nearly gone. There had been few casualties but the men were very weary. Had the Mexicans launched their first attack as quietly as they had moved into position for it, that onslaught might have told the tale, as the Texans were sound asleep. The three pickets stationed outside the walls to observe the enemy must have been bayonetted for they gave no warning. The alarm was given by a captain on the walls. Travis was on his feet instantly. Snatching up a rifle and his sword he called to Joe, his negro servant, and ran across the plaza to a cannon at the northwest corner of the wall. "Come on, boys, the Mexicans are here!" The cheer for Santa Anna and the notes of *Deguelo* helped to rouse the men. A clink of equipment, the pat-pat of running feet and the ghostly lines took shape in the moonlight.

After two repulses the Mexican officers had some difficulty getting their men in a mood for a third attack. But the ranks were reformed, the bugle sounded and the wave surged forward, officers beating the laggards with the flats of swords. Profiting by experience, the Mexicans varied their mode of assault. Having met with no success on the fronts assigned to them, the east and west columns swung over and joined the north column to storm that rampart. The consolidated force charged across the space swept by the Texans' cannon and reached the shadow of the wall where the cannon could not be trained to play upon them. "Nor could the defenders use their muskets with accuracy," wrote a Mexican general, "because the wall having no inner banquette, they had, in order to deliver their fire, to stand on top where they could not live for a second."

The wall was cleared and the scaling ladders flung up. Mexicans tumbled over "like sheep," according to Travis's Joe. The Commander of the Álamo fell with a ball through his head as he stood behind a useless cannon and made ready to fire his rifle. The Texans met the onrush with rifles, pistols, knives and their fists, but the Mexicans were too numerous. The defenders retreated across the plaza to the barracks that formed the east wall and to the church, also on the east side.

Meantime the southern column, which had always struck vigorous blows, breached the wall and came through. A desperate fight ensued. The Mexicans fell in heaps. The Texans took refuge in a barrack building forming the west wall of the plaza and fought from room to room until not a man of their number remained alive.

On the east side of the plaza the fight went on in the barracks there. The Mexicans ended it when they dragged inside a howitzer filled with grape, which they fired through the length of the building. Fifteen Texans were found dead in front of the gun and forty Mexicans behind it. This building was used as a hospital and according to one account, Jim Bowie perished there propped up on his cot and defending himself with two pistols.

The last point taken was the church. With his rifle "Betsy," Davy Crockett and the twelve from Tennessee held the inner gate to the little churchyard, firing until they no longer had time to load. Then clubbing their rifles and drawing hunting knives from their belts, they dispatched twenty-five more of the enemy before the last backwoodsman fell. Inside the church there was a brief struggle. The most plausible account says that Bowie died there, whence he had been carried so that his sister-in-law might attend him. Both versions of Bowie's death declare that he fought from his bed to the last and that his body was pitched about on the bayonets of the soldiers.

It had been agreed that the last Texan soldier alive should blow up the powder magazine in the church. A Mexican shot down Major Robert Evans as he attempted to apply a match. This seemed to complete the conquest. Across the corpse-strewn floor in a far corner huddled a little knot of women and children and a few slaves. The soldiers began to fling them about roughly. Mrs. A. M. Dickinson, the wife of a lieutenant who had perished on the walls, held her fifteen-months-old baby girl at her breast. At the woman's side crouched young Asa Walker, a wounded gunner. Mrs. Dickinson pleaded for his life, but the Mexicans ran him through, tossing "his body on their bayonets as a farmer would handle a bundle of hay."

The slanting sunlight, driving through holes in the roof, made irregular islands on the bloodstained western wall. It was eight o'clock in the morning and the Álamo had fallen.

8

General Santa Anna gave Mrs. Dickinson a horse and sent her eastward to spread the story of the Álamo and to say that such

would be the story of any and all who opposed the Mexican
General. Sam Houston was the first person of consequence that
Mrs. Dickinson encountered.

Houston had learned of the Álamo's plight at Washington-on-
the-Brazos, whither he had returned from the Indian country to
help form a new government for Texas. Independence had been
declared and Houston restored to the command of the armies.
With four followers he set out for the front an hour after Travis's
message reached Washington. Mrs. Dickinson told him it was
too late to save Travis. Houston then sent for Fannin, hoping to
lead that force—the only one now remaining in Texas—against
the Mexicans. Again Fannin moved reluctantly and the Mexicans
cornered him. He surrendered and, with his entire command of
four hundred and twenty men, was lined up and shot.

To the rallying cry of "Remember the Álamo!" Sam Houston
raised eight hundred men out of the ground and ruled them with
a discipline that Texans never before had known. With the new
government and the entire rebel population of Texas in panic and
in flight, Houston managed his makeshift "army." Outmarching
and outmaneuvering the Mexicans, only six weeks after the Álamo,
Houston defeated Santa Anna at San Jacinto in one of the extraordinary battles of modern times.

THE PLOT THAT FAILED

VIII

THE PLOT THAT FAILED

I

WHILE their neighbors filed through to shake hands with her husband, Mrs. Lincoln and her three boys stood apart with a group of friends in the Great Western Railway station at Springfield. Outside a cold, vertical February rain fell from a heavy morning sky and the smell of wet clothing and shoe-leather contributed to the discomforts within.

At seven fifty-five the train was announced and the official party of the President-elect went aboard. The people flowed upon the tracks and about the cars. The bell of the locomotive was clanging, the conductor's hand was on the bell rope ready to signal the engineer, when Mr. Lincoln appeared upon the back platform, removed his stove-pipe hat and raised his hand. He looked very weary.

"My friends, no one not in my situation can appreciate my feeling of sadness at this parting. To this place and the kindness of these people I owe everything. Here I have lived a quarter of a century and have passed from a young to an old man. Here my children have been born and one is buried. I leave now, not knowing when or whether ever I may return."

In life he never returned.

2

That evening the train reached Indianapolis amid scenes of tumultuous demonstration: bonfires, bands, salutes, a parade and a ceremonial welcome by the Governor and the Legislature. All day when the train had halted or merely slowed its pace there had been smaller copies of such scenes.

The North was falling in behind this tall Lincoln of whom it really knew so little. The feverish months that had intervened since the election in November had seen seven Southern States repudiate the Union. And now, as Mr. Lincoln rode eastward to take the oath of office, southern men rode toward Montgomery to unite the estranged commonwealths as a rival Confederacy. The South acted, as it seemed from a distance, with undivided resolution, while disparities of view enfeebled the North. Writing in his influential *Tribune,* Horace Greeley had suggested that difficulties could be solved by letting the erring sisters go. But this did not seem the proper remedy and the distracted northern people, yearning for a leader who would point the way to something better, rushed to the side of the man they had chosen President.

When Mr. Lincoln's route to Washington was published, a cloud of invitations and pledges of loyalty came from every state—save one—through which he should pass. The state that sat in silence was Maryland, which the South claimed as its own, and whose secession would have isolated Washington. No word from the Governor, from the Legislature, from any city or town. Only two invitations from all Maryland, one to a private dinner by the president of the Northern Central Railroad, over whose line Mr. Lincoln's train was announced to pass from Harrisburg, Pennsylvania, and one from the proprietor of the Eutaw House, in Baltimore, where the official party was to stop.

In many parts of the South the threat was heard that Mr. Lincoln should never take the oath of office in Washington City. The only route to Washington City from the North was through Maryland. But at a time when there was much irresponsible talk on both sides, the cooler heads, in the North at least, paid little attention to these extravagant threats. Mr. Lincoln himself refused to dignify them by discussion, even privately.

The demonstrations along the line of the President-elect's progress grew in fervor. In a corridor of the State-House at Columbus, Mr. Lincoln was nearly crushed by admirers. The stampede of a cavalry escort, while attempting to hold back the cheering throngs, endangered the lives of those in the personal carriage of the President-elect at Pittsburgh. At Buffalo, Major Hunter of Mr. Lincoln's staff suffered a broken arm while trying to stem a charge of the crowd that nearly smothered the distinguished guest in an effort to shake his hand.

Nevertheless, in the face of this public acclaim, before the entourage left Buffalo, Norman B. Judd, whose counsel had more weight with Lincoln than that of any other member of the party, received a warning that the President-elect's life might be in serious jeopardy if he should attempt to pass through Baltimore. The warning came in a letter from a friend of Mr. Judd, Allan Pinkerton, the detective. As yet he was not sure of his facts, Mr. Pinkerton admitted, but said he would continue his investigations and report further. Mr. Judd spoke of this communication to no one. He knew too well Mr. Lincoln's droll indifference to stories of personal danger.

3

Allan Pinkerton was in the employ of the Philadelphia, Wilmington & Baltimore Railroad, one of the two lines connecting Washington with the North, the other line being the Northern Central from Harrisburg, over which Mr. Lincoln was scheduled to pass. The strategical importance of these roads had been called to the attention of the South some few weeks previously when General Winfield Scott, the aged hero of the Mexican War, transported a few Regulars over them for the security of Washington. Southern hotspurs openly advocated measures to prevent the use of these railroads by the military forces of the Union.

The first inkling that action had been suited to the word had come from Dorothea Lynde Dix, a wealthy spinster in her latter fifties, whose fame as a social worker was international. Miss Dix was New England born, and intensely loyal to the Union.

Of recent years she had spent much time in Baltimore. Six weeks before Mr. Lincoln started on his way to the inaugural, she had gone to Philadelphia to tell the president of the Philadelphia, Wilmington & Baltimore that secession sympathizers in Maryland were organizing to seize his railroad. Her visit resulted in the employment of Mr. Pinkerton.

As J. H. Hutchinson of Charleston, South Carolina, the detective had opened a brokerage office in Baltimore. At the same time a well-dressed man with a cavalier air had registered at Barnum's fashionable hotel as Mr. Howard of New Orleans. He was often seen in the company of an attractive young woman. The man was Harry Davies, of the Pinkerton office, born in Louisiana, connected by blood with a well-known Creole family and educated for the priesthood—wanderer, adventurer and gallant. His companion was Mrs. Catherine Warne, the most celebrated woman detective of her day.

Other plausible strangers also appeared in Baltimore and along the Maryland line of the Philadelphia, Wilmington & Baltimore Railroad.

The first acquaintance Mr. Hutchinson made in Baltimore was that of a fellow-broker who occupied an office across the hall from him. It became their habit at the close of the business day to have a glass together at the bar of Barnum's Hotel. There Mr. Hutchinson's circle of acquaintances expanded, Barnum's bar being a rendezvous of the social and professional élite, of whom Hutchinson's broker friend was a popular member. Mr. Howard of New Orleans also usually dropped in for apéritifs with a party of gay young companions. His conquest of Baltimore society had been a swift one, and now he went to many of the best houses, thanks to an impression he had made upon an aristocratic idler named Hillier.

In this milieu a man less observing than Mr. Hutchinson would have been aware that the sympathy of Baltimore, and for that matter most of Maryland, was with her sister states of the South which had seceded. This is not to say that there was an equal ardor in favor of the secession of Maryland. If the North chose to fight, and Maryland was not so certain as South Carolina that the North would not fight, the shores of the Chesapeake would be a battle-ground. But there was much secession sentiment and its proponents were active. Among these were men highly placed in public life, including the Governor of the state, and most of the city administration of Baltimore. The Marshal of Police, Colonel Kane, later a brigadier general in the Confederate Army, was quite outspoken in his views. Much was said by curbstone strategists of safeguarding the two lines of railroad for the southern cause and the impression got about that this was being done.

By the first of February, 1861, several military companies had been formed and equipped in Baltimore for "home defense." Their purpose of serving the South, in case of war, was an open secret. One similar company was formed by Union adherents. Along the line of the two railroads, other companies were formed and drilled with little show of secrecy. Mr. Hutchinson knew all of these companies, saving one, to be for the South. He knew this because he had a detective in each one of them. The out-of-town companies were mostly comprised of railway employees, and upon a given signal were to burn bridges and take charge of the rolling stock.

Perhaps the most important project was delegated to the cavalry company at Havre de Grace, where trains were carried over the Susquehanna River on a steam ferry. Mr. Hutchinson's man at Havre de Grace was a young daredevil, Timothy Webster, whose usefulness, like that of Mr. Howard in Baltimore, was enhanced by a woman assistant.

By degrees, Mr. Hutchinson was being admitted to the real secrets of the schemers in Baltimore when the announcement that Lincoln's intended passage over the Northern Central raised a question of procedure.

One evening Mr. Hutchinson lingered at Barnum's bar with a Mr. Fernandina, who had taken a drop too much. Mr. Fernandina occupied a curious position. His acquaintance with the notables of Baltimore had been formed at a chair in the barber shop of Barnum's Hotel.

This barber had seen better days. The story was that he had been an officer in the Italian Army. In any event the present crisis enabled Mr. Fernandina to improve his social standing. He became captain of one of the volunteer companies. Conscious of the fact that he had risen in the world, he sought to impress Mr. Hutchinson with his knowledge of important secrets.

"Lincoln shall never, never take the oath of office," said he. "My life is of no consequence. I am willing to give it for his. As Orsini gave his life for Italy, I am ready to die for the rights of the South!"

"Are there no other means," asked Mr. Hutchinson, "of saving the South?"

"No!" exclaimed the ex-barber. "Die he must and shall!" A waterfall of impassioned language fell from the lips of the Italian. "Mr. Hutchinson, if I alone must act I shall not hesitate! Lincoln shall die in this city!"

The conversation was overheard by a resident of Baltimore, whom Allan Pinkerton, in his notes, identified only as "Captain T." On the following day Hutchinson encountered Captain T. and asked him how much there was to this talk of Fernandina.

"It is determined," said T., "that that God damned Lincoln shall never pass through here alive!" The Captain added that he had "seen" Colonel Kane. "He is all right. In one week from to-day the North shall want a new President."

The reports that Mr. Howard submitted to his chief supported the declarations of Fernandina. Exhibiting a gold badge as the insignia of his rank as lieutenant in the Palmetto Guards, Hillier, the society man in search of adventure, had gradually disclosed to Howard the particulars of the conspiracy.

The itinerary of the President-elect, as announced by the newspapers, called for his arrival at the Calvert Street depot of the Northern Central at midday. There his party would take carriages and ride a mile and a half to the Baltimore & Ohio depot to entrain for Washington. The deed was to be done during the passage through the town.

As the days passed the thing preyed upon the mind of Hillier.

He drank to excess, his sleep was disturbed by unpleasant dreams. Howard was now his closest confidant.

"I am destined to die shrouded in glory. Let us have another Brutus. I swear I will kill Lincoln before he reaches the Washington [Baltimore & Ohio] depot, not that I love Lincoln less but my country more. I am ready to do the deed and then will proudly announce my name and say 'Gentlemen, arrest me. I am the man!' "

Five years later another young megalomaniac was to sway against Barnum's bar, his unstable brain reeling under the force of almost identical reverberations. His name was John Wilkes Booth.

4

Mr. Lincoln was in New York City, and in a few days was due to be in Baltimore. The time had come for Allan Pinkerton to communicate to Norman B. Judd a confirmation of the serious posture of affairs.

This was a matter the detective hesitated to confide to the mails. His first thought was to go to New York in person, but the Baltimore situation was too acute. Accordingly, he sent Catherine Warne, with a letter to E. S. Sanford, president of the American Telegraph Company, to arrange an interview with Judd. Pinkerton himself went to Philadelphia to receive a code message from Mrs. Warne as to the outcome of her mission. Instead of one telegram he received three. Mrs. Warne, Sanford and Judd each wired to Pinkerton to meet Judd in Philadelphia on the arrival of Mr. Lincoln's party.

Meantime as Hutchinson, the broker, the detective returned to Baltimore, where events moved swiftly. The conspirators had dispatched agents north to watch the movements of the President-elect and to report any change of route or plans. Should the party come by way of the Philadelphia, Wilmington & Baltimore Railroad, which necessitated no change of trains, the blow was to be struck at the steam ferry at Havre de Grace.

No such change was anticipated, however, and plans were made

THEY HAD THEIR HOUR

in view of an arrival at the Calvert Street depot and a ride through town. All events favored this procedure. A sullen crowd would be on hand. Newspaper reports of the North's reception of the President-elect had incensed the South. Police arrangements for keeping the crowd in check would be inadequate. This, however, is no proof of the hinted complicity of Marshal Kane, an honorable man and not a partner of assassins. Police arrangements in the North had everywhere been inadequate.

As reported by Howard the arrangement was this: When Mr. Lincoln should emerge from the depot through a narrow passage where the carriages awaited, a fight would be started among some roughs to distract the police. Lincoln would be quickly enveloped by a hostile crowd, and the blow struck. A small, swift steamer lying in an inlet of the Chesapeake would carry the assassin to a southern port.

But who should do the deed?

According to Howard twenty men, including Fernandina and Hillier, had taken an oath to kill Mr. Lincoln, if designated to do so. The President-elect was to be in Baltimore on February twenty-third. On the night of February twentieth, these conspirators met, and drew ballots from a hat in a dark room. No one was to disclose his ballot, but the holder of a red ballot was to strike the blow, choosing his weapon. Eight red ballots were placed in the hat, instead of one as supposed.

5

The following day Pinkerton took a train for Philadelphia, registering at the St. Louis Hotel as J. H. Hutchinson of Baltimore. Mr. Lincoln arrived amid tumultuous scenes, admirers nearly overwhelming his carriage before it reached the Continental Hotel, in Chestnut Street, five or six blocks from Pinkerton's lodgings. Judd and President Felton of the Philadelphia, Wilmington & Baltimore Railroad met Pinkerton in his room.

The immediate difficulty confronting the conferees was to convince Mr. Lincoln of the seriousness of the situation. Political assassination was then a crime unknown in the United States. Judd emphasized the almost boundless confidence Lincoln had in people. Moreover, he wished to do nothing to indicate that he suspected the southern people of bad faith.

After much discussion it was decided that Pinkerton should meet the President-elect and support Judd in his statement of the case.

Years later both Judd and Allan Pinkerton recalled the tussle they had getting through the crowd that surrounded the famous Continental Hotel. Mr. Lincoln was holding a reception in the spacious parlors on the second floor. It was eleven o'clock at night before he could get away to join the two in Judd's room.

"Though plainly exhausted from the fatigue of travel and receptions he greeted us in his usual kindly and gracious way," Mr. Pinkerton wrote in a letter to Judge Herndon, of Springfield, the former law partner of Lincoln. Mr. Judd, who was a well-known railroad attorney and presently became United States Minister to Prussia, made the opening statement, marshaling his facts expertly. "Mr. Lincoln," wrote Pinkerton in his note-book after the interview, "listened very attentively but did not say a word, nor did his countenance, which I closely watched, show any emotion."

The detective then spoke, giving additional particulars—the state of popular feeling in Baltimore and the actual details of the contemplated murder. In conclusion he said that he did not believe Mr. Lincoln could traverse that mile and a half in an open carriage alive.

Lincoln said nothing. Judd pressed him to take the train that night and, under guard, slip through Baltimore in secret.

Parrying this suggestion Lincoln asked a series of questions. Why not give the whole story to the newspapers? he urged, thinking that publicity would kill the plot. Pinkerton replied that it would mean the lives of some of his detectives.

"Will you," said Judd at length, "on *any* statement that we can make consent to leave for Washington on to-night's train?"

"No," said Mr. Lincoln, "I can not consent. I shall hoist the flag on Independence Hall to-morrow morning, and go to Harrisburg and meet the Legislature. Then I shall have filled all my engagements. After this if you, Judd, think there is positive danger in my attempting to go through Baltimore openly, according to the published program, I will place myself in your hands."

6

The three separated at one o'clock in the morning. Pinkerton spent the rest of the night making arrangements for the morrow. At six o'clock, with the sun just rising, the detective went to Independence Square, which was filled with people. Lincoln ran up the flag and endeavored to retire but the people cried for a speech.

The President-elect responded with a brief plea for a return to the principle of equal rights as guaranteed by the Declaration of Independence. "But if this country cannot be saved without giving up that principle . . . I would rather be assassinated on this spot than to surrender it."

The speaker paused. The lines of his tired face were deep.

"My friends," he added, "this is wholly an unprepared speech. I may have said something indiscreet. But I have said nothing but what I am willing to live by, and if it be the pleasure of Almighty God, to die by."

Mr. Lincoln's party was preparing to leave for the Harrisburg train when a slender young man, obviously nervous, appeared. He identified himself as Frederick Seward, son of the man whom Lincoln had chosen to be his Secretary of State, saying he had a communication from his father which he could place only in the hands of Mr. Lincoln. The President-elect opened the letter and read:

"My son . . . will show you a report made by our detective to General Scott. . . . I deem it so important as to dispatch my son to meet you wherever he may find you. I concur with General Scott in thinking it best for you to reconsider your arrangement. No one but General Scott, myself and the bearer is aware of this communication . . . WILLIAM H. SEWARD."

The report contained a description of the Baltimore plot, gathered by agents of the War Department, who had worked entirely independently of Pinkerton, and, indeed, without knowledge of his activities. Mr. Lincoln was now convinced of the need for caution.

That afternoon Lincoln addressed the Legislature at Harrisburg, and rode from the capitol to a reception at the Jones House. The reception was to be followed by the Governor's dinner at the hotel, which was set for an early hour to enable the President-elect to retire to the Executive Mansion for a good night's rest. Allan Pinkerton had remained in Philadelphia and arrangements in Harrisburg were in the hands of Judd and a few railroad and telegraph officials. Their program was that Mr. Lincoln should leave the Jones House ostensibly for the Executive Mansion. But actually he should be conducted to a special train which would speed him to Philadelphia in time to catch the regular night express to Washington, where he should arrive at an hour when the world believed him still in bed in Harrisburg.

To accomplish this would seem a problem for a magician. It proved a great problem for Mr. Judd who, at the close of the reception, whispered to Lincoln that it would be necessary to impart the secret to a few additional members of the staff. Up to this time only Mrs. Lincoln and Ward H. Lamon had been told. The plan called for Mr. Lincoln to travel with one companion from his suite, Pinkerton providing other guards who would be answerable for his safety. Lincoln had chosen Lamon, an athletic young Virginian practising law in Illinois.

Five or six of the principal members of the official party were summoned to a small room opening off the parlors in which the reception had been held. Mr. Lincoln was present. Judd presented the case, and outlined the course of action proposed. A warm discussion ensued. Colonel E. V. Sumner was especially critical. "Say the word and I'll get a squad of cavalry, sir, and *cut* our way through." That had been his method in the Mexican War.

What particularly ruffled the Colonel was that Lamon and not he had been chosen for the post of danger. As the meeting broke up Sumner said, "*I* have undertaken to go to Washington with Mr. Lincoln and shall do it!" The members separated to take their places at the dinner, Judd walking beside the Colonel trying to explain that the presence of an additional man would be an added risk, but the old soldier's mind was made up.

At a quarter to six o'clock dusk had fallen. A locomotive and one passenger coach, without lights, waited on the main line at the edge of town. But the dinner was not more than half over and a thousand people encircled the hotel.

Mr. Lincoln was seated next to Governor Curtin who, at the last moment, had been informed that quite possibly before the dinner was over his guest would have to leave Harrisburg upon a "secret mission." The Governor was instructed to give out that Mr. Lincoln had retired to the Executive Mansion on account of a headache.

A closed carriage drew up to a side entrance to the hotel. A few minutes later Ward Lamon, in evening clothes, strolled into the dining-room and caught the eye of Mr. Lincoln.

Those seated near heard the President-elect murmur something about a headache and a breath of fresh air. Protesting that Governor Curtin must not think of deserting his guests, Mr. Lincoln took Lamon's arm and slipped through a doorway.

In a remote part of the room the military figure of Colonel Sumner, splendid in blue and gold, also arose and left the dining hall.

But he missed Lincoln and Lamon, who had ascended to a private room, to make a partial change of clothing. He caught sight of them, however, in a corridor on the ground floor hastening toward the door where the carriage stood.

Judd was there. "Hurry," he called softly.

Mr. Lincoln stepped inside. Lamon followed. Colonel Sumner reached to grasp the handle of the carriage door.

"One moment, Colonel," said Judd, laying a hand on the officer's shoulder.

Sumner turned to see who had spoken. The door slammed and the carriage was off.

The telegraph wires out of Harrisburg, except those used in the operation of trains, had been cut. Railroads wires were tapped and messages not relating to the movement of trains were held up.

Seated in the dark coach, Mr. Lincoln opened a satchel and abstracted a manuscript which he carefully buttoned in an inside pocket of his vest.

"You know," he said, in his deliberate way, "I had a scare to-day. This"—he tapped the bulge in his vest—"is the only existing copy of my certificate of good moral character, written by myself"—in other words, his inaugural address, which two continents were waiting to hear. "I thought I had lost it."

Mr. Lincoln went on to say that he had entrusted his valise to his eldest son, Bob, a boy in his teens. Not appreciating the value of its contents, Bob had left the satchel in the baggage room at the Jones House and, when his father sent for it, he was given a bag that looked like his but contained only a soiled shirt, a few paper collars, a deck of cards and a bottle of whisky. Mr. Lincoln chuckled over the mistake, but said that he was really disturbed until his own grip was found.

Allan Pinkerton met the train with a carriage at the West Philadelphia Station of the Pennsylvania Railroad. There was nearly an hour to spare before the Philadelphia, Wilmington & Baltimore express left for Washington from another depot at ten-fifty o'clock. The time was spent driving about the city.

At exactly train time Lincoln, Lamon and Pinkerton left the carriage in a dark street a square from the station. The President-elect wore an overcoat, a plaid muffler and a soft black hat. Passing through the station, he stooped a little to dissemble his height which seemed all the greater beside the squat figure of Pinkerton.

At the train-side were Catherine Warne and George D. Bangs, of the Pinkerton force, who had arranged to have a "sick friend" taken into the sleeping car by the rear entrance.

Three adjoining sections had been engaged. Mr. Lincoln, Lamon and Pinkerton took their places in the middle one, drawing the curtains although the berth was not made down. Lincoln and Lamon occupied one seat, and Pinkerton sat facing them. Mrs. Warne and Bangs were in the sections on either side. Both were armed. When Conductor Litzenberg came through, Bangs produced tickets for the party.

8

None of the five slept that night, and they hardly spoke, except Mr. Lincoln who fell into his natural rôle of a story-teller. In a voice that was inaudible outside the berth, he related one anecdote after another in his usual manner. "I could not then," said Pinkerton, "nor have I since been able to understand how any one, in like circumstances, could have exhibited such composure."

The first critical stage in the journey was at the Havre de Grace ferry. As the train began to slow up Pinkerton quietly made his way to the rear platform. Two beams from a dark lantern flashed from beside the track. It was daredevil Tim Webster signaling that all was well. A year later daredevil Tim died on a scaffold in Richmond—the first Union spy to pay the penalty.

The train reached Baltimore at three-thirty o'clock, and lay over half an hour. Again Mr. Pinkerton left the car. One of his men paced the station platform. The city was asleep.

Dawn brought into view the steel frame outlining the unfinished dome of the Capitol as the train rolled into Washington.

Mr. Lincoln arose to straighten his clothing.

"Well, boys," he said, "thank God this prayer-meeting is over!"

There was just time for another Lincoln story:

A river steamboat, grounded on a bar, had resisted all attempts to float her. There seemed to be nothing to do but wait for a higher stage of water. A religious revival meeting was in progress in a tent on shore, and the captain said that it might adjourn to the boat's salon. The weight of the worshipers rocked the craft so that she slid into deep water. One good brother was on his knees delivering a prayer in a loud voice when the captain rushed in.

"Off this boat, every damned one of you!" he shouted. "This prayer-meeting's over!"

THE STOLEN RAILROAD TRAIN

IX

THE STOLEN RAILROAD TRAIN

I

On Sunday evening, the sixth of April, 1862, a tall, carefully dressed civilian with a heavy black beard and the inflection of the South in his speech, presented himself to the pickets of Mitchel's Division, encamped near Shelbyville, Tennessee. His papers were in order and he was admitted.

Major General O. M. Mitchel and the spy sat down over a map and it was daylight before they reached an agreement. The scheme offered by the secret agent was such that even a soldier as bold as Mitchel drew back. But step by step the civilian justified the proposal. Audacity would promote its success, he said, and success would be worth any risk. General Mitchel's caller asked for thirty picked men from whom to make his personal selections, and at length Mitchel agreed he should have them.

That forenoon thirty volunteers were culled from the veteran Second, Twenty-First and Thirty-Third Ohio Infantry Regiments, the colonels passing upon the qualifications of each man who was told that a detail was being made up for duty involving great personal peril. Though occupied with plans for a military advance, General Mitchel himself took the time to look over a few of the applicants. In the afternoon the chosen thirty were sent to Shelbyville to purchase civilian clothing and to report to J. J. Andrews, a tall civilian with a heavy beard who would be found on the streets of the town.

Shelbyville was full of soldiers, and, as soldiers often laid off their uniforms when going home on furlough, the thirty made their purchases without exciting comment. J. J. Andrews was easily identified. He sauntered about the streets, frequently entering a store to take an apparently idle interest in a soldier who was buying clothing. In the course of the afternoon all thirty approached him, singly or in small groups, for they were generally unknown to one another. He would ask what they were to report to him for. The soldiers would say that they did not know, or something of the sort. Andrews would ask them a few questions. Then in a casual tone he would say, "You may meet me to-night shortly after dark on the Wartrace Road a mile or so from town." To five or six he said, "There must be some mistake. I am not the man you are looking for." Their demeanor had not satisfied the Union spy.

Nor was Sergeant Major Marion Ross altogether satisfied with his interview. "A mile or so from town." "Shortly after dark." The instructions were so vague that he asked his friend Corporal William Pittenger what he thought of this Andrews. "I answered with enthusiasm," the Corporal related in after years. "The strong influence this singular man never failed to exert over those who were brought in contact with him was already at work. His pensive manner, his soft voice, not louder than a woman's, his grace and dignity made me at once declare him above the ordinary type of manhood. He was more like a poet than an adventurer, but I would have trusted him to the end of the earth."

2

Such whole-hearted endorsement put Ross in entire agreement with his friend's estimate. In fact, his curiosity was now aroused and he wished that he knew more about their new leader. And General Mitchel himself would have liked to know more about James J. Andrews, but all he knew or ever learned was that he was a good spy and described himself as a resident of Flemingsburg, Kentucky.

This town was equally unsatisfied with the scope of its knowledge. Andrews had come there two years before the war—from

Virginia, as he said, but he gave no particulars. Something about the man suggested an interesting past. Flemingsburg believed he "had a story."

Perhaps one person in Flemingsburg really knew. She was Elizabeth Layton to whom Mr. Andrews, after a long courtship, had just become engaged. They were to be married in two months, and a part of the bargain was that Andrews should abandon his perilous profession as a Union secret agent. The service he had proposed to Mitchel was intended to be his last. It was calculated to reveal to the world where his true loyalties lay, for in the South Andrews was known as a confidential agent of the Confederate armies.

The night following the interviews at Shelbyville was pitch dark and the rain fell in sheets. Twenty-four men, singly or in small parties, trudged through the mud of the Wartrace Road. Several of them were hopeless of meeting Andrews or any one on such a night. Yet twenty-three of the twenty-four found him as readily as if they had had daylight and explicit directions to guide them. Andrews led them into a patch of woods near the road and began to speak in a quiet voice, stopping when the thunder was too loud for him to be heard distinctly.

He said that the expedition for which they had volunteered would take them into the enemy's country in disguise, which meant that any one captured and detected would probably be hanged as a spy. Therefore, any one unwilling to take the risk might now withdraw. Mr. Andrews paused. No one stirred and in a few sentences the speaker outlined the undertaking. In bands of two to four, the party would proceed to Marietta, Georgia, in the heart of the Confederacy, arriving on Thursday, four days hence. The following morning they would capture the north-bound mail train from Atlanta to Chattanooga, and run it to Bridgeport, Alabama, burning bridges behind them and rendering useless a hundred and thirty miles of railroad and telegraph. At Bridgeport, the party would meet Mitchel in the course of his southward advance. The destruction of these communications would paralyze the movement of southern armies in the Central West and embarrass Lee's operations in Virginia.

"I shall be in Marietta with you or before you," said Mr. Andrews, "and there will tell each man what to do."

The route from Shelbyville to Marietta was long and difficult, and Andrews gave his men a few pointers on travel. If questioned, the best thing to say was that they were Kentuckians on their way to join the southern armies. But the men were to use their heads. They had been selected because they were thought capable of independent action.

"But what if they take us at our word and insist that we enlist?" asked one.

"Oh, be looking for a special regiment that is some place else. But if diplomacy fails do not hesitate to enlist any place."

"What if they won't take us?"

"No danger about that," replied Andrews. "The difficulty is not to get in but to stay out of the rebel army."

Andrews distributed seven hundred dollars of Confederate money and shook hands with each man. "Good-by. Good-by, Sergeant. Marietta not later than five, Thursday afternoon. Now, move out, men. Not more than four together."

3

On the appointed Thursday—April 10, 1862—two of the twenty-three reached Marietta. They strolled about town until late and went to bed uneasy. All day Friday they waited without a sign of one of their comrades, so far as they were able to recognize, the party having been together but once and then in the dark. The evening train from Chattanooga, however, brought Andrews and the remainder of his men, except two who were never heard from.

Incessant rain had made traveling difficult. When the party converged at Chattanooga to take the train for Marietta, Mr. Andrews had passed the word that the raid should be postponed one day. Thus all but the two men who had outstripped their schedule by a few hours had lain over at Chattanooga. Andrews's reason for the delay was that he felt it better to run the captured train into Bridgeport a day late rather than risk getting there ahead of Mitchel whose advance, he figured, would be retarded by the weather.

At Marietta the men slept in different hotels and at dawn met Andrews in his room for final instructions. As usual the leader did not waste a word. "Buy tickets to different points up the line. Take seats in the same car. When the train stops at Big Shanty remain seated until I tell you to go. When the signal is given, if anybody interferes, shoot him."

The ranking soldier present was Sergeant Major Ross, whose courage was well known. Respectfully asking permission to speak, he suggested that the whole project be dropped or delayed for a reconsideration of all the factors involved. The delay of one day had altered everything, said Ross. Big Shanty was surrounded by troops; the line was congested by rolling stock being hurried out of Mitchel's reach; should Mitchel get to Bridgeport on time, the raiders, a day late, might miss him. Very courteously Mr. Andrews took up Ross's objections. He said the excitement and confusion caused by Mitchel's drive into Alabama would facilitate, not hinder, the flight of the fugitive train. "Boys," he concluded after dismissing the last of the sergeant major's arguments, "I will succeed in this or leave my bones in Dixie."

That was the nearest to an heroic speech that J. J. Andrews ever made. He closed his watch and picked up his tall silk hat. The depot was just across the street and there was barely time before the train came in to buy tickets.

An hour later Conductor William A. Fuller walked through the coaches. Fuller was a wiry young fellow, with a blond goatee and steady gray eyes.

"Big Shanty!" he called. "Twenty minutes for breakfast."

The sleepy passengers began to scramble toward the door. Andrews rose and beckoned to William Knight, who had been designated as engineer. The station was on the right side of the track. Four Georgia regiments were encamped on the left side and a bored sentry walked his post within a few feet of the cars. Andrews and Knight got off on the side next to the camp. They strolled forward and took a look at the engine. The cab was empty. Behind the tender were three empty freight cars. Andrews stopped beside the last one.

"Uncouple here," he told Knight.

He walked to the coach where the other men were waiting. Strolling part of the way down the aisle, Andrews paused and said in an ordinary tone, "Come on, boys, it's time to go."

4

Wilson W. Brown, the relief engineer, and George D. Wilson, the fireman, swung off and darted toward the locomotive. Knight was in the cab with his hand on the throttle. Andrews signaled the others to tumble into the box-cars—all the work of probably twelve seconds. Knight pulled the throttle half-way open. The wheels spun on the track but the train did not move. Then the wheels "bit" and the engine, the three box-cars attached, shot forward with a bound that piled the box-car passengers in a heap.

They scurried to their feet to look from the doors and cheer. The start had been propitious beyond expectation. The picket, near enough to have used his bayonet, was staring in open-mouthed amazement—which, after all, was a fortunate negligence on the part of this green recruit as each of Andrews's men carried a cocked pistol in his coat.

The feeling of triumph was short-lived, however. Less than a mile from the Confederate camp the engine began to falter, which was strange, for this locomotive, the General, was rated one of the best on the Western & Atlantic road. Shortly this excellent engine stopped dead and Andrews, who was in the cab, called to the men in the cars to cut the telegraph wires. While John Scott, the smallest man in the party, was shinning up the telegraph pole, the trouble with the engine was located. The draft was shut off and the fire nearly out. Wood doused with oil soon had the fire-box roaring and they were on their way again.

Nothing now, said Andrews who was not given to strong statements, could defeat them. Cutting the wires at this point was an excess precaution. There was no need for it so soon as Big Shanty lacked a telegraph office. Pursuit would be a matter of hours, the nearest engines available for this purpose being at Atlanta on the south and Kingston on the north, each about thirty miles from Big Shanty. Three south-bound trains from Chattanooga must be dealt with, but Andrews had arranged for that. He would adhere to the regular time on the mail train until Kingston was reached, and pass there a local freight, the first of these trains. After burning some eleven bridges beyond Kingston and keeping the wires cut to prevent word from getting ahead of them, the raiders could skirt Chattanooga by means of the "Y" below the town, and dash westward into Alabama where Mitchel would be waiting.

The schedule of the fast mail from Atlanta was sixteen miles an hour and Andrews had difficulty in holding his engineers down to that speed, even though the track was crooked and soft from the rains, and the rails light and worn by the constant travel of military trains. The local freight must be passed at Kingston and it would be better to take it easy en route than to get to Kingston early and have to wait. So they jogged along, stopping once to relieve a track repair gang of its tools, and again to cut wires and lift a rail. The rail-lifting was slow work as the tools they had taken were not the proper ones.

Half-way to Kingston Andrews received a surprise. Slowing up for a private switch that led to the Etowah Iron Works, five miles off the main line, he saw a locomotive fired up not forty feet from the main track. It was the veteran Yonah, owned by the iron works, and, carefully as he had explored the road, Andrews had not learned of its existence until now. Knight put on the brakes.

"We had better get rid of that," he suggested.

Andrews hesitated. "No," he said, "go ahead. It won't make any difference."

Andrews did not wish to risk a delay in meeting the freight at Kingston. Beyond Kingston he could destroy track and thwart pursuit by the Yonah as effectively as by attacking its crew and the iron works gang at the switch. The decision reveals an important difference in temperament between Andrews and his men. The men would have preferred to disable the Yonah on the spot. They were soldiers, the pick of a first-class division, and accustomed to direct methods. Andrews's way was otherwise—to avoid clashes and to finesse his way through tight places where the flick of an eyelash might mean death.

5

Seven miles from Kingston was Cassville, a wood and water stop. The box-car doors were closed while the engine crew replenished the tender. The wood-yard foreman strolled up, curious to know about the small train running on the schedule of the morning mail, with the mail's locomotive but none of the regular hands. Mr. Andrews had put on his silk hat in place of the cap he wore while the train was under way. This was a powder train, he said, being taken through to General Beauregard, who was in a bad way for ammunition. The wood-yard foreman wished the powder-bearers luck.

Kingston was a good-sized town. The station platform was filled with people. The branch train for Rome was there, waiting for the Atlanta mail. Knight stopped alongside it and the Rome engineer called out:

"What's up? Fuller's engine and none of his men on board."

"I have taken this train by Government authority," said Andrews, "to run powder through to Beauregard." He waved his hand toward the box-cars in which his men were shut up.

The local freight was late. Andrews could get no information beyond that. Five minutes passed. Ten, fifteen minutes. To the men in the dark box-cars they seemed like hours.

Mr. Andrews walked up and down the station platform. One or two persons recognized him and saluted respectfully. He would stop and chat for a moment, belittling the alarming stories of Mitchel's advance into Alabama. People spoke of his poise in the face of the vexatious delay of the powder train.

Finally the freight came in. Andrews hastened to ask the conductor to pull up so that the powder train could move. The conductor was willing to oblige, but indicated a red flag on the end of his train. Another train was behind, made up, the freight conductor said, of everything on wheels that could be gleaned out of Mitchel's path. "And where," asked the conductor, "did you say you were to deliver this powder to Beauregard?" "At Corinth, Mississippi," repeated Andrews. "Why, you can't get through," explained the conductor. "Mitchel is on the line at Huntsville." Andrews said he did not believe it, but the trainman said he knew, having just come from there.

Twenty minutes, thirty minutes dragged by. Andrews patrolled the station platform within ear-shot of the telegraph key. With one hand he raised his tall hat in polite greeting. The other hand enclosed the butt of a pistol in the pocket of his long black coat. Any attempt to send a suspicious message and the telegraph operator would have been a dead man. Andrews told Knight to get word to the men in the cars as to how the land lay and have them ready to fight.

Knight and his crew oiled their engine. An old switch tender who had spent a lifetime on southern railroads, hung around asking questions. The powder-train story did not concern him. The strange crew in the General's cab interested the veteran whose mind was an encyclopedia of southern railway personnel. Where had they worked? Road? Division? Knight and his helpers answered in monosyllables. Fortunately Brown had once run a locomotive on the Mobile & Ohio, but there was no evading a certain discomfort in the old-timer's boring cross-examination.

Forty minutes is a long time to wait for a train under any circumstances. There was a whistle around the curve and Andrews met the refugee train as it pulled in, shouting directions for it to take its place on the already crowded sidings. This conductor also pointed to a red flag on his last car. The refugee train was running in two sections.

Fifty minutes. One hour—and a whistle that was music to the ears of twenty-two men. Section two rumbled in. Two regular trains from the north were now overdue. A prudent conductor would not have entertained a notion of leaving Kingston then. But Andrews said he would have to take the chance of passing the trains at Adairsville, ten miles farther on.

He waved for the switch admitting his train to the main line to be opened. But the old switch tender refused to budge. He had hung up his keys in the station and said that Andrews would have to show his authority to get them. The men inside the box-cars heard the old man's defiance and got their pistols ready. Not so the mannerly Mr. Andrews whose life was filled with escapes from apprehensive moments. He laughed at the veteran's distemper and said he would get the keys. He did so, and the General was off after a delay of one hour and five minutes at Kingston, making in all an elapse of three hours and thirteen minutes from Big Shanty, thirty-two miles away.

"Push her, boys, push her," Andrews urged, and the General simply flew.

6

Well for Mr. Andrews that he had taken a chance and left for Adairsville. Four minutes after the General cleared the Kingston yards, a screaming whistle was heard from the south. The impatient passengers thought Fuller's train was coming and picked up their valises. It was Fuller—but he had not brought his train. The old Yonah rolled in, wheezing and blowing. Fuller swung off with the stunning story of the capture of the General at Big Shanty, and while the tracks were being cleared of the four trains congesting them, he managed to give a few of the details of his almost incredible pursuit.

At Big Shanty—now the town of Kenesaw—Fuller had just sat down to breakfast when a shout went up that his train had been stolen. He was on the platform in time to see the General and three box-cars glide around a curve. The station and camp were in an uproar. The dumfounded sentry stammered his story. It flashed on Fuller that the engine had been seized by deserters who would run it up the track for a few miles and take to the woods.

"Let's get her back before we are badly out of time," he shouted and, with Engineer Cain and Superintendent Murphy of the machine shops, started up the track at a dead run. Two miles out the three were winded and about to give up when they met the track gang whose tools Andrews had appropriated.

"If we can find the old Yonah at our end of the branch, we will get the scoundrels at Kingston where those extras will hold them up," said Fuller.

Before any one could reply to this observation push-car and riders, sailing down a grade, were pitched into a ditch, having struck a lifted rail.

The Yonah was overtaken just as she started to leave the main line. This old engine was full of complaints, but she had had her day, and on this day she turned back the calendar. The sixteen miles to Kingston were covered in thirteen minutes.

The crowd at the station told Fuller that his quarry had eluded him by four minutes. The conductor dashed into the telegraph office and sent a message north. He came back to the platform to hear the powder story, but, of course, did not learn that the "powder" cars were filled with armed men. Otherwise, he and his few helpers would have proceeded much more cautiously. The trains still were in a snarl on the tracks and, rather than lose any more time in switching, Fuller decided to abandon the Yonah. He uncoupled the engine of the Rome train and was off in a little better than six minutes, or about eleven minutes behind the Yankees.

The message telegraphed from Kingston did not get through because Andrews had stopped above the town in a blinding rain and cut the wires. Here the men also started to lift a rail, but their ineffective tools made clumsy work of it. Two-thirds of the rail was loose from the ties and the fugitives were about to give it up as a bad job, when the unmistakable whistle of a locomotive was heard from the south. Pursuit! It could be nothing else. The lifting of the rail became a matter of life or death. Most of the members of the party were large muscular men. They grasped the loose end of the rail, and with the strength born of peril heaved and pulled and heaved and pulled again. The iron rail snapped and the men tumbled in a heap. In an instant they were on their feet, in the cars and away.

At Adairsville the raiders were cheered by the sight of the south-bound freight waiting on the siding. At the depot Andrews received positive information that Mitchel held several miles of the railroad in Alabama. To Andrews, the Yankee raider, this was welcome news. To Andrews, the Confederate powder-train official, it presented complications. The story of the powder train was rendered absurd on its face, but the marvelous address of the spy covered up the inconsistency long enough for him to get away. This took a little time, too. He tarried to reassure the freight crew and send them south with their train. With the pursuers coming north, the freight going south, and a broken rail between them, Andrews expected his adversaries to be delayed long enough to give him the lead he needed.

To accomplish this he took further risks. The south-bound passenger train, following the freight, was overdue. The station officials advised Andrews to wait for it. Quite truthfully Andrews said he could not afford to wait, but he promised to run slowly, sending a flagman ahead on curves. Thus Andrews hoped to reach Calhoun, nine miles farther on, and deal with the passenger train there.

So as not to arouse suspicion, the General rolled cautiously away from the Adairsville depot. A quarter of a mile of this and Andrews told Knight to let her go.

7

The Yonah, ancient as she was, had been a faster locomotive than the engine Fuller took from the Rome train, but it was this fact—and an element of luck, as the conductor himself admitted—that averted disaster to the pursuit. Having struck one broken rail he was on the lookout for others, although the rain made it almost impossible to see anything. Nevertheless Fuller did see, or thought he saw, where the track had been tampered with in time to have his engineer throw the engine into reverse and stop it on the brink of the gap.

The conductor leaped from the useless locomotive and, motioning to his men to follow again, started another foot-race up the track, sliding and slipping in the mud. He had not gone far when he saw the through freight headed toward him. He flagged it down and backed it into Adairsville. The freight engine was the Texas and there was no better locomotive on the line. It was detached and with a small party of armed men started, tender forward, toward Calhoun.

Fuller believed he had the Yankees now. Andrews was thought to be running slowly for fear of colliding with the south-bound passenger train. If so, Fuller's quarry was boxed between two trains. But if Andrews had succeeded in reaching Calhoun before the passenger left, Fuller himself would risk a collision—unless he took care. Fuller did not take care. The scent was hot and he sent the Texas racing ahead.

8

To this day Knight probably holds the speed record between Adairsville and Calhoun, Georgia. The nine miles were behind the stolen engine in seven and one-half minutes—over a track on which safe running was reckoned to be sixteen miles an hour. At that the Andrews party escaped destruction by thirty seconds. The passenger train had just pulled out from the station when the wild General was seen roaring toward it. The two locomotives, screaming under the pressure of their brakes, were stopped within a few yards of each other. The passenger engineer was trembling with fright—and he was angry. He refused to back up and let Andrews pass. A crisis seemed at hand, for Andrews literally did not have a moment to lose, as he had not yet cut the wires beyond Adairsville.

The rain still fell. The passenger conductor came up to see what was the trouble. Andrews addressed him in a tone of authority. He said he had requested the removal of his passenger train in order that powder for the front might not be delayed. Now he had no alternative but to issue orders. Without a word the conductor obeyed.

The spraddling hamlet of Calhoun diminished in the distance and the Yankees breathed more easily. Sergeant Major Ross had been right about a day's delay altering things. Yesterday it would have been smooth sailing—no extra trains, no excitement on the line, the powder-train story perfection itself. By now the raiders should have been near their triumphant journey's end. But to-day difficulties had been encountered only to be overcome. Five trains passed, a pursuit shaken off by a matter of minutes, and now they were on the main line once more with an open road ahead and a broken track behind.

9

Fuller covered the nine miles to Calhoun in ten minutes—which still leaves the Yankee Knight in possession of the record, however. The passenger train was still waiting. One scare in a day had been enough for the engineer. Andrews had tried vainly to send him on his way, which would certainly have been the end of Conductor Fuller. Instead, the raider's Nemesis, saved by another stroke of luck, rushed the Texas, running backward, out of Calhoun. Fuller himself perched on the tender where he could get a better view of the track.

The General and crew were within a few minutes of the first bridge to be burned—a covered wooden structure over the Oostanaula River. Here Andrews planned to render his success secure. He stopped a couple of miles in front of the bridge to cut wires and take up track. While some of the men tugged at a rail, others collected wood to fire the bridge. This would not be easy as the downpour continued and everything was soaking wet. The toiling rail crew was having its usual difficulties when they saw a sight that would not have startled them more had it been a ghost. A locomotive whistled and hove in view, burning up the track from the south. For the first time during the chase, Fuller sighted his quarry. Those at the rail yanked like men possessed. They could not break the rail, but they bent a yard of it some inches out of line. That seemed sufficient to wreck any train and the men jumped into the box-cars and the General started off.

It did not, however, wreck the mysterious pursuer. As far as the fugitives could see the oncoming engine shot over the bent rail as if nothing was wrong. On the tender Fuller had been so engrossed in observing the men in possession of the General, that he overlooked the rail until it was too late to stop. Actually the rail had nearly thrown the pursuing crew from the cab and they thought they were lost. Not until afterward did they learn how fortunate they had been. The bent rail was on the inside of a curve and the weight of the swiftly moving engine was on the outside rail. The bent rail simply straightened and the train kept on the track.

As for the Yankees, all their chances of getting away now depended on firing the bridge, and Andrews attempted a dramatic expedient to gain time for that. He reversed the General and charged his pursuers. When going full tilt the rear box-car was uncoupled, and the General was started forward leaving the box-car to continue the assault.

The bridge was reached. On a fair day a little oil and a faggot or two would have finished it, but it was raining harder than ever. Every stick of wood was soaked and the men kept their pistol ammunition dry with difficulty. Nevertheless a fire was kindled and coaxed to burn in one of the remaining cars. The plan was to leave the car in flames on the covered wooden bridge, but before the fire seemed the least encouraging here came the pursuers—pushing the raider's box-car in front of them. The southerners had had some more luck. On a down-grade the flying box-car might have driven them back for miles. But the hard-pressed Andrews was compelled to let it go on a level stretch. Fuller simply had reversed the Texas for a short distance, and, when the car slowed down, coupled it on and renewed the chase.

When he came in sight of the bridge, Andrews was forced to flee, and, for the first time, a feeling that the fates were not on their side overtook the Union adventurers.

Certainly all the advantages of chance had gone against Andrews. Still, Fuller's pursuit had been intelligent and daring and he had made no mistakes. None can question the daring of Andrews, but he had made a grave mistake in not destroying the Yonah.

On the bridge the Texas picked up the smoking car that Andrews had tried to convert into a firebrand. Both cars were side-tracked at Reseca, a station a few hundred yards beyond the bridge.

Passing Reseca the General did not run very fast. It was plain that there was no eluding the Texas by speed alone. The Yankees tried wrecking her. As there was no time to stop and dismantle the track, a hole was rammed in the rear end of the remaining box-car, and ties and sticks of fire-wood were dropped out in the hope of obstructing a rail. The wood showed a maddening disposition to roll off the track, but now and then a piece stayed on and Fuller was forced by the protests of his men to slow up.

The desperate expedient was effective as long as the wood lasted, but presently it was all gone, except a few sticks which were crammed into the fire-box for a sprint to the next wood-yard. There about half a load had been thrown aboard when the Texas hove in sight, but fuel was so precious that the men continued to pile it on and Fuller had to check speed to avert a collision. Before the hard-pressed General pulled out, Andrews's men had made a barrier of ties across the track, and, while Fuller removed it, the fugitives gained a few minutes' headway in their race to the water tank a few miles farther, for the General's boilers were almost dry. When the General left the water tank, the Texas was again in view.

Andrews was now ten or twelve miles from Dalton which was a large town with a complicated arrangement of switches. Somehow the hard-pressed Yankees must gain a few minutes to take care of possible delays there. It was also equally important to cut the wires before a message could get into Dalton to raise enemies in his path. A tremendous spurt was made. Then a sudden stop by throwing the engine into reverse. Before the wheels had ceased to revolve, the diminutive Scott was out of the car and up a pole. Another party was building a barrier across the track. Another was frantically trying to wrench up a rail. Corporal Pittenger, a young law student who had got in the army with difficulty because of his thick spectacles, approached Mr. Andrews.

"We can capture that train if you are willing," he said.

"How?" asked Andrews.

Without hesitating for a word the Corporal outlined an excellent plan of attack. "Block the track and place our party in ambush. Run our engine out of sight to disarm suspicion. When they stop to remove the obstruction we'll seize their engine and reverse it against any other trains that may be in this pursuit."

Mr. Andrews said nothing for a moment. "It is a good plan," he conceded. "It is worth trying." He glanced about as if studying the landscape. His survey was interrupted by the inevitable whistle of the pursuers. His glance shifted to the men who were vainly straining to force the rail.

"All aboard, boys," he called, and the dash to Dalton began.

10

The Texas was not in sight when the General halted a hundred yards in front of the Dalton depot which was a large structure with a shed enclosing the track. Several local railwaymen came up. The powder story was useless now—what with one battered car which had been literally peeled for fire-wood and a company of correspondingly battered men. Andrews dropped from the cab to see if the switches were set for a clear track. They appeared to be. "I am running this train through to Corinth," he called out in general acknowledgment of a flood of inquiries, and, signaling Knight to proceed, caught on the engine step as it passed.

The General tore through the station shed and through the town to the great consternation of the citizens of Dalton. This consternation had not diminished when, five minutes later, Fuller's

Texas rolled in merely slowing up to drop a man who bolted like a shot from a gun and literally fell upon the telegrapher's key.

At the same instant, a mile from Dalton, in plain sight of a Confederate regiment, John Scott was climbing a telegraph pole. One minute later the wire was cut, putting a period where no period was intended in Conductor Fuller's message from Dalton. But this much got through:

"GEN LEADBETTER COMMANDER AT CHATTANOOGA. MY TRAIN CAPTURED THIS A M AT BIG SHANTY EVIDENTLY BY FEDERAL SOLDIERS IN DISGUISE. THEY ARE MAKING RAPIDLY FOR CHATTANOOGA POSSIBLY WITH THE IDEA OF BURNING. . . ."

The Chattanooga commandant understood. What chance now for Andrews and his band? Every mile of flight from Fuller brought them a mile nearer to the open arms of the waiting Leadbetter.

Some distance from Dalton the road passed through a tunnel. Here was the place to turn and fight if they were ever to do it. But Andrews signaled to keep on. He meant to stake everything on the destruction of the Chickamauga River bridge. He ordered a fire built in the remaining box-car. This was hard to do. The car had been picked clean. Inside and out, it was wet and rain was still falling in torrents.

By drawing on the last quart of oil and almost the last stick of fire-wood a blaze was started. It crackled encouragingly and the spirits of the men rose with it. The little train stopped under the shelter of the bridge. As the oil burned from the surface of the wet wood the fire drooped a little. Still, the interior of the bridge shed was fairly dry and given time the flames in the car would do their work.

A fire always holds an attraction, and, as this fire meant so much to its guardians, they half forgot their peril, and tarried to watch it. It was midday and the strain since dawn had been great. It was worth the price to relax. If the fire failed a few minutes would not matter.

The blaze picked up again. It took possession of the car and tongues of flame licked the half-dry timbers of the bridge. No one had said a word for what might have been a full moment when the lookout called that the smoke of the Texas was in sight.

The burning car was uncoupled rather deliberately and one of Andrews's men, who was brave enough to tell the truth, said that his heart sank. The General limped through the village of Ringgold. Wood was gone and oil was gone, but Andrews dared not stop.

Fuller picked up the blazing car on the bridge and dropped it at Ringgold. A few miles from there he sighted the Yankees drilling along at fifteen miles an hour. They were burning their clothing to keep moving and the journals on their engine were melting from want of oil. Their last fragment of hope was a wood-yard several miles ahead.

Fuller guessed their straits and their plan, but he lagged back. He knew that he was dealing with men who would be desperate at bay. With the whole country behind him aroused and other engines in pursuit by now, Fuller felt no call to precipitate a battle.

The General's speed fell to eight miles an hour and Fuller slacked accordingly, keeping a good quarter to half a mile in the rear.

Knight said he could not make the wood-yard. Andrews did not delay his decision.

"Jump and scatter, men, and be quick."

The men began to jump, rolling over and over until they vanished in the dripping woods beside the right-of-way. When all were off Knight reversed the engine and jumped. The old General moved off toward the pursuers, but the steam was too low for it to obtain any speed. Fuller simply reversed, ran back away and let the General come up gradually and couple on.

A troop train which had joined the pursuit was soon on the spot and the country was smothered with searchers under orders to take the "train thieves," dead or alive.

All were taken, the captures requiring from a few hours to ten days.

Nothing the soldiers of the North did during the war aroused the South to a greater pitch than the exploit of these twenty-one men. The newspaper *Southern Confederacy* of Atlanta declared the preservation of the railroad bridges a victory equal to Bull Run. "The mind and heart sink back at the bare contemplation of the consequences that would have followed the success" of the raid. It resulted in a reorganization of railroad administration in the South.

Mr. Andrews left his bones in Dixie. He was hanged in Atlanta, ten days before the date set for his wedding. When his Kentucky fiancée read an account of it in a newspaper, the shock killed her.

The following week seven others were executed, but the sudden thrust of a Federal column interrupted the court martial of their fourteen comrades, eight of whom eventually escaped and reached the Union pickets. By this time the cry for vengeance had modulated and a few southerners went so far as to show publicly their admiration for the Yankees' valor. A year later the six who remained in Confederate hands were exchanged for their weight in important political prisoners held by the North. President Lincoln received them at the White House and listened to an account of their adventures.

"A little luck with the battles now and the war will be over," he said.

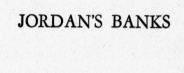

JORDAN'S BANKS

X

JORDAN'S BANKS

1

THE night was so very dark and still that the glow of their camp-fires a mile away made the Yankees seem nearer than they really were. A horseman approached watchfully—up the driveway to the large rock which stood as high as his horse. Dismounting behind the boulder, he crept across the lawn and stepped noiselessly up on the square-columned portico of the big farmhouse. His rap was answered by a stout gentleman in a night-shirt.

"Father."

"Sam!"

The boy explained that he owed the Yanks the pleasure of this unexpected call. They were crowding him pretty close. He had left his last hiding-place without his boots.

Mother bustled after something to eat. Father went for a pair of boots. Sam ate and, throwing himself on a couch, was asleep in a minute. Mother picked up the mud-stained overcoat he had flung aside. A Union Army coat! She took it to the kitchen and tried to dye it gray, but gray does not "take" on blue. Then she sat down beside her husband and for the rest of the night watched the face of her sleeping boy. Before daybreak they called him. He put on the boots. Mother held up the coat. Sam kissed her and glided into the dark.

2

Mother had forgotten to change the buttons, but no matter. If captured with the papers he carried, the style of his coat would have little influence upon the fate of Private Sam Davis, of Captain Coleman's scouts.

Captain Coleman was General Braxton Bragg's intelligence officer. The accuracy with which he kept his chief posted on the plans of the Federals had won him a reputation in both armies. He was a tall man with piercing blue eyes, a short, chestnut-colored beard and a cavalier air. Before the war he had been a doctor. His true name was Shaw, H. B. Shaw, but the Captain's work was such that he thought it advisable to conceal his identity even in the Confederate lines.

In October, 1863, Grant directed General Grenville M. Dodge, who was in Mississippi, to start north, comb the country, capture Coleman and break up his scouts. Dodge set out with the Sixteenth Army Corps—about ten thousand men.

At the time Captain Coleman and a few of his men were in Nashville which had fallen into Federal hands. They had in their possession plans of the fortifications of the city and other items of vast interest and importance to General Bragg. One night they met to put the finishing touches to their labors for him.

A custom of the scouts was for one man to carry all dangerous papers so that, in the event of capture, there would be no evidence against his comrades. On this occasion Captain Coleman handed the papers to Sam Davis who had just passed his twenty-first birthday. He was a quiet young fellow, very boyish-looking, with light hair, comprehending gray eyes and a winning smile. Two years as an infantry private in continuous campaign and six months as a Coleman scout had little altered this schoolboy who had enlisted during the first week of the war.

Sam tucked the papers in his boots and shook hands around. Then the little band scattered to meet at Bragg's headquarters outside of Chattanooga where the southern general had bottled up a Federal army. The route to Chattanooga lay, by air line, through one hundred miles of hostile territory and directly in the path of Dodge's broomsweep which, a couple of evenings later, forced Sam's unscheduled visit to his home in Rutherford County.

On November 17, 1863, a few days after his farewell to his parents, the young soldier rode down the Lambs Ferry Pike in the sunlight. Sam had quit slinking about at night. It seemed to arouse less suspicion when he made little pretense of hiding. He had concocted a casual story of a Federal soldier looking for his regiment, and even the washed-out appearance of his overcoat had caused no embarrassing investigations. In another day, with luck, Sam would be at Bragg's headquarters and his boot relieved of its incriminating secrets.

But this was not to be. With only one day between him and his goal, Sam had the misfortune to meet a troop of Dodge's Seventh Kansas Cavalry. These Yanks were different from the other easy-going Federals to whom the boy had given a friendly hail and passed by. The story of the lost regiment was received with cold and questioning stares, and with businesslike caution Sam was taken to the county jail at Pulaski.

He was locked up with twenty or thirty other suspicious characters that the vigorous Dodge had gathered in. Among these was a tall man with a short brown beard. His sharp blue eyes met those of the new prisoner, but not a shadow of recognition crossed the countenance of Sam Davis—or of his Captain.

3

A guard conducted Sam to the corps headquarters, where an officer sat studying the documents which had been taken from his boots by the Kansas cavalrymen. General Dodge raised his eyes to the boy who stood before him—"a fine, soldierly-looking young man"—these are the General's words—"dressed in a faded Federal coat and an army soft hat. He had a fresh, open face, which was inclined to brightness. In all things a true soldier." General Dodge received Sam amiably and asked him how he had come into possession of the papers. Sam courteously replied that that was something he would not tell.

General Dodge sketched to Sam the predicament he was in. A Confederate soldier, one of Coleman's scouts, taken within the

Federal lines in Federal uniform with dispatches to General Bragg—a more complete definition of a spy was not contained in the manuals. Yet the General said he was prepared to offer Sam a chance for life. Captain Coleman was the man he wanted. Possibly Sam knew where his captain could be found. If so, and if he would assist the General's men to find him, the General could promise that Sam's life would be spared.

Sam thanked General Dodge for his interest, and then by his silence signified that the interview could terminate at the General's pleasure. The General signed to the guard to take the prisoner away.

Sam was escorted back to the jail and turned in with the other people Dodge's men had rounded up—including the tall man with brown beard who was detained simply on general suspicion.

Three days later Sam stood before General Dodge again. Motives of policy solely had prompted the corps commander's first offer of clemency, but this was no longer true. The fact remained, of course, that the capture of Coleman was more important than the death of his subordinate. But the Federal authorities now desired Sam to speak, not so much on account of the information he could give, but to enable his captors to save the life of a boy who had won their hearts. All of the officers who had been sent to talk to Sam—Chaplain James Young, Eighty-First Ohio Infantry, Provost Marshal Armstrong, Captain Chickasaw, chief of Dodge's scouts, and others—were so taken with his manner that they instinctively desired to save him, and made extraordinary efforts to persuade Sam to provide them with an admissible military excuse for doing so.

"Davis met me modestly," said General Dodge. "He was a most admirable young fellow, with the highest character and the strictest integrity. I tried to impress on him the danger he was in. I made a direct appeal to him to give me the information I knew he had. I pleaded with him with all the power I possessed to give me some chance to save his life. He replied, 'General, I will not tell. You are doing your duty as a soldier, and if I have to die, I shall be doing my duty.'"

[184]

It was useless. A court martial sentenced Private Samuel Davis, First Tennessee Infantry, to suffer death by hanging on Friday, November 27, 1863.

4

The twenty-sixth was Thanksgiving Day. That night Chaplain Young and Sam prayed together and sang *On Jordan's Stormy Banks I Stand*.

In the morning the Chaplain returned early to renew his plea to Sam to talk. Captain Armstrong came at ten o'clock to lead the prisoner to the gallows. The Chaplain asked Sam for a keepsake and the boy took off the blue-gray overcoat. Mr. Young kept that coat for forty years and then, after cutting off a button for himself, presented it to a Confederate museum.

Between the files of the execution guard, Sam walked out of the jail. A wagon with a coffin in it was waiting. Sam got in and sat on the coffin and, between lines of soldiers, was driven to the scaffold which had been set up beside a large tree on a conspicuous ridge. Nearly the entire Sixteenth Army Corps was grouped about it when Sam got out of the wagon and sat down under the tree.

"How long have I to live, Captain Armstrong?"

"About fifteen minutes, Sam," said the Captain.

"What is the news from the front?"

Captain Armstrong said Bragg had been defeated at Lookout Mountain.

"I am sorry to hear it," said Sam.

The preparations went forward fumblingly. The soldier detailed to spring the trap was trying to beg off. He offered all the money he had to hire a substitute. There were no takers, and finally everything was ready. With tears streaming down his face Captain Armstrong approached the doomed boy.

"Sam, I swear to God I'd rather die myself——"

"Never mind, Captain," was the gentle reply, "you are doing your duty. I thank you for all your kindness."

A shout from the ranked soldiery suspended proceedings. A horseman galloped up and leaped from his saddle. It was Captain Chickasaw. The Federal scout leader hastened to where Sam sat and crouched beside him, speaking earnestly in a low tone. Ten thousand men looked on and wondered. Sam listened for a few moments and then rose and, in a tone which carried a touch of rebuke, exclaimed:

"Do you suppose I would betray a friend?"

Captain Chickasaw took out his watch. He said he had come with the final proposals of General Dodge, and was authorized to give the prisoner five minutes in which to reconsider his answer.

Without speaking Sam took a note-book from his pocket and began to write. When he finished he tore out the leaf and handed it to Chaplain Young. The Chaplain glanced at the paper. The others crowded around, expectantly. They read:

"Dear Mother—

"I have five minutes to live and will spend them writing to you. I don't want you to grieve after me. I don't only feel that I am doing my country's bidding but that all heaven is sanctioning the act I am about to take. I have asked the Chaplain to sing

"On Jordan's stormy banks I stand
And cast a wistful eye
To Canaan's fair and happy land
Where my possessions lie. . . ."

Captain Chickasaw said the five minutes were up, and turned away. Sam Davis faced the provost marshal.

"I am ready, Captain," he said.

5

Not long after Sam Davis had been buried, a file of prisoners was marched from the Pulaski jail and put aboard a train bound for an internment camp in Chicago. Among them was Dr. H. B. Shaw, looking very much a member of the medical profession with his chestnut-colored beard. As a matter of fact, he had answered truthfully many of his captors' questions about himself, even to giving them his real name. He told them he was a physician and, when asked to do so, was able to substantiate his claim to a knowledge of medicine. Nevertheless, something about the doctor determined the Federals to hold on to him a little while longer. But when the prison train reached Chicago, Doctor Shaw was missing, having escaped en route.

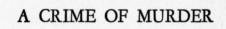

A CRIME OF MURDER

XI

A CRIME OF MURDER

I

LEWIS PAYNE turned up the collar of his threadbare coat and breasted the chill March wind that whipped along Calvert Street in Baltimore. He was homelesss, penniless and hungry; and he was in some danger. A few days before he had applied at a house for work in exchange for something to eat and had been impertinently refused by a colored servant. On Payne's feet were the remnants of a pair of Confederate cavalry boots and beneath his rags a world of southern pride. The line had to be drawn somewhere. Payne was a giant in size and in strength. He collared the negro and told him to mend his manners.

For this Payne had been arrested. The provost marshal was familiar with his kind. At the beginning of the war, Baltimore was frank in its sympathy for the southern cause. During the war, it was a haven for southern refugees and a convenient abiding-place for southern spies. Now that the struggle was all but over, the swarm of destitute Confederates became a minor public problem. The armies of the South were losing hope, their ranks melting not from battles entirely. A piece of Confederate uniform worn with a thin show of disguise was no extraordinary sight to Baltimore in the winter of 1864-65. The provost marshal discharged Payne with a curt order that the boy betake himself north of Philadelphia and not show himself in Baltimore under penalty of unpleasant consequences.

This seems a lenient and sensible disposition of the case, but Payne did not find it so. He had sold the army horse that had brought him from Virginia and spent the proceeds in search of employment. He had no money with which to travel.

At the corner of Fayette Street the anxious boy came abreast of Barnum's Hotel, which was Baltimore's most distinguished hostelry. A slice of the gay dining-room was visible through a window. The lobby with its groups of fashionably-dressed guests was in full view. These people were warm and well-fed and among friends; they inhabited another world. Payne passed the great door which a proud old negro opened and a gentleman in a splendid overcoat with a fur collar stepped forth.

Something about the stranger arrested Lewis Payne. He saw a man in his middle twenties, of medium height, graceful bearing and a handsome countenance with flashing dark eyes. The stranger passed an acquaintance and called out a cordial word of salutation. When Payne heard the voice he felt that he could not be mistaken. He stepped up and, touching his tattered hat, addressed the man in the splendid coat. Lewis Payne knew how to speak to a gentleman. He had gone to war from a good home.

For a moment the two conversed beside the hotel door. Then the man in the fine coat and the ragged young giant walked away together.

2

John Wilkes Booth was not an ungenerous man by nature. He made his money easily and spent it freely, and the petition of a needy southerner was a fairly sure passport to his purse. But a surer passport was flattery. Admiration was as the breath of life to him. On the stage Booth, the actor, was a personage. He said grand things, he did grand things, and audiences acclaimed him. John Wilkes did not distinguish between Booth, the actor, and Booth, the man. Off stage he must also be important. What he said must be grand, what he did must be grand; and he must be acclaimed. This weakness fattened a corps of unblushing sycophants.

Booth bought Payne a meal, found him lodgings and listened to his story.

Four years before, in the spring of 1861, a sixteen-year-old soldier of the Second Florida Infantry named Lewis Thornton Powell had arrived in Richmond with his regiment. Payne said that his true name was Powell, but, in search of the beginnings of a new life, he had called himself Payne only since leaving the army. Richmond was full of wonderful sights to the country clergyman's son who had never seen the inside of a theater. Booth was playing in Richmond. Lewis went and, in an inexpensive seat in the gallery, he was thrilled by Booth's acting. When the play was over he hung around the stage door for another look at his hero. When the actor appeared the captivated boy all but fell at his feet.

From Richmond Payne went to the war proper and fought through the great campaigns of 1861, '62 and '63 under Lee. At Gettysburg as a sergeant, he was wounded in Pickett's charge and taken prisoner. He escaped and joined a Virginia cavalry regiment, and fought on until January of 1865, when southern hopes were drooping. Payne's two brothers had been killed in battle and he could get no word from home. He gave up and rode his horse to Baltimore. Several times during the war Payne had seen Booth act, but he had not spoken to him since that night in Richmond, every detail of which he treasured in his memory.

Much as this meeting signified for Lewis Payne, it meant no less to the romantic egotism of John Wilkes Booth, who could give a veteran a dollar and become a participant in his battles. Here was an admirer whose sincerity was unimpeachable, and Booth's pulses tingled at the thought of having had the image of his artificial grandeur borne upon fields of fire by this simple chevalier of the South. That was ample to spread the protecting mantle of John Wilkes Booth's easy wealth over Lewis Payne.

Yet there was something more. Booth observed the newly found friend he was feeding. His muscular frame was well-proportioned, with broad shoulders, narrow hips and a bull-like neck supporting a massive head crowned by a thatch of tawny hair. His countenance seldom changed expression. The under jaw was heavy and cruel, the mouth firm. Beneath contemptuous brows were still gray eyes that had looked at death. Here was a man—a boy, rather, for the freshness of Lewis Payne's tanned complexion kept him from looking older than he was—to whom desperate hazards were as casual as coffee. Now it chanced that the elegant John Wilkes Booth needed a man who would not flinch at a desperate hazard.

3

On the following day Lewis Payne, with money in his pockets, took the steam cars for Washington, and twelve days later—on the evening of March 13, 1865—he ascended the steps of a cheerful-looking two-story brick house on H Street and pulled the bell. The household of Mrs. Surratt's boarding establishment was at home with the exception of the landlady's son John. Miss Anna Surratt and Miss Fitzpatrick were at the piano. Mrs. Surratt and other guests were playing euchre. A boarder named Louis J. Weichmann answered the bell.

Payne was well-dressed and well-groomed. He introduced himself as an acquaintance of John Wilkes Booth. A friend of the distinguished Mr. Booth was welcome at Mrs. Surratt's, and Payne was presented to the circle in the parlor. He spent the evening there, and being shown a room, retired when the others did.

Louis Weichmann was a clerk in the War Department, and when he came home from work the next evening he met Payne in the hallway. Payne also had just come in. The two mounted the stairs together. Through the half-open door to Weichmann's room a young man, lying on the bed, was visible. Payne asked if this were John Surratt, the landlady's son. Weichmann said that he was, and that he and young Surratt shared the room. Payne requested an introduction to Surratt and the two entered the chamber.

The following evening when Weichmann returned from his work he noticed a false mustache on a table in his room. Not finding his roommate Surratt about, he went up to the attic where he saw Surratt and Payne seated on a bed examining revolvers and knives. So engrossed were the pair that they did not hear the approach of the War Department clerk, who tiptoed down-stairs and informed Mrs. Surratt of what he had seen. The mother was not alarmed. She reminded Weichmann that when her son went "into the country" he needed such things for his protection.

Weichmann knew what Mrs. Surratt meant by John's going "into the country." John Surratt was a courier for the Confederate Government. He made regular trips between Richmond and the North, sometimes carrying dispatches as far as the Confederate "embassy" in Montreal. The secret route between Washington and the southern capital was a thoroughly established one and was traveled nearly every day. From Washington the route led almost due south into Maryland through Surrattsville and Beantown to Port Tobacco on the Potomac, slightly under forty miles below the capital. There was a ferry to the Virginia shore whence it was a matter of sixty-odd miles to Richmond by way of Port Royal and Bowling Green. The Maryland end of the route presented hardly any more difficulties than the Virginia end, especially in the latter days of the war. All Maryland was heavily southern in its sympathies, and the isolated section below Washington was almost solid for the Confederacy.

John Surratt had been born in Surrattsville, thirteen miles from Washington. When the war came, John's brother Isaac joined the Confederate Army. A tavern owned by John's father became a station on the underground to Richmond and John drifted into the courier service at the age of seventeen. In 1862 Mr. Surratt, senior, died. In 1864 the widow leased the tavern and the family farm to a Washington ex-policeman named Lloyd and took the house in H Street. Before the war Louis Weichmann and John Surratt had been chums at St. Charles College, and, during the war, Louis had often visited John in Surrattsville. Abandoning his studies for the priesthood, Weichmann had taught school in Baltimore, and while there had affected no concealment of his southern leanings. From Baltimore he had come to Washington to work in the War Department, and in the H Street house Mrs. Surratt treated him more as a son than as a boarder.

Weichmann's concern over the guns and knives was not such as to cause him to shun the company of his roommate or of the new lodger Payne. When he heard that Booth, who was to play at Ford's Theater that night, was placing a box at the disposal of some of Mrs. Surratt's guests, he hoped to be included in the number. He was not included, however. The only tickets sent were two each for John Surratt and Payne, who took with them Miss Honora Fitzpatrick and nine-year-old Appolonia Dean. They occupied box number seven, which was known as the President's box, although actually, when the President attended, the partition separating this box from number eight was removed, throwing the two boxes into one.

Between acts Booth came up from the stage and called Surratt and Payne from their chairs into the passageway where the three whispered excitedly. When the play was resumed, Surratt and Payne returned to the box. When the entertainment was over they took Miss Fitzpatrick and Appolonia home, and retraced their steps to Gautier's high-toned saloon on Pennsylvania Avenue.

There they found Booth and three other men whom Booth introduced as Sam Arnold, Michael O'Laughlin and George Atzerodt. It is possible that a fourth person, besides Booth, was there— a boy of nineteen named David A. Herold. But the chances are that Davy Herold would have been omitted from such a conference. He was willing and he was an abject worshiper of Booth. He was wild and adventuresome, but too talkative and he had been spoiled by his widowed mother and seven adoring sisters.

The others present were of a different stamp. Sam Arnold and Mike O'Laughlin had been Confederate soldiers. They were about Booth's age—twenty-five—and bore evidence of fair education and good rearing. Their families had been neighbors of the Booths at Bel Air, Maryland, where the celebrated tragedian, Junius Brutus Booth, had made his home on a farm and reared his family of ten children. John Wilkes was the youngest but one. The elder Booth had died when John was a boy. He remembered his father only as a garrulous eccentric who had wrecked his mind with drink. John, Sam and Mike had gone to school together, and seven months before this meeting at Gautier's, when the South believed that its sole chance to win the war lay in the defeat of President Lincoln by General McClellan in the election of 1864, Booth had approached his two boyhood friends with a proposal to make this a certainty. They told Booth they were with him.

The plan had been to kidnap the President and carry him to Richmond by way of the underground. While exploring this route and arranging for the passage of the carriage containing the captured Executive, Booth had met George Atzerodt, a carriage painter by trade and a fierce-looking little fellow with a German accent. Atzerodt had been engaged to ferry the kidnapping party and their victim across the Potomac. During this reconnaissance, Booth had heard of John Surratt, the fleet Confederate courier. He had sought him out in Washington, and thus had become an occasional caller to flutter the hearts of Miss Anna Surratt and the other young ladies at the house in H Street.

This had been the plot, but delay followed delay due, for one thing, to Booth's preference for theatrical rather than practical methods. His vanity was the axis about which everything else must be made to revolve. The election came and Lincoln defeated McClellan by a small margin. The conspirators then worked to execute their coup before Lincoln should be inaugurated for his second term, their object now being to obtain, in exchange for the captured President, the release of all Confederate prisoners-of-war, and other military advantages. A date in January, 1865, was set, but nothing came of it, and Booth's associates began to sicken of his management of the affair. It was at this time that Booth met the resolute Lewis Payne. Here was valuable acquisition to his forces.

4

The meeting at Gautier's was stormy. John Surratt opened proceedings with the startling announcement that the plot was known to the Government and had better be dropped. Booth raged against giving up, and the discussion, growing more heated, turned to ways and means. Booth insisted on a spectacular seizure while the President was attending a theater, but there were no adherents to this plan, except possibly Payne who said nothing. Arnold proposed to waylay the President while driving in the suburbs. Booth lost his head and hinted at the murder of Lincoln, declaring he would shoot any man who tried to back out before some sort of blow was struck. The ex-soldier Arnold replied that he himself had done some little shooting in his day and Booth apologized. At five in the morning the meeting broke up with a suburban kidnapping agreed upon.

Five days thereafter, on Monday, March twentieth, Booth, Surratt, Atzerodt and Payne mounted horses in front of the Surratt house and rode in pairs out Seventh Street toward the country. Arnold and O'Laughlin started from another point and fell in behind. Davy Herold had gone on ahead to meet the party and their prospective prisoner with arms and ammunition at a hamlet called Tee Bee on the underground six miles beyond Surrattsville.

No sooner had the four left the H Street house when Louis Weichmann unexpectedly arrived and learned of their departure from Dan, the colored kitchen boy. The clerk found Mrs. Surratt in tears. "John is gone away! John is gone away!" she sobbed.

In a wooded stretch of road near where Seventh Street crosses the District of Columbia line, the horsemen met and made their dispositions. It was two o'clock, and in a few minutes the President's carriage was due to pass en route to the Soldiers' Home. Not more than one guard would attend Mr. Lincoln as the President was a fatalist and believed that when his end was due it would come. The plan was to do away with the driver and guard and seize the President. Surratt would then mount the box and drive away over the road so familiar to him.

Wheels were heard on the gravel. The desperadoes crouched in their places. A carriage swung into view. It was the President's carriage—but the President was not in it. Another man was there, whom the plotters recognized, or thought they did, as Chief Justice Chase.

Louis Weichmann sat on the bed he shared with John Surratt, turning over in his mind what seemed to him the curious circumstance of Mrs. Surratt's grief. He had not seen her so affected when John had left on other mysterious errands. Just then Surratt, greatly agitated, burst into the room. Payne hurried up to his own room and began to pack his belongings. Down-stairs Booth paced the parlor carpet, slapping his boots with a riding whip. The three retired to the attic for a confab and presently left the house together. Weichmann still wondered vaguely what the fuss was about.

After supper Weichmann also left the house. He looked up Captain D. H. Gleason, an employee of the War Department, and related what had happened. They discussed the advisability of notifying the Secretary of War, but without, it appears, entertaining any serious intention of doing so. Weichmann was a man bold in whispered talk, but timid in action.

The parties to the conspiracy were frightened by their failure and they scattered. Booth and Payne went to New York. O'Laughlin and Arnold returned to their homes in Maryland where Arnold wrote Booth withdrawing from "the enterprise" in favor of a job in a Union Army sutler's store at Old Point Comfort, Virginia. Surratt went to Richmond for the Confederate Government. Atzerodt hung around town to spend some money Booth had given him. Davy Herold did likewise, bedeviling his mother and sisters, who tried to get him to go to work. Davy was a pharmacist's clerk when he worked. Abraham Lincoln left for the front to see General Grant.

5

On Saturday, April first, the Confederate Secretary of War gave John Surratt two hundred dollars in gold and dispatches for Montreal, and on Sunday the southern capital was evacuated. On Monday afternoon John arrived in Washington during the demonstration over the fall of Richmond. He changed his clothes at his mother's house, bought Weichmann an oyster supper, and took a train north. The following Sunday night, April ninth, President Lincoln returned to the capital by boat and was greeted with the glorious news of Lee's surrender, which had taken place that afternoon. That same evening Booth arrived from New York, Payne having preceded him. Washington celebrated the victory all night long.

On Monday the rejoicing continued and an impromptu parade with a band serenaded the White House. President Lincoln showed himself for a few minutes and asked the band to play *Dixie*. He said he had always liked the tune, and that we were again all one country. On Tuesday Mrs. Surratt's presence in Surrattsville was required by business concerning the settlement of her husband's estate. She asked Weichmann if he would borrow Booth's horse and buggy and drive her out. Booth said that he had sold his horse and buggy only the day before. He handed Weichmann ten dollars, telling him to hire a rig and accommodate Mrs. Surratt. As a matter of fact, Booth had not only disposed of his driving horse and buggy, but also the saddle horses he had kept most of the winter for the kidnapping. All he had left was one horse that was blind in one eye, which no one apparently wished to buy.

All day Monday and all day Tuesday Booth stalked about Washington with the grim Payne at his side. The celebration of victory continued, which Booth took as a personal affront, having, as he imagined, or at any rate desired Payne to imagine, borne an heroic part for the lost cause. Every peal of a bell and every torchlight marcher reminded Booth of the failure of his abduction plot. And the cruel part of this was that some of his own men had reproached him as responsible for this failure. Booth must have wondered what was going on in the brain that lay behind the inscrutable mask of this Payne boy's face.

The star and the satellite sauntered aimlessly upon the White House lawn, where a band was playing and crowds were calling for the President. Mr. Lincoln appeared. In the victory manifestations there had been a note that Mr. Lincoln did not like: too much hang-Jeff-Davis talk and similar vaporings of the curb-stone patriots, of whom, on the South's side, John Wilkes Booth was an eminent example. In his remarks Mr. Lincoln spoke tenderly of the South and of the sufferings of its people. The seceding states should be taken back and treated as if they had never been away. Then he touched upon a delicate subject, even for the North. Northern extremists were loudly advocating the franchise for former slaves—more as a measure of revenge than anything else. Lincoln said he was opposed to this and believed that only the "very intelligent" negroes and those who had been Union soldiers should vote.

Either Booth misunderstood this utterance or he was insane. In any event he seized Payne's arm and told him to shoot Lincoln on the spot. Payne refused, saying it was needless to run such a risk. As the two walked away Booth muttered, "That is the last speech he will ever make."

6

Two days later General Grant arrived in the capital and Michael O'Laughlin came over from Baltimore to see the welcome.

The day after that was Friday, April fourteenth. At two A.M. Booth wrote a letter to his mother, who was a staunch Union woman. He tried to appear philosophical over the outcome of the war. Then he went to bed and about noon appeared at Ford's Theater and asked for his mail. Harry Ford, the proprietor's younger brother, handed the actor a letter with some word about its being for the handsomest man in Washington. Booth sat down to read the letter and Ford began to twit him about the Union victory.

"By the way," said Ford, "your friends Lincoln and Grant are coming to the theater to-night, and we're fixing to bring Lee in handcuffed and show him off."

Booth made a hot retort to the allusion to Lee and then asked if it were really true that Lincoln and Grant would attend the evening performance. Ford said it was, and the actor folded his letter and walked away.

Seeking out George Atzerodt and Davy Herold, Booth directed them to hire horses. He then hired a mount for himself and put it in a stable behind the theater where the one-eyed horse also was kept.

While these things were being done Mrs. Surratt received another summons to Surrattsville on estate business. Weichmann volunteered to do the driving as before and the widow gave him money to hire a conveyance. As the two were starting out, Booth appeared at the boarding-house carrying a small parcel. On learning of Mrs. Surratt's trip into Maryland, Booth asked her to hand the package to Lloyd, her tenant, and to tell him that Booth would call that night for those two carbines that Lloyd had been keeping for him. Mrs. Surratt promised to execute these commissions and drove off with Weichmann.

Booth then returned to the theater. The auditorium was dark and it was empty. Harry Ford and Ned Spangler, a scene shifter, had completed the decoration and appointment of the presidential box. This box was on the right side of the house, as one faced the stage. From the main floor it was reached by a stairway which led to a passage extending behind the boxes. The passage was separated from the rest of the theater by a door, and from each box, including the President's, by other doors.

Booth ascended the stairs and entered the President's box. He noted the arrangement of the soft chairs that Ford had brought from the theater's reception-room to replace those ordinarily used in the boxes. He surmised that a big red plush rocker was intended for the President.

The lock on the door of the President's box was out of order, but Booth took no chances on its being repaired before nightfall. He stooped and sighted a line from where the head of a tall man would show above the back of the chair to the door, and with a gimlet bored a hole large enough to admit the muzzle of the small Derringer pistol that he carried. As the gimlet was a small one it was necessary to work the hole a little larger with a pocket knife. With the upright of a music stand, Booth next improvised a bolt on the inside of the passage door, so as to shut off the main part

[202]

of the theater from the box. Then sweeping up the gimlet shavings and some plaster he had knocked from the wall during his preparation to bolt the passageway door, Booth stole from the theater unseen.

From Ford's Theater the actor rode on horseback to Grover's Theater, where he wrote a letter. "For a long time I have devoted my energies, my time, and money to the accomplishment of a certain end. The moment has now arrived when I must change my plans. Many will blame me for what I am about to do; but posterity will justify me." The letter was signed: "Men who love their country better than gold or life. John W. Booth, Payne, Herold, Atzerodt."

Booth addressed the letter to the editors of the *National Intelligencer,* stamped the envelope and remounted his horse. On Pennsylvania Avenue he met an actor named John Mathews whom months before he had ineffectually tried to involve in the kidnapping plot. Mathews remarked that Booth's nerves appeared to be unstrung. Booth laughed at the idea and asked Mathews if he would do him a "little favor." When Mathews assented Booth handed him the letter. "I may leave town to-night. Unless you hear from me by ten o'clock to-morrow will you mail this letter?"

While they were talking a band of Confederate prisoners marched past under guard, and presently General Grant passed in a carriage. After the General had gone by, Mathews again asked his companion what made him so nervous.

7

General Grant was returning from the White House, where he had called to say that he had canceled his theater engagement. He intended to leave that night for New Jersey, to spend the week-end with his daughter Nellie, who was attending school there, and whom he had not seen for a long time. The President was reluctant for Grant to go. Mr. Lincoln said that he had seen the play at Ford's before, but would be there because the people expected him. He said that the public would be greatly disappointed not to see their victorious general. Grant was a battle soldier and few civilians, even in Washington, had seen him.

It was a beautiful spring day, and enjoying the first relaxation from the burdens he had borne for four years, the President had spent as much of it with his family as he was able. Captain Robert Lincoln, the President's son, had surprised them by walking in during breakfast. He had come straight from the front and for an hour the family sat over their breakfast dishes while Bob told of the surrender of Lee. Little Tad Lincoln listened with his mother and father—all ears. Captain Lincoln exhibited some mementoes of the event, including a photograph of General Lee, which the President took from the hand of his son and studied it carefully. "It is a good face," he said, "the face of a noble, brave man. Now, Robert," he added, "you must lay aside your uniform and go back to college and in two or three years I will try to tell you whether you will ever make a lawyer or not."

In the forenoon there was a Cabinet meeting. The President urged that no resentment be shown the South. "No persecution, no hanging or killing those men, even the worst of them." Secretary of War Stanton, for one, heard these words in silence. Mr. Stanton was bitter against the South.

Until the middle of the afternoon the President was busy with callers and papers. He pardoned a Union soldier, sentenced to death for desertion, and a Confederate soldier under similar sentence as a spy. In the afternoon he and Mrs. Lincoln went for a drive. "Mary," the President said, "we have laid by some money, but it is not enough to support us. We will go back to Illinois, and I will open a law office in Springfield or Chicago."

Returning from the ride, the President brushed the dust from his clothing and was washing his hands when the Assistant Secretary of War, who called on a plea of urgent business, was shown in. The Assistant Secretary said that the Provost Marshal of Portland, Maine, had telegraphed that he had located Jacob Thompson, a notorious Confederate agent in the North. Thompson was fleeing the country and the Provost Marshal asked for instructions.

"What does Stanton say?" Lincoln asked.

"He says to arrest him," replied the Secretary's subordinate.

Mr. Lincoln reached for a towel. "No-o-o," he said. "When you've got an elephant by the tail and he is running away, just let him run."

Later the President said something about liking to get out of that theater engagement if he could. Some one had given him a new book by Artemus Ward, which he would have preferred to read rather than see *Our American Cousin* again. But Mrs. Lincoln said the President could not disappoint the audience, especially since General Grant had rather unceremoniously done so. Mr. Lincoln sat chuckling over the pages of Artemus Ward and had to be called two or three times to come to dinner.

After dinner last-minute visitors kept the carriage waiting. As the President started to leave the library, two gentlemen were announced. They wished passes to Richmond. Mr. Lincoln picked up a card and wrote hastily:

"No pass is necessary now to authorize any one to go and return from Petersburg & Richmond— People go and return just as they did before the war. A. Lincoln."

It was after eight o'clock. With Mrs. Lincoln and the other members of the theater party who were waiting, the President passed down the stairs and through the doorway to the carriage.

8

At this moment four men were whispering in a room in the Herndon House on Pennsylvania Avenue. Booth said that the departure of Grant had simplified matters. Instead of taking Payne with him to the theater, the southerner could assassinate Secretary of State Seward. Payne would ride the one-eyed horse and Herold would show him the way to the Seward residence. Herold would then post himself so as to join Booth on his flight. Payne accepted the new assignment without a word. It was a hazardous mission. As a result of a buggy accident, Seward was in bed with a broken jaw and carefully guarded against the intruders who would give a public man no peace.

There was no change of plan for Atzerodt. He would kill Vice-President Johnson, who was alone in his hotel room doctoring a cold. But Atzerodt had weakened. He declared he had been employed to kidnap and not to kill. Booth persuaded; he stormed. He told Atzerodt that if caught he would "hang anyhow," and left the miserable little German sick with terror and indecision.

The play had been under way for some minutes when the President arrived. In his party were Mrs. Lincoln, Miss Clara Harris and her fiancé, Major Henry R. Rathbone. A single guard, John Parker, took his post by the door to the passage back of the box—the door that Booth had prepared to bar from within. The orchestra struck up *Hail to the Chief,* the audience cheered and on the stage Laura Keene left off her lines and made a sweeping curtsey. Mr. Lincoln stood for a moment in acknowledgment of the greeting and, still smiling, seated himself in the red rocking chair.

At twenty minutes of ten o'clock Booth appeared at the stage door and called for some one to hold his horse. Entering the stage door he passed through a private way to Tenth Street in front of the theater. Captain William Williams of the Washington mounted police recognized the actor and asked him to have a drink, but the invitation was declined. The White House carriage was in front of the theater with a small crowd about it, as there had been a report that the President would leave after the second act. Booth joined the crowd and his restless actions attracted the attention of Sergeant Dye of the provost guard, who nodded to a fellow-sergeant, and the two watched Booth narrowly. He was conversing in low tones with a man who has never been identified. When the second act ended and Mr. Lincoln did not appear, Booth went alone into a saloon next door to the theater and drank a glass of whisky.

The third act curtain had been up for a few minutes when Booth playfully took hold of the hand of John Buckingham, the door-keeper, and asked him if he wanted a ticket. Buckingham admitted the actor, who went in, looked around and came out almost immediately. As he passed out, Buckingham was talking to an acquaintance and he introduced Booth. The actor made a few genial remarks and asked for a chew of tobacco. Ten minutes later he again passed out the stage door and had another drink of whisky. As he reentered the theater, Buckingham heard him humming a little tune.

Booth knew the situations of *Our American Cousin,* and the one he was waiting for would be at hand in about five minutes. Unrecognized by any one, he climbed up the stairs and went along the corridor to the door of the passageway behind the President's box. The guard, Parker, was not at his post. He had taken a seat in the balcony where he could obtain a better view of the stage. Booth moved softly to the door of box number seven. The lock had not been repaired; there would be no occasion to use the gimlet hole. Booth stepped back and barred the passageway door with the bolt he had made from the music stand, thus cutting off interference from that direction. There were now perhaps three minutes and a half to wait in the dim corridor back of the boxes.

On the stage the designing "Mrs. Mountchessington," who had been rallying the shrewd Yankee "Asa Trenchard" on his unfamiliarity with the ways of London society, delivered a parting shaft and flounced off the stage. Trenchard was alone on the boards, and but two players were in the wings, awaiting entrance cues. "Society, eh?" said Asa, looking after the retreating Mrs. Mountchessington. "Well, I guess I know enough to turn you wrongside out, you darned old sockdolaging man-trap!"

At this sally the audience laughed so heartily that no one outside of the box heard the report of the small pistol that Booth held a few inches from the back of the President's head.

Major Rathbone was the first to realize what had happened. He lunged at Booth who slashed Rathbone with a long knife, and, shouting "Revenge for the South!" vaulted the rail of the box. Rathbone grappled after the assassin and deflected his leap, so that Booth caught his spur in the frame of Washington's picture and the folds of a Treasury Department flag that formed a part of the decorations.

The stage was fourteen feet below and ordinarily the leap would have been nothing for one of Booth's athletic training. He alighted in a sort of crouching heap and was up instantly. Brandishing his knife he shouted something that was not clearly understood and started to run off the stage.

Before the nonplused spectators could think, a heart-piercing scream from Mrs. Lincoln filled the theater. Leaning over the box rail with the blood dripping from his sleeve, Major Rathbone shouted:

"Catch that man!"

PURSUIT

XII

PURSUIT

I

WHEN John Wilkes Booth declined his invitation to have a drink, Captain Williams of the Washington mounted police went un-accompanied to Doc Claggett's café a few doors from Ford's Theater. He was there twenty-five minutes later when some one shouted that the President had been shot.

Williams dashed to the theater and heard that the assassin had escaped by the stage door. Taking charge of a policeman or two and some soldiers of the provost guard, the Captain began to handle the crowd that was pouring from the playhouse. He had cleared a path when a group of men, followed by an hysterical woman clinging to an army major in a bloody blouse, emerged bearing a window shutter on which lay the inert form of Abraham Lincoln. The President was carried into Mrs. Peterson's boarding-house across the street.

A moment later news came that the home of Secretary of State Seward had been invaded by a frenzied giant who slashed his way through a ring of attendants, wounding four of them, and delivered at the bedridden Secretary a knife-thrust that would have been fatal had not the steel frame binding his broken jaw deflected the blade. And like the man who had shot the President, this demon had thrown off those who tried to seize him, leaped upon a horse and vanished into the moonless night.

It appeared as though a conspiracy to exterminate the personnel of the Government was in motion. Captain Williams received orders to gather up his men and guard the Kirkwood House, where the Vice-President was asleep. The orders came from the Peterson house, where the fierce and instantaneous energy of Secretary of War Stanton radiated from a room adjoining that in which the President was dying.

Stanton was drastic. He placed the capital under martial law. He roused regiments from their slumbers and sent them galloping to guard the exits of the city and residences of officials, and to scour the town for the conspirators. Ford's Theater was seized and every person in its employ arrested. Three colonels were rolled from their beds to interrogate those who were brought in from the theater and elsewhere.

2

Before the first of Stanton's soldiers was bugled from his blankets, a man riding rapidly was halted by the Regular Army sentry at the Navy Yard Bridge on the eastern edge of the city. The sergeant of the guard, Silas T. Cobb, was making his round of inspection.

"Who are you, sir?" asked Cobb.

"My name is Booth," said the horseman.

"Where are you from?"

"From the city," said the horseman.

"Where are you going?"

"I am going home."

In response to further questions Booth said he lived on a farm in Charles County, Maryland. Sergeant Cobb asked if he did not know that no one was allowed to pass the barriers after nine at night, and the man said that that was news to him. He added that he had waited purposely to have the moon, which was about to rise, to ride by. Cobb permitted the man to go.

Ten minutes later a young fellow presented himself to the sergeant, and, giving the name of Smith, was passed also.

A little later John Fletcher, a liveryman, turned up. He described a young man and his horse and asked if they had passed. The description suited Smith, and Fletcher was told that such a man had passed. The man's name was not Smith, the liveryman said, but Herold, and the horse that he had hired was overdue at the stable. Fletcher asked permission to pursue Herold and Cobb offered to let him pass on condition that he not return until daylight. This stipulation the liveryman declined to accept and rode back to town to tell his troubles to a policeman.

One was not hard to find. By the time Fletcher reached town, every policeman in Washington was on duty and the hunt for the President's assailant was on. Between tiptoeings in and out of the next room to gaze into the face of his unconscious chieftain, orders flew from the firm lips of the Secretary of War. Some hurly-burly in their execution was natural. Persons were snatched before the three colonels with such rigor that they were frightened half out of their wits. Actors and theater attachés who were morally certain that the assassin was John Wilkes Booth qualified their assertions in the face of awful warnings against telling anything but the absolute truth, and the identification of the actor was momentarily clouded. A sheer guess as to the man who had struck down Mr. Seward fixed upon a Confederate desperado named Boyle.

About one o'clock in the morning Lieutenant John F. Toffey was on his way to report for duty at a military hospital a mile from the Navy Yard Bridge when he noticed a riderless horse. Its body was quivering in every nerve and sweat was pouring from it in a stream.

The horse was taken before the three colonels, who found that it was blind in one eye. The liveryman Fletcher identified the animal as belonging to John Wilkes Booth. He said that it had been ridden lately by George Atzerodt and David Herold, friends of Booth. Fletcher also told of his pursuit of Herold on the hired horse and of his colloquy with Sergeant Cobb.

One squad of men was already searching Booth's room at the National Hotel. Others now descended upon every livery-stable in town.

The hotel squad brought in a gimlet and a letter signed "Sam" that they had found in Booth's trunk. The letter was dated Hookstown, Maryland, March 27, 1865. It explained the writer's failure to keep an appointment with Booth in Washington, saying that he was no longer a party to Booth's "enterprise" and had promised his parents to seek employment. The writer warned Booth against rashness, and censured him for his previous conduct. Booth was advised to "go slow. . . . See how it will be taken in R——d [Richmond]." The letter contained a reference to "Mike."

From the liverymen the three colonels learned of the horses that Booth had hired the afternoon before, and also of his horse deals during the winter. These revelations brought in the name of John Surratt.

At three A.M. Mrs. Surratt's house in H Street was surrounded by detectives. The boarder and friend of the family, Louis Weichmann, answered the bell and was told by the officers that they were searching for John Wilkes Booth and John Surratt. The detectives followed Weichmann up-stairs, saying that Booth had shot the President and that Surratt had stabbed the Secretary of State. Weichmann told the detectives they were mistaken about Surratt, as he was in Canada. The party trooped back downstairs and when Mrs. Surratt came from her room, which was on the first floor, Weichmann related to her what the detectives had said about Booth.

"My God, Mr. Weichmann," the woman exclaimed. "You don't tell me so!"

3

Mrs. Surratt assured the officers of her son's absence in Canada and exhibited a letter that she had received from him on the day before. The detectives departed after Weichmann had promised to report at headquarters at eight o'clock.

Weichmann was there before eight o'clock and was taken into custody. A party of detectives carried him to Surrattsville. The roads were alive with troops. By sunup a brigade of infantry, a thousand cavalry, and two hundred detectives had been thrown into Maryland.

From a liveryman the authorities had learned of Weichmann's

two trips with Mrs. Surratt to the tavern at Surrattsville—the last one on the day of the President's murder. Lloyd, the tenant of the Surratt property, was questioned. Being a former Washington policeman, Lloyd knew one of the detectives. The hour was a little early for the inn-keeper who seldom felt well in the morning, but he told the same story of Mrs. Surratt's visits that Weichmann had told. This account confined itself to Mrs. Surratt's legal business in the village, and made no mention of the Booth parcel or of Booth's message to have the guns ready on the night that the murder was committed. Although reminded by his former associates on the force of the immense rewards that would be forthcoming for information leading to the capture of Booth, the ex-policeman clung to his story. Specifically he denied that Booth or any traveler had called at the inn on the preceding night. Everything had been normal, including the fact that Lloyd had gone to bed drunk. No other evidence was obtained in Surrattsville to cast doubt upon this story.

The next day was Easter Sunday. The hat and overcoat of Mr. Seward's assailant had been found. Weichmann continued to urge the impossibility of the guilt of his roommate, John Surratt. He said the hat and overcoat of Seward's attacker might possibly belong to one George Atzerodt, and accompanied the detectives to Baltimore in an effort to find Atzerodt. They did not find him, and the detectives began to grow suspicious of the good intentions of their willing helper. Weichmann was extremely nervous and the hat and overcoat story must have seemed rather curious on its face, as the best available descriptions of Atzerodt indicated that this apparel was intended for a man about twice his size. The officers concluded that Weichmann was misleading them to protect some one. Their surmises turned to the house in H Street.

On Monday Michael O'Laughlin surrendered to the authorities in Baltimore and Sam Arnold was arrested in Old Point Comfort, Virginia, where he was working. They had been traced by the letter from Arnold found in Booth's trunk.

That night at half past eleven o'clock a party of army officers arrived at the Surratt house and Major W. H. Smith pulled the bell. A tall, genteel appearing woman of middle age responded.

"Are you the mother of John H. Surratt, Jr.?" the Major asked.

"I am, sir," said Mrs. Surratt.

"I have come to arrest you and all in your house," announced Major Smith.

Mrs. Surratt did not say a word and the officers stepped inside. In the house were the landlady, her daughter Miss Anna, her sister, who was visiting in Washington, and one boarder, Miss Fitzpatrick. The other boarders had left when the Surratt house became involved in the national tragedy. Major Smith sent for a carriage. While they were waiting for it to arrive the door-bell rang.

Captain Wermerskirch answered it. A large man stood on the stoop. He was unshaven and dirty and his clothing was torn and covered with mud. Over his matted hair, in place of a hat, was drawn the sleeve of an undershirt. On his shoulder he carried a pick. The man saw the officers and the little group of bonneted women in the parlor.

"I guess I am mistaken," he said, and started to walk out.

An officer barred the way. "Whom do you wish to see?" he asked.

The man said he had come to see Mrs. Surratt. He was asked why he wished to see Mrs. Surratt.

"To dig a gutter," replied the man with the pick.

He was reminded that it was a strange hour to dig a gutter. The man said that he had not come to work but to find out at what hour to begin in the morning. The officers asked him other questions. His first replies were plausible. He was a poor man, with no home, who slept where he could lay his head and made his living with his pick. But in a few minutes he had contradicted himself and Major Smith asked Mrs. Surratt to step to the door.

"This man says he has come to work for you. Did you ever see him before?" asked the army officer.

Mrs. Surratt was near-sighted. In the dim light of the hallway, she peered at the unkempt figure, and raising her hand replied:

"Before God, sir, I never saw him before."

The carriage had come. Mrs. Surratt asked for a moment in which to pray. When the widow arose from her knees, the women and the rough-looking stranger were taken before the three colonels, who were reenforced now by a general.

The four women looked at their fellow-prisoner and each declared that he was unknown to her. One of the officers ventured an opinion that he was John Surratt, and Miss Anna wept so bitterly that her mother was obliged to comfort her. Finally the stranger was ordered to remove the shirt-sleeve from his head and Miss Fitzpatrick exclaimed that he was Mr. Payne!

Mr. Payne, however, meant nothing to the inquisitors. On their long list of suspects and of possible and of probable suspects, this name did not appear. The women were taken to the Carroll Prison and the officers went to work to fit the mysterious Payne into their scheme of things. They had astounding success. In the small hours of the morning he was identified by a negro house-boy as the iron-armed savage who had strewn a trail of blood through the residence of the Secretary of State.

4

Lewis Payne was taken aboard a navy ironclad, anchored in the middle of the Potomac, and chained in the hold. Double irons were then put on his hands and feet. His head was enclosed in a bag with a small hole to admit air. In the floating prison he was presently joined by O'Laughlin, Arnold and Ned Spangler, a scene shifter at Ford's. They were likewise bagged and ironed, except that they were not chained down. Three days later—the sixth day after the murder—George Atzerodt was pulled from a bed at the home of a cousin in Maryland, and he and the cousin were added to this hooded company.

Nor were these all of the arrests. It is doubtful if any one man knew how many arrests had been made up to this time, but the number was over a hundred and fresh detentions took place almost every hour. The principal quarry, however, were still at large.

Maryland was the logical place to look for them, but the discoverable traces were faint. The best evidence amounted to this: Following the church service at Bryantown on Easter morning, thirty-six hours after the murder, Dr. George A. Mudd had told an army lieutenant that his cousin, Dr. Samuel Mudd, had set a broken leg for a man early the morning before, which in the light of subsequent disclosures looked suspicious. The injured man was accompanied by a younger companion. Dr. Samuel Mudd had requested that his cousin communicate this to the authorities.

This clue was strengthened by Atzerodt, who told of the abduction plot, and of the preliminary trips of Booth through southern Maryland along the route of the old underground to Richmond. From Atzerodt, or from some of the many residents of Maryland who were questioned, it was learned that Booth had met Dr. Samuel Mudd on these travels, and through him had purchased the one-eyed horse.

Lloyd, the Surrattsville tavern-keeper, was arrested and subjected to strong pressure. The sot broke down and confessed that sometime after midnight on the night of the murder Booth and Herold had been at the tavern. Booth had remained outside while Herold roused Lloyd from a drunken sleep. Herold bought a bottle of whisky and carried off a carbine from among the weapons that John Surratt had stored at the inn following the collapse of the kidnapping plot. Herold also carried off the parcel that Mrs. Surratt had left at the inn the afternoon before. The parcel contained a pair of field-glasses. While Herold was thus engaged, Booth had sat on his horse drinking whisky. As they rode away Booth tossed down the empty bottle exclaiming, "I have murdered the President," and Herold said, "I fixed Seward."

The confession unnerved Lloyd. When he had finished he broke down, crying, "I am to be shot! That vile woman has ruined me!" He was taken to Washington and locked up in the Carroll Prison.

On the same day, Friday, April twenty-first, Dr. Samuel Mudd was arrested and taken to Bryantown, five miles from his home, where he answered questions freely and told this story:

At four o'clock in the morning after the murder, he was awakened by a young man who asked for medical attention for a companion, who was on a horse in the yard. The man on the horse wore a thick beard. Doctor Mudd and the young fellow, who said his name was Tyson, carried the injured man into the Mudd parlor, where it was discovered that the small bone of the left leg was broken. The flesh about the wound was much lacerated, apparently from hard riding. Doctor Mudd set the limb and accepted a fee of twenty-five dollars. Tyson did all the talking. He said his companion's name was Tyler. Doctor Mudd made no further inquiries. Discretion is a part of a doctor's profession, and, in southern Maryland in war-time, it was a part of every one's profession. The physician granted the injured man's request for a little rest and Tyson carried him up-stairs. Doctor Mudd retired to his chamber down-stairs and went back to sleep.

The young man had breakfast with the family and talked a great deal. He gave the Mudds the impression of a harum-scarum boy who was trying to show off. A servant carried food to the patient up-stairs. In the afternoon Mrs. Mudd took a tray containing some dainties to the sick-room. The patient declined the refreshments and asked for whisky. A little vexed, Mrs. Mudd returned to the kitchen to superintend the preparations for Easter. A noise on the stairs brought her from the kitchen and she was surprised to see the young man helping the sick man down-stairs. It was awkward work and the invalid's whiskers skewed around so that Mrs. Mudd could see that they were false. The injured man's face was so drawn by pain, however, that Mrs. Mudd felt compassion for him and said that they were welcome to remain for a while longer, if they desired. The young man thanked her and made some flip retort about having a lady-love near by who would care for them.

An hour later Doctor Mudd returned from Bryantown with the news of the President's assassination and the arrival of troops in search of the assassin. Mrs. Mudd told of the departure of the two men and of the false beard. "Those men were suspicious characters," the doctor said to his wife. "I shall go back to Bryantown and tell the officers." It was supper-time and Mrs. Mudd persuaded her husband to wait until morning and inform the officers when the Mudds went to church.

Doctor Mudd admitted his previous meetings with Booth. He had seen him three times. But Mudd seemed so willing to assist the authorities that they gave him twenty-four hours in which to prepare to submit to arrest. The doctor went home, arranged his affairs and returned alone to Bryantown, from whence he was removed to the Carroll Prison. At the prison Doctor Mudd examined photographs of Booth and of Herold and said that it was possible that the injured man was the actor. All doubt on this score was removed, however, when the boot that the surgeon had cut from the broken leg was found in Mudd's house. It bore the lettering "J. Wilkes ——." Doctor Mudd's composure was a little shaken when the boot was handed to him to identify. He said he had not examined the boot previously and had meant to give it to the authorities but had forgotten to do so.

5

These events established Booth's flight into Maryland. Was he still there? This was the question now troubling the authorities.

The question had also troubled Captain William Williams of the mounted police as early as Wednesday, April nineteenth, two days before the disclosures of Doctor Mudd and the confession of Lloyd. Captain Williams was in Port Tobacco, Maryland, on the Potomac forty miles below the capital, where the Richmond underground crossed the river into Virginia. Here it was thought that Booth would attempt to cross, if he had not already crossed. Sixteen hundred cavalry had swept the surrounding swamps and countryside. They were ordered to dismount and sweep again.

Captain Williams was in the barroom of Brawner's Hotel in Port Tobacco when a tall man entered. He had a weatherbeaten look and a lean hard face. Williams knew the tall man. His name was Thomas A. Jones and he had been the chief agent at the Maryland end of the underground.

Looking at Jones as he spoke, Captain Williams said that he was authorized to announce that three hundred thousand dollars would be paid for information as to the whereabouts of Booth. Mr. Jones was conversing at the bar. For an instant his steady eye caught the glance of the policeman and presently he sauntered from the room.

For two more days the troops and detectives continued their fruitless search about Port Tobacco. Then on what seemed to be a hot scent they began to draw off into St. Mary's County adjoining. Thomas A. Jones was one of the first to be aware of this maneuver. He stole from his house and cautiously approached a little pine woods a mile away, giving a low whistled signal. In the thicket he came upon two miserable human beings shivering under a wet blanket.

"To-night," said Jones, "you cross the river."

For five days and six nights, Booth and Herold had lain in the woods while searchers passed and repassed within a few yards of them. The broken leg had unsettled the contemplated plan of flight. Surrattsville had been reached within two hours, or a little more, after the crime. This was one-third of the way to the river, which under ordinary circumstances would have been crossed before daylight. But the splintered bone was tearing the flesh of Booth's leg at every jump and the pair, riding slowly, turned from the prearranged line of escape toward Doctor Mudd's.

Leaving Mudd's the next evening, the fugitives almost ran into the arms of the troops at Bryantown. A negro guided them around the village or they should have done so. The negro acted as their pilot nearly all night, taking them as far as the plantation of Colonel Samuel Cox, a prominent man whose house was not three miles from the Potomac River.

Herold knocked at the door and requested shelter for himself and a disabled friend. Cox had been an open Confederate sympathizer, but he was shocked at the news of the President's murder, which he had received just before going to bed. He questioned Herold closely and the boy refused to give his name. Cox said that with the President's murderer at large and soldiers apt to appear at any moment, he could not in the middle of the night take in strangers who declined to explain themselves. In terror the fugitives passed the rest of the night in a little ravine on Cox's farm.

While riding about his place the next morning—Easter morning—Colonel Cox came upon the outlaws. Booth's plight was pitiful and Cox promised to help them to the river. He led the way to the pine thicket, which was on a neighbor's land, and told the fugitives to remain there until a man appeared and gave a certain whistled signal; then to do as this man should direct.

6

The man with the whistle signal was Cox's foster-brother, Thomas A. Jones. He told the pair that his instructions were to get them out of Maryland as quickly as possible. He brought them food and newspapers. But before Jones could move his charges the country swarmed with troops, and Jones was obliged to steal out and shoot the mounts of Booth and Herold for fear that they would answer the neighs of the cavalry horses.

Booth's sufferings were terrible, and he was not tortured by the pangs of the flesh entirely. In the newspapers he read of the universal horror at his deed, and of its repudiation by the South.

In a note-book that he carried Booth penciled his defense. He raged against a world that had misjudged a patriotic deed. "For doing what Brutus was honored for—what made William Tell a hero . . . I am looked upon as a common cutthroat;" and much more in the same vein. He complained of the Government's injustice in suppressing the letter that he had written to the *Intelligencer*. (It was Booth's conclusion that the Government had suppressed this letter in which, a few hours before the murder, the megalomaniac had sought to glorify his deed. Mathews, the actor to whom Booth had given the letter to mail, had opened it when he heard of the President's assassination. Fearing he might be unable to explain the possession of such a document, Mathews destroyed it and kept his silence for two years. The quotation given in the previous narrative is from Mathews's memory.) Booth further wrote that for six months he had "worked to capture" the President and, only on the day of the deed, had determined to kill him. The laborious scribblings also cleared up the dispute over what Booth had shouted when he leaped to the stage of Ford's Theater. It was *Sic Semper Tyrannis.* Herold, Booth wrote, was spending a good deal of time in prayer.

The night that Jones came to remove the fugitives was made miserable by a cold rain blown by the wind. Booth was lifted astride a horse. He begged to be taken to the house for a cup of hot coffee, but Jones said he was risking enough. The horse was led through a swamp to the river's edge. A flat-bottomed boat was there. It was so dark that the men could not see one another, but went about their business by the sense of touch. Booth was helped into the stern of the boat. He insisted on paying Jones for his trouble, and, finally consenting, Jones reckoned up the score item by item. It came to seventeen dollars. Jones would take no more, and Booth counted out the sum of seventeen dollars, fumblingly transferring the money to his protector's hand in the darkness.

The river was three miles wide, but Booth must take a slanting crossing, turn a point of land and ascend a creek on the Virginia side, a passage of about eight miles. Jones did his best to explain the directions to Herold. The boy took the oars and Jones shoved them off.

"God bless you, my dear friend," called Booth. "Good-by, good-by!" And the sound of the oars was silenced by the wind and the rush of the rain on the water.

7

Herold lost his sense of direction and rowed all night, landing at daybreak on the Maryland side, fifteen miles by shoreline from the starting-place. But the next night he crossed to Virginia.

By one means and another the pair made their way eight miles inland to the home of Dr. Richard Stuart, whose fervent devotion to the southern cause recommended him to the fugitives as a protector. But Doctor Stuart had laid down his arms, and he declined to harbor two such suspicious-looking characters. He gave them some food, however, and directed them to a negro's hut where Booth wrote a note and sent it to the doctor:

"Forgive me, but I have some little pride. I was sick, tired, with a broken leg, and in need of medical assistance. I would not have turned a dog from my door in such a plight. . . . The sauce of meat is ceremony, the meeting were bare without it. Be kind enough to accept the enclosed five dollars, although hard to spare, for what we have had. STRANGER."

Next morning the negro drove the outlaws twelve miles to Port Conway on the Rappahannock River. While waiting for a fisherman to ferry them over the river, three paroled Confederate officers rode up. Herold called one of them, a Captain Jett, aside. He disclosed his identity and threw himself on the southerner's mercy. Jett was greatly agitated but presently he promised to do something to help the fugitives. They crossed the Rappahannock and three miles farther Captain Jett introduced "John William Boyd," a wounded fellow-Confederate, to the household of a rather imposing Virginia plantation manor. Jett rode on to Bowling Green to call on a young lady.

The name of Booth's hosts was Garrett. The following afternoon—Tuesday, April twenty-fourth, the ninth day after the crime—at about five o'clock Booth, Herold and the Garrett family were seated on the front gallery when a platoon of Federal cavalry galloped past. Booth and Herold slipped from the porch and hid in a thicket behind the barn. Some persuasion was necessary to induce them to come out for supper. The explanations they gave for their conduct did not satisfy their hosts. The Garretts became further suspicious when Booth offered young Jack Garrett one hundred and fifty dollars for his horse. It was Jack's army horse and the young man would not sell.

Booth and Herold asked permission to sleep in the barn. It was granted, but when they were inside Jack Garrett locked the barn door and he and his brother went to sleep in a shed near by, believing the strangers meant to steal horses and depart during the night.

At two o'clock in the morning there was an imperious rap at the door of the Garrett homestead. When Mr. Garrett, senior, appeared in his night-shirt, he was seized by a man in the uniform of a Federal lieutenant who pressed a pistol to the old man's head. Another soldier dangled a rope. In the background were the indistinct forms of some thirty cavalrymen. Among them was a disheveled man whom Mr. Garrett, unless he was too greatly startled, may have recognized as Captain Jett.

8

Jack Garrett ran up calling to his father to do anything the soldiers asked. These troops were commanded by First Lieutenant Edward P. Doherty, Sixteenth New York Cavalry, whose energy and resourcefulness were largely responsible for tracking Booth to the Garrett place. But when the quarry had been located Lieutenant Luther B. Baker, a nephew of the chief of the United States Secret Service, attached himself to Doherty's little command and began to wave pistols and make himself conspicuous.

The barn was surrounded. Baker unlocked the door and one of the younger Garretts went in to demand Booth's surrender. He came out saying that Booth had threatened his life.

Presently Booth called to Baker. "Captain," he said in a distinct voice, "I know you to be a brave man, and I believe an honorable one. I am a cripple; I have but one leg. If you will withdraw your men one hundred yards I will come out and fight you."

Next Booth proposed that the men be withdrawn fifty yards and lastly he offered to fight the entire command singly. "Give me," he cried, "a chance for life!"

A party of soldiers who had dropped asleep from weariness were aroused to pile brush against a corner of the barn.

Booth was heard cursing Herold for cowardice, after which the actor shouted to those outside:

"There's a man in here who wants to come out!"

Davy Herold thrust his arms through a chink in the wall beside the barn door, was manacled and dragged forth, Booth calling out that "before my Maker he is innocent of any crime."

The barn was set on fire, and Booth could be seen through the chinks by the door. He rose from a bed of straw, with a crutch under his left arm and a carbine in his right hand. He took a hop or two toward an old table. He took hold of the table and made as if to throw it at the fire in an attempt to put it out. The flames licked higher. Dropping the crutch the actor passed the carbine from his right to his left hand, drew a revolver and took two or three hops toward the door, where Baker was lying in wait beside the chink.

There was a shot. Sergeant Boston Corbett had violated Doherty's explicit order not to fire without command. Booth gave a little spring upward and fell on his back. Baker was on him in an instant, wrenching the revolver from his hand.

This was at three-fifteen o'clock in the morning. They laid Booth on the Garrett lawn. He spoke twice. The first time he asked whether his captors would communicate a message to his mother. Lieutenant Baker stooped and wrote it down. "Tell her I did—what I thought—was—best." Later he indicated by a look that he wished his arms, which had been paralyzed by Corbett's bullet, raised so that he could see his hands. It was done, and Booth looked at them and said:

"Useless—useless!"

At seven o'clock he died.

EXPIATION

XIII

EXPIATION

I

A RADIANT May sun slanted through the bars of the low-ceilinged room in the old Washington Penitentiary and cast their latticed shadow upon the floor. The fragrant spring air of the Potomac neutralized the odor of the fresh whitewash that came from the blank walls. Behind a long table with a green cloth top sat the court martial consisting of nine officers of the army—seven grave-looking men with beards, and two with mustaches.

In front of the court were other tables. Three army judge advocates were busy at one with books and papers. About another, with their heads together, bent the counsel for the accused. At a third table were the newspaper men with their pencils behind their ears, as little of note had happened yet. In one corner of the room were a few rows of spectators, whose presence was a mark of exceptional privilege.

These groups filled the calcimined chamber, save for a railed-in platform against the wall opposite the court. On the platform were eight vacant chairs.

A door opened and the room was very still, which accentuated the sound of shuffling feet and the clank of iron without. A civilian entered followed by a soldier. The civilian's wrists were handcuffed together, and as he walked he stooped under the load of the seventy-five-pound weight at the end of a two-foot chain clamped to his left ankle. He took his place on one of the platform seats. The spectators discerned a mild-looking young man about twenty-five years of age, of medium size, rather genteel face and a high

forehead. His brown eyes blinked from the unaccustomed brightness of the room, for the bag tied over his head since his arrest
had just been removed. This was Booth's schoolmate, Samuel
Arnold. He was nervous and fidgeted in his seat.

Arnold was followed by Dr. Samuel Mudd, likewise manacled
and accompanied by a soldier. Doctor Mudd's beard, his prema-
ture baldness and his dignity made him look older than his thirty-
two years. He sat down in a chair next to Arnold and the soldier
stood between them.

Then came Edward Spangler, the scene shifter at Ford's, a
loutish, simple-looking fellow in working man's clothes. He did
not seem greatly worried, or to have much capacity for worry.

Next to enter was Michael O'Laughlin, a small man to whom
the seventy-five-pound weight was a real burden. He had a bright
alert face and a neat black mustache and goatee, but his dandified
attire had lost its air of spruceness. O'Laughlin had surrendered
to the authorities in Baltimore. His quick glance jumped about
the courtroom as if he were still eager to please.

Except in the case of Doctor Mudd, the parts these four had
played in the great conspiracy were obscure to the popular mind.
That was something to be brought out at the trial. Vague also
was the popular conception of the rôle assumed by George
Atzerodt, who followed O'Laughlin to the prisoner's dock, but
the impression was that Atzerodt must be a desperate character,
and though small of build, his fierce-looking countenance seemed
to justify the worst suspicions. He was more heavily ironed than
the others.

The sixth in the line was the gigantic scowling Payne, also
fettered with extra irons. Every one had heard of the savage aspect
of the assailant of Secretary Seward and a buzz of interest swept
the room. Payne took no notice of it, but crossing his legs gazed
over the heads of the onlookers at a patch of landscape visible
through a window.

Then came young Herold. In this prisoner—Booth's companion in his flight—great interest had been aroused, but the
actual appearance of the culprit did violence to many bloodcurdling

illusions. Davy's round weak face looked sorely troubled; the muscles of his mouth twitched; and he had neglected to shave.

The last prisoner was Mrs. Surratt, a tall woman in her middle forties and inclined to stoutness. She was dressed plainly in black, with an old-fashioned brooch at her throat. Mary Surratt had never been beautiful, but as a girl she must have been undeniably attractive, because she was still attractive under the least favorable of circumstances. Her chestnut hair was parted in the middle and combed close to her head. Steady blue eyes looked from a countenance which, though pale and tense, faced an unfriendly world with a quality of tranquillity that came from the well-springs of character—and every eye turned on Mary Surratt that morning appreciated as much. Mrs. Surratt was not ironed but like the others was attended by a soldier.

The prisoners stood while the charge against them was read. Severally and jointly they were accused of "maliciously, unlawfully, and traitorously . . . combining, confederating and conspiring together with one John H. Surratt, John Wilkes Booth, Jefferson Davis, George N. Sanders, Beverly Tucker, Jacob Thompson, William C. Cleary, Clement C. Clay, George Harper, George Young and others unknown to kill and murder . . . Abraham Lincoln, . . . Andrew Johnson, . . . William H. Seward, . . . and Ulysses S. Grant; and in pursuance of . . . said . . . conspiracy . . . unlawfully and traitorously murdering the said Abraham Lincoln, . . . and traitorously assaulting with intent to kill and murder the said William H. Seward, . . . and lying in wait with intent to . . . kill and murder the said Andrew Johnson and the said Ulysses S. Grant."

To this each prisoner pleaded not guilty, and the court adjourned to reconvene on the following day—May 11, 1865—at ten in the morning.

2

Thus swiftly had the wheels of justice turned. Fifteen days following the death of Booth and the capture of Herold, eight prisoners had been winnowed from the sheaf of prospects and brought to trial, while the search for the others went forward. The complicity of Jefferson Davis and those whose names followed his in the formal charge had been guessed at because of their supposed connection with John Surratt. Like him, these others were Confederate agents who had operated for the most part in the Northern States and in Canada.

The scope and speed of this tremendous effort to vindicate justice attested the energy of Edwin M. Stanton, Secretary of War. From the first Stanton had believed the crime to be a Confederate plot. The conclusion suited the forces of his mind. Mr. Stanton had been very bitter against the South and had shown his bitterness in speech and in deed. During the feverish small hours of the morning of April fifteenth, when the President was dying, the first evidence that incontestably linked John Wilkes Booth with the assassination, simultaneously seemed to support the theory of Confederate participation. This was the letter of Sam Arnold advising Booth to "go slow" and take matters up with Richmond. Stanton accepted this as proof. He directed La Fayette C. Baker, Chief of the Secret Service, to uncover the facts.

Baker was another man of enormous energy. Already he had determined the apportionment of the Government's reward of fifty thousand dollars for the capture of Booth. His nephew, Lieutenant L. B. Baker, headed the list with an award of seventeen thousand five hundred dollars. The quiet Lieutenant Doherty, actually more responsible than any one else for the capture, trailed along behind several other of Baker's favorites with two thousand dollars. Eventually, however, Congress took a hand in the matter, raising Doherty's award to seven thousand dollars and reducing that of L. B. Baker to four thousand.

But for the time being La Fayette C. Baker's prestige remained supreme. With Stanton's complete confidence and power practically unlimited, no secret was deemed immune from his net of spies which spread everywhere. Almost instantly, it seemed, Baker reported to Stanton that everything in the sweeping charge was proved. From Canada, from Richmond and elsewhere, Baker's men brought evidence involving the Confederate President and his personal agents in the murder of Abraham Lincoln. The Secretary of War was assured that John H. Surratt had been in Washington on the night of the murder, and not in Canada, as his friends would have the authorities believe.

This beginning seemed promising, but Mr. Stanton met obstacles to his passionate efforts to uncover the guilt of the criminals. Though hunted everywhere John Surratt had not been caught. Baker's evidence represented him as ranking among the moving spirits of the plot. They had his mother, but the evidence against her was incomplete. Under pressure John Lloyd, tenant of the Surratt property at Surrattsville, somewhat strengthened the net of circumstantial proof against his landlady, but pressure on other prisoners produced no such encouraging results.

In this connection the prisoner Weichmann became an object of especial attention. He was a member of the Surratt household and shared a bed with John. This placed a War Department clerk in an equivocal situation, which other considerations failed to redeem. Weichmann's eagerness to demonstrate that Surratt was in Canada when Mr. Baker declared positively that he had been in Washington at the time of the murder; the personally conducted wild-goose chase after Atzerodt and the ridiculous misidentification of the garments of Payne—these circumstances were damaging. The fact that some time before the crime Weichmann had confided his suspicions of Booth and Surratt to an office mate, but had gone no further, did not balance the score.

The officials bore down upon this prisoner very severely, and at length conducted him before Secretary Stanton. Mr. Stanton was a hard man for a culprit—or for any subordinate—to face. The Union generals had found him so, excepting Grant, who called his superior a blusterer. What Grant took for bluster most men assumed to be the evidences of an extraordinarily forceful personality, and so it appeared to Louis Weichmann. Mr. Stanton subjected the clerk to an examination that lasted for two hours. Weichmann was led from the Secretary's presence a cringing wreck, but he clung to his story. Pressure was not relaxed, and a few days later, given the choice of amplifying his admissions or facing a court martial, Weichmann pieced out the story that had sent Mary Surratt to the dock.

After the pleas of the eight prisoners had been heard, the introduction of evidence began. The first testimony was given by Baker's men, who claimed to have proof of the complicity of Jefferson Davis and the Confederate agents named in the charge. This had been previously announced to the press, and the North accepted their guilt as a fact. All that Baker's men were required to make plausible was something that nearly every one already believed, and in this they were given great latitude. There was no cross-examination and they were permitted to introduce testimony which ordinarily would not be entertained even by a military court, whose rules concerning the admissibility of evidence are much broader than those applying to civil tribunals. Still they failed. Their evidence was inconclusive, and the court turned its attention to the prisoners at the bar.

3

Payne had no defense and attempted none, although a lawyer who had volunteered his services went through certain formalities. Herold might as well have attempted no defense. Atzerodt was little better off. That he made no attempt on the life of Vice-President Johnson because he had lost his nerve amounted to little in the way of mitigation; Atzerodt knew of Booth's intention to kill Lincoln in time to have forestalled it. At no time was there a doubt as to the penalty these three would pay.

The cases against Doctor Mudd and Ned Spangler were not so clear, and the prisoners were skilfully defended by General Thomas Ewing, a brother-in-law of General Sherman. The evidence against Mudd established that he had sympathized with the South during the war. While working on details of the abduction plot, Booth had seen Mudd on his tours of southern Maryland, and it seemed possible that the doctor may have known of this plot. Mudd admitted setting Booth's leg. Such was the evidence against the doctor, but the court was lenient in the admission of testimony for the prosecution and strict in its rulings as to what the defense might present. As an example, General Lew Wallace, a member of the court, reprimanded one of the defending counsel for endeavoring to impeach the testimony of a Government witness—an elementary right in ordinary courts of law.

The evidence in Mudd's favor was this. He had repudiated his southern preferences some months before the crime and at the last election had supported the Union ticket. His meetings with Booth and his acquaintance with Surratt were not shown to be connected with the crime. Mudd denied that he had recognized Booth when he set his leg. Nothing was proved to the contrary. On hearing of the assassination, Mudd had notified the authorities of his suspicions of Booth and Herold, though not so promptly by some eighteen hours as he might have done.

Ned Spangler was a shiftless but amiable character of low intelligence. For years he had done odd jobs for Booth, and thought it a kind of honor. He had cared for the horses Booth acquired for the abduction plot. While decorating the presidential box at Ford's on the afternoon before the murder, he was reported to have said, "Damn the President and General Grant." When Booth leaped to the stage after the deed and made his escape through the stage door, Spangler yelled to another scene shifter, "Don't say which way he went!"

The defense of Arnold and O'Laughlin was that neither of them had seen Booth for nearly a month before the murder and did not know that it was contemplated. As for the abduction plot—that was not what they were on trial for. Arnold had written Booth withdrawing from that enterprise, but the letter held out the hope that if Booth would change his dramatic tactics and consult with the Confederate authorities in Richmond, he might come back in. Arnold was in Old Point Comfort, Virginia, clerking in a Union Army canteen on the night of the crime and was arrested there some days later. O'Laughlin was in Washington on the night of the murder. He said he had come from Baltimore to see the celebration of the surrender of Lee. His time was fully accounted for by witnesses of unquestioned loyalty. He did not see Booth, although he made some attempt to find him for a friendly visit.

The Government contended that the murder conspiracy and the kidnapping conspiracy constituted the same offense, notwithstanding the fact that no mention of abduction appeared in the comprehensive charge. The defense was unable to introduce satisfactory evidence that the abduction plan was abandoned, the participants to it had dispersed and the assassination conspiracy was thereafter erected on a new basis. Booth's note-book would have established this, but Secretary Stanton did not turn the note-book over to the court. He submitted everything else that was found on Booth's body, however, and many things that were found in his trunk.

The cases for and against these prisoners were interrupted from time to time by the introduction of additional evidence against Jefferson Davis and associates. But proof of their connection remained elusive.

4

The first witness against Mrs. Surratt was Louis Weichmann. He testified that Booth had come to the Surratt house the first time in January, 1865, in the company of John Surratt, and thereafter was frequently at the house. He always asked for John, and, if John were absent, for his mother. Weichmann had observed Booth and Mrs. Surratt in private conversation several times, but without hearing what passed between them. Herold had visited the Surratt home once; and Atzerodt had been there once, staying all night. The witness had never seen Arnold or O'Laughlin. Weichmann described Payne's stay at the Surratt residence, and told of finding Payne and John Surratt in the attic examining knives and guns. He also told of returning home unexpectedly on the day of the attempted kidnapping of the President to find Mrs. Surratt weeping. This seemed significant to him, as Mrs. Surratt had never wept before when John was away on his missions as a Confederate courier, although the witness tactfully avoided an open admission of his knowledge that his roommate was a rebel agent. Weichmann described the two trips to Surrattsville with the prisoner, the last one being on the day of the murder. He said that on both occasions Mrs. Surratt had held conversations with Lloyd, her tenant, which he did not overhear. There was an appearance of furtiveness about the conversations, the witness said.

The next witness for the prosecution was the drunkard John M. Lloyd. He told of a visit to Surrattsville by Herold and John Surratt to stow away carbines after the failure of the kidnapping. He said that on her first visit Mrs. Surratt had inquired about these "shooting irons," adding they would be needed soon. On the second visit Lloyd said that Mrs. Surratt told him to have the guns ready as they would be called for that night. At the same time she handed him a parcel, which Lloyd found to contain Booth's field-glasses and which were picked up by the assassin during his flight.

Other Government witnesses related the dramatic story of Payne's return to her house and of Mrs. Surratt's failure to identify him; also that a search of the premises had disclosed a small lithograph of Robert E. Lee, one of General Beauregard and a tintype of Booth. A point was made of the fact that, when told that she was under arrest, Mrs. Surratt did not ask why she was being detained.

This completed the Government's case against Mary E. Surratt. The defense sought to divest it of value as evidence by the cross-examination of the prosecution's witnesses and by fresh testimony.

Weichmann was cross-examined by United States Senator Reverdy Johnson, Maryland's most distinguished lawyer. Mr. Johnson had joined Mrs. Surratt's counsel after the start of the trial, having become convinced of the prisoner's innocence during a conversation with her in her cell. His appearance caused a commotion among the members of the court. On vaguely expressed grounds, General Harris, one of the members, challenged his right to appear, implying that during the war Mr. Johnson had not supported the Union as loyally as he should have done. The language of General Harris was intemperate and discourteous. Mr. Johnson replied with some spirit that he was eligible to appear before the United States Supreme Court and challenged the intimation that he had been unfaithful to his oath as a senator, or to his obligations as a citizen. He was permitted to appear before the court, but the hostility of several members remained undisguised. Under Mr. Johnson's cross-examination, Weichmann admitted that Mrs. Surratt was a hospitable, generous and devout woman. On Sundays Weichmann usually accompanied her to mass. He admitted that he had heard no word of any conversation between her and Booth or Lloyd. By further cross-examination of Weichmann and by the direct testimony of several other witnesses, it was brought out that Mrs. Surratt's visits to Surrattsville were in response to urgent summonses to attend to private legal business.

On cross-examination Lloyd confessed that he was drunk when he talked to Mrs. Surratt during her last trip to Surrattsville. Others testified that Lloyd was so drunk as to be irresponsible. Additional witnesses were found to her conversations in question. They had not heard what was said, but they swore that the conversations appeared to be of a casual nature.

The defense produced several witnesses who had seen nothing suspicious in Booth's visits to the Surratt house. Also it was shown that likenesses of Grant and of Sherman were in the house and that the daguerreotype of Booth had been purchased at a photographer's gallery by Miss Anna Surratt, the prisoner's daughter. Character witnesses testified to Mrs. Surratt's good reputation and to her kindnesses to Union soldiers.

While the defense of Mrs. Surratt was under way Weichmann, who had been released from prison, met a friend named Lewis J. Carland. In a sworn statement Carland later related what had happened. Weichmann, he said, declared himself to be miserable on account of his testimony against Mrs. Surratt and said that he was going to confession to relieve his conscience. The two young men walked to the rooms of a mutual acquaintance, John P. Brophy, a college student. Weichmann asked Brophy what effect his testimony had had. Brophy was indignant. He accused Weichmann of trying to hang an innocent woman, and Weichmann admitted his belief in Mrs. Surratt's innocence, but said that he had been forced to give his testimony by threats of hanging. He said that the Government agents had told him he had been talking in his sleep and that if he did not make a clean breast of it there would be no hope for him. "And I did not want to be hanged," said Weichmann.

Carland advised Weichmann to make an affidavit of his statements, but Weichmann did not do so. Brophy, however, reduced them to writing and visited the defense counsel, offering to take the stand and swear to Weichmann's admissions. With a feeling that they had overthrown the Government's case, Mrs. Surratt's attorneys asked permission to call Brophy as a witness. The judge advocates objected and the court sustained them. Brophy was not permitted to testify. He then wrote an account of the matter for the *National Intelligencer,* but the newspaper declined to publish it.

5

The trial dragged through May and through June. The introduction of evidence against Davis and his colleagues was renewed several times. Witnesses went far afield, but their testimony missed the point. This spectacular phase of the promised revelations quietly faded from the proceeding and interest centered upon Mrs. Surratt. At the beginning her complicity had been taken for granted. But when the trial closed on its fifty-third day, something akin to doubt had begun to surmount the grief-stricken rage of the North.

On June twenty-ninth the court met with the judge advocates, who had conducted the prosecution, to render its verdict. Over Herold, Atzerodt and Payne there was no debate. They were found guilty and sentenced to be hanged. O'Laughlin was next on the list. Assent of the six members necessary to inflict the death penalty was wanting, and O'Laughlin was sentenced to life imprisonment. The simple Spangler was found guilty as accessory after the fact and given six years' imprisonment. Arnold was given a life sentence.

Then came Mrs. Surratt. The court adjudged her guilty. At least six of the nine members voted for death, but to the record was appended a petition to the President to commute her sentence to life imprisonment. The petition was signed by five members, or a majority, of the court. It was now six in the evening of a long, hard, hot day and the court deferred sentence on Doctor Mudd until the morrow, when he was given life imprisonment.

The first four days of July were a period of suspense. The verdicts and sentences could not be made public until reviewed by the President, who was ill. On July fifth Judge Advocate General Holt carried the findings to Mr. Johnson, together with a digest containing the salient features, with one astonishing exception, of the various cases; there was no hint of the petition for clemency for Mary E. Surratt.

6

The Judge Advocate General left the White House with the sentences approved and the date of execution set for July seventh between the hours of ten A.M. and two P.M., or in less than forty-eight hours. Further than that twenty-four of these hours elapsed before the public or the defense counsel were informed of what had taken place. At five P. M. on July sixth John W. Clampitt, one of Mrs. Surratt's attorneys, was startled by a newsboy's cry in the street, "Execution of Mrs. Surratt!" The newsboy exaggerated. The paper merely contained news of the President's approval of the death-warrant, but Mr. Clampitt was so shocked that he hardly knew which way to turn.

With some of his colleagues he hastened to the White House. Two senators and a file of soldiers guarded the stairway to the President's study. Senator King of New York told the lawyer that it was useless to try to see the Executive, but Mrs. Stephen A. Douglas, widow of the statesman from Illinois, thrust aside the bayonets of the soldiers and gained the presence of Mr. Johnson. Her plea for a delay of the execution was futile.

Joined by Miss Anna Surratt, almost hysterical with grief, the lawyers called on Judge Advocate General Holt. The girl fell on her knees as the attorneys entreated the prosecutor to intercede for three more days of life for her mother. Judge Holt promised to do so and made an appointment for Clampitt and Miss Surratt to meet the President on the following morning.

At eleven o'clock that night, Mr. Clampitt sent a telegram to Reverdy Johnson in Baltimore. Because of the attitude of the court, Senator Johnson had virtually withdrawn from the case, believing his advocacy harmed rather than helped his client. Reverdy Johnson suggested a writ of habeas corpus to transfer Mrs. Surratt from the custody of the military to the civil courts. The papers were prepared and, as a church clock tolled two in the morning, the attorneys pulled the bell at the home of Justice Andrew Wylie of the District of Columbia Supreme Court.

The Justice received them in his night clothes, took the papers and retired to another room. Presently he returned. "Gentlemen," he said, "my mind is made up. I am about to perform an act which before to-morrow's sun goes down may consign me to the old Capitol Prison." With that he signed the writ. At four o'clock Mr. Clampitt placed in the hands of the United States Marshal an order directing him to obtain from General Hancock, Military Commandant of the District, the person of Mary Surratt.

When day dawned General Hancock was at the White House to report the unexpected turn of affairs. Thither also hastened Secretary of War Stanton and Judge Advocate General Holt. While they conferred with the President, a soldier from the penitentiary arrived with a message.

"The prisoner Payne has just told me that Mrs. Surratt is entirely innocent of the assassination of President Lincoln, or of any knowledge thereof. He also states that she had no knowledge whatever of the abduction plot. . . . I believe that Payne has told the truth."

The note was signed by Major General J. F. Hartranft, commandant of the prison.

At the hour appointed for their audience with the President, Mr. Clampitt and Anna Surratt arrived. They met Judge Holt coming from the Executive's chamber. "I can do nothing," he said. "The President is immovable."

Miss Anna threw herself at the feet of the guardians of the President's door, imploring them to admit her. The broad hallway of the White House was filled with distinguished persons, not a few of whom turned their heads. Secretary of Treasury McCulloch said this sobbing girl—"an amiable and accomplished young lady"—was "the most pitiable object that I ever beheld." She asked for a respite of three days, and for the promised interview with the President. Interview and respite were refused. John Brophy was one of a number of other callers also turned away.

Mr. Johnson had been closeted with Holt and "two eminent statesmen" who have not been formally identified, but the accepted presumption is that Mr. Stanton was one of them. Judge Holt said that they counseled the President that clemency for Mrs. Surratt "would amount to an invitation to assassins hereafter to employ women as their instruments."

The writ of habeas corpus was returnable before Justice Wylie at ten o'clock, the hour set for the execution. The justice was in his chambers, but the writ was not returned. For an hour and a half he waited. At eleven-thirty General Hancock, accompanied by the Judge Advocate General, appeared before Judge Wylie. Mrs. Surratt was not with them. They reported that the President had suspended the writ of habeas corpus.

In another part of the city a crowd was gathering about the penitentiary, where a high brick wall patroled by soldiers concealed the scaffold. Those who found points of vantage on the roofs of surrounding buildings and the tall masts of ships in the river could obtain a view. The scaffold was empty. General Hartranft was taking advantage of the latitude permitted by the death warrant to delay the execution.

7

Meantime, under General Hancock's orders, a squadron of cavalry formed a line stretching along Pennsylvania Avenue from the White House to the penitentiary, miles away, in readiness to transmit by signal notice of a reprieve. The day was stifling hot and the horses pawed the cobble-stones. One hour, two hours, they stood there. At the penitentiary General Hartranft glanced at his watch time and again. Regretfully at one-thirty he was obliged to put his machinery in motion. The legal hour for the conclusion of the execution was two o'clock.

Anna was with her mother at the parting. Herold was surrounded by his seven sisters. A slattern who had been his mistress clung to Atzerodt. Payne stood alone with a scornful curl on his lip. He had slept soundly all night.

It was a walk of fifty feet from the penitentiary building to the steps of the scaffold in the yard. Mrs. Surratt went first, on the arms of two soldiers, followed by two priests of the Catholic Church, and a man who held an umbrella above her head.

Before the scaffold was aligned a company of veteran infantry. In front of the soldiers stood a knot of officials and newspaper men under umbrellas. Four graves were near by. More soldiers looked down from the top of the wall. At the gallows steps Mrs. Surratt hesitated. "Holy Father, can I not tell these people before I die that I am innocent?" The sacrament of extreme unction had been administered. "No, my child," Father Walter said, "the world and all that is in it has receded for ever. It would do no good and might disturb the serenity of your last moments."

Payne stepped forward next, ironed hand and foot. His step was light and steady, for the great chains on his limbs were nothing to his enormous strength. "His face might have been likened to that of a builder of castles in the air," wrote the New York *Herald* correspondent, adding that the spectators were unable to suppress a visible show of "admiration" for one who could face death so calmly. This quality of sheer and absolute courage had struck all who came in contact with Payne as one of the remarkable features of the dreadful episode. By orders, Payne's confinement had been more rigorous than that of the others. At no time had he complained or asked a favor of his jailors. To their questions, some frankly sympathetic, he returned brief but always courteous answers; the scowl on his countenance did not go very deep. He had shown no remorse for his act, no sense of degradation at his fate, no bravado. His one regret, he said, was that he should have unwittingly been a party to the conviction of Mrs. Surratt. He mounted the gallows stairs with more composure than the military attendants and with an ironical gesture of politeness bowed his tall head to the noose. It seemed incredible.

Herold walked with slight help, though transfixed by fear. Atzerodt gibbered on the point of collapse and was half carried.

At one-twenty and one-half o'clock General Hartranft dropped his sword and the trap fell. The bodies were cut down at five minutes of two.

8

John H. Surratt read of his mother's death in a newspaper in Canada and fled to Europe where he enlisted in the Papal army under the name of Watson. There he was recognized several times but Washington, after the first phases of the frenzied hunt, showed a singular disinclination to take him into custody. It was finally done, however, and in 1867 he was brought home for trial.

Meantime, a hearing before a committee of the House of Representatives had revealed the existence of Booth's note-book, which Stanton had suppressed. This caused a flurry. The bearing of the note-book upon the trial of Mrs. Surratt was plain to all who recalled or should consult the record, but the subject slept until John A. Bingham, special assistant to Judge Advocate Holt during the trial, and now a member of the House, saw fit to direct a shaft of satire at Representative Benjamin F. Butler of Massachusetts. Ben Butler had been a Union general, an advocate of firm measures against the South and a champion of military courts for the trial of civilians. To say the least, the point of Mr. Bingham's ridicule was not well taken, but few were prepared for the retort it drew from Butler.

"The gentleman has had the bad taste to attack me for the reason that I could do no more injury to the enemies of my country. I did all I could, but the only victim of that gentleman's prowess that

I know of was an innocent woman hung upon the scaffold, one Mrs. Surratt."

Reverberations of this sensation brought to the ears of President Johnson the report that a petition for clemency formed a part of the record of the case against the condemned woman. The proceedings of the trial were in print, with a War Department certification of their accuracy. But the bulky volume contained no reference to a petition for commutation. The President sent for the original papers. Among them he found the petition, and, returning to his private secretary, dictated the following communication to the War Minister of Abraham Lincoln:

"August 1, 1867.
"Sir: Public considerations of a high character constrain me to say that your resignation as Secretary of War will be accepted.
"Very respectfully yours,
"ANDREW JOHNSON.
"To the Honorable Edwin M. Stanton, etc."

Seven days thereafter the trial of John Harrison Surratt terminated in a disagreement of the jury, which stood eight to four for acquittal. The prisoner was released without a second trial.

9

Thus the narrative of a crime of murder so foul and so futile that it set a grief-blinded world to seeking undiscriminating revenge. The assassin had struck down not only a man, but also the qualities that his life embodied—human kindness, rationality, justice amid a tempest of the passions.

The Judge Advocate General claimed that President Johnson had seen the clemency petition when he approved the sentences. The President said he had not seen it, and the best evidence supports his contention. Yet Mr. Johnson suffered from the arrows of remorse because he had suspended the writ of habeas corpus; and in the impeachment proceedings brought against him he suffered from insinuations, principally the spurious coinage of La Fayette Baker, the baseness of which have no parallel in our annals. The crime that elevated Andrew Johnson to the Presidency also helped to destroy him, as it destroyed others. The two United States Senators who guarded the President's door against those who approached it on errands of mercy killed themselves within a year. The Chief of the Secret Service left public life shorn of character. Hardly any one escaped.

Michael O'Laughlin died in prison on the barren island of Dry Tortugas, off Florida. Mudd was pardoned in 1868, although he would not have been had Mr. Johnson been able to avail himself of the accumulation of sixty-five years of evidence, which indicates that the surgeon had recognized Booth when he set his leg. Spangler and Arnold were released from Dry Tortugas in 1869, and so closed, with an act of mercy, the record of the mad murderer's deed and all that came in its train.

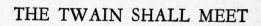

THE TWAIN SHALL MEET

XIV

THE TWAIN SHALL MEET

I

At "Moving Town," that is to say, Julesburg, Colorado, the chief engineer of the Union Pacific Railroad swung from his private car as it came in from End of Track with the empty supply train. The chief's form was square and stocky, his clothing rough and soiled with dust, his countenance weathered by the suns and storms of many climes.

Jack Casement, the construction boss, was on hand to give him greeting.

"Are the gamblers quiet and behaving?" asked the engineer, whose singularly soft and deliberate voice indicated an unruffled mind directing his tireless body.

"You bet they are," replied Jack Casement. "They're out there in the graveyard."

Jack Casement, who had commanded an infantry brigade in the Civil War, added that this small difficulty, incident to the building of the first transcontinental railroad, had been overcome with the aid of two companies of Regulars. Grenville M. Dodge, the chief engineer, waved his approval and asked how the reserve of ties and fish-plates was holding out. Then going to the telegraph office he requested of the contractors in Chicago a report on the parts for the big bridge over the Dale Creek gulch. Next he paused before a mountain of mail to read slowly a letter from his wife in Council Bluffs, Iowa, and write out in a smooth rapid hand the reply of a lonely man who saw little of home.

Jack Casement's assurance concerning the decorous attitude of the gamblers was true, of course, only by a comparison of their present behavior with what it had been before his intervention. Naturally, they were not all in boot hill. But some of the boldest of their number were there, and this had a sobering effect upon the conduct of affairs at The Big Tent, the fanciest citadel of chance in Moving Town. The moral tone of Moving Town had gone up several pegs and was about what it had been at the birth of this celebrated auxiliary to the construction of the U. P., at Kearney, Nebraska, one hundred and eighty-seven miles down the track.

2

Kearney, the first advance base of operations, was one hundred and ninety-six miles west of the grand base at Omaha. It flourished during the closing weeks of 1866. Two long trains a day came from Omaha, feeding the great dumps of rails, bolts, fish-plates, lumber, ready-cut timbers for the bridges and the commissary, quartermaster and ordnance stores necessary to the army of six thousand men that was driving the pathway of the iron horse westward. Two other daily trains carried material to the End of Track. The town of Kearney was a haphazard pattern of shacks and tents on the bank of the Platte, swarming with track gangs, graders, bridge men, tie choppers and trainmen; Boston Irish, Mexicans, busted forty-niners, Indians, silent old plainsmen in leather shirts and Regular soldiers in blue, a considerable portion of whom had lately worn the Confederate gray. To provide entertainment for these were dives of every description.

When the advance base moved a hundred miles west to North Platte the camp followers moved with it. In the spring of 1867 the base shoved on to Julesburg and the trek of the parasites became a matter of routine that made "Moving Town" a part of the vocabulary of railroad construction. The East refused to believe what it read in the papers: at any rate, no regular trains could ever be run over a track laid down so fast.

In the fall of 1867 Engineer Dodge pushed his base to a place he called Cheyenne, in Wyoming Territory, five hundred and seventeen miles from Omaha and six thousand and sixty-two feet above the level of the sea. A day or so later a long, chartered freight train pulled in at the new station, laden with frame houses, tents, picket fences, household goods, roulette wheels and liquor. A brakeman saluted the world at large:

"Well, gents, here's Julesburg!"

The Big Tent and all that went with Moving Town enjoyed a brisk season in Cheyenne; so brisk, indeed, that the conviction took hold that Cheyenne was another San Francisco in the making. This was a conviction common to most new urban communities in the West, and traces of it survive in the mushroom oil camps of to-day. It had obtained at Kearney, North Platte and Julesburg, where fortunes had been lost in real estate as well as at faro. Moving Town grew in size and riotousness with every move. When the bewildering avalanche descended upon Cheyenne, the forlorn objects of its deserted predecessors meant not a thing to those who, with true western buoyancy, proclaimed that *here* was to be the great permanent city of the Rockies. Was not the U. P. putting up its shops there?

Within a month there were three thousand people at Cheyenne, in two months six thousand. Lots were sold for fabulous sums. The pay of ten thousand men whose money burned holes in their pockets was the circulating medium.

But the railroad marched on. With a construction organization which to this day excites the admiration of the engineering world, Grenville Dodge pushed the line over Lone Tree Pass, hitherto believed insurmountable. End of Track brought up at a place Dodge marked for a station which he named Laramie City, and the rumor came back to Cheyenne that it was to be the next advance base. Some of the more long-sighted citizens of Moving Town leased patches of sage-brush in this Laramie.

Cheyenne was less than six months old when Dodge moved his base. The Big Tent followed immediately and that was a signal for a scramble among the lesser fry for choice locations. But so much had been invested in the prospects of Cheyenne that the situation was different from what it had been before.

Cheyenne was not going to be superseded without a fight. A vexed group of civic boosters called on Dodge. They did not get very far with the quiet young man who at thirty-four had won his major general's stars in battle under U. S. Grant.

"No one can prevent an exodus from an old base to a new one. You know that. I have said this will be the headquarters of the mountain division of the road. The shops will be here and a branch line to Denver. That's what you had to bank on in the beginning and what you have to bank on now."

But Thomas C. Durant, the vice-president of the road and a master of the art of political finance by which it was being built, was on from the East. At Cheyenne he gave the citizens small satisfaction. He wasn't certain about the shops. Proceeding to Laramie, he assured the local enthusiasts that he saw the beginnings of a great city. The shops, he said, would have to go to Laramie. The telegraph clicked and a grim-looking delegation waited on Grenville Dodge at Cheyenne.

"If Durant said that about the shops, well, he lied," observed the chief engineer in his reflective way.

Dodge's car was attached to the next train to Laramie. He encountered Mr. Durant in the dusty main street and told the vice-president that he, as chief engineer, was building the road. "The men working for it will take orders from me and not from you. Interfere and there will be trouble." Mr. Durant faded away to the markets of the money-changers in the East, and the shops stayed at Cheyenne, which girded itself for a return to prosperity. Immigrants were promised a law-abiding community to which they could bring their families in safety, Colonel Murrin, the mayor, promulgating an ordinance which declared that any person shooting at another would be fined ten dollars "whether he hit or missed."

Laramie sowed its wild oats in a hurry. In three months the base pushed to Benton, named for the Senator from Missouri, who, in 1849, had delivered a grand oration about bridging the continent with a railroad. On the peak of the highest mountain, intoned the Senator, there should be carved a gigantic likeness of Columbus with arms outstretched toward India. Benton, Wyoming, six hundred and ninety-eight miles from Omaha and eleven hundred and fifty-five miles from San Francisco, proved to be the most notable stand of Moving Town. In two weeks it had a population of three thousand with one newspaper, five dance-halls and twenty-three saloons.

At Benton, Moving Town reached the pinnacle of its glory. Thereafter the problems of the chief engineer became such that to overcome them, and above all to increase the speed with which the iron trail forged toward the sunset, he decentralized his organization of base camps so that Hell on Wheels, as Moving Town had come to be known, diminished to a shadow of its former splendors.

3

Of an array of difficulties that beset the cool-headed ex-soldier one rose to dominate: the Union Pacific had a rival for the enormous Government subsidies without which no railroad in the West could be built. The Central Pacific of California, begun on the coast and building eastward, was no longer a subject of ridicule, even though every pound of material, excepting ties, was brought from the Atlantic seaboard around the Horn, a voyage of twelve thousand miles.

Seven years before, in the summer of 1860, Theodore D. Judah, who had come out from New York State to construct the twenty-two-mile Sacramento Valley Railroad, rode down the mountains with his young wife and a few friends. Mrs. Judah had cooked for the party because her husband could not afford to hire a servant. The proprietor of Strong's Drug Store in Sacramento gave the engineer the use of a desk in his back room to transform his notes into a profile map. He took the map to the hardware store of Huntington & Hopkins in K Street where his dreams and schemes of building a railroad to the East had always been received without derision. The hardware dealers looked at the map and called in the Crocker brothers, dry-goods merchants and wealthy men. The Crockers consulted with Leland Stanford, wholesale grocer and one of the solid political and financial rocks of the valley.

Judah had something tangible this time. Unless his figures were wrong, he had found a pass in the Sierra Nevadas only one hundred and twenty-eight miles from Sacramento, through which it might actually be possible to build a railroad. Stanford sent the engineer to San Francisco to endeavor to interest some of the capitalists there. Money-raising was not Judah's forte, however, and he returned empty-handed.

The following year, 1861, Leland Stanford was elected governor and the Central Pacific Railroad Company of California was incorporated with a capital of one hundred and twenty-five thousand dollars. Stanford was president, C. P. Huntington, vice-president, Mark Hopkins, treasurer, and T. D. Judah, chief engineer. There was a plan to get subsidies from the Federal Government, but the Civil War deferred hopes in this direction. And so a start was made with the hundred and twenty-five thousand dollars. While loungers laughed Governor Stanford pitched a shovelful of sand from a cart into a mud-hole at the end of K Street in Sacramento and track-grading was inaugurated. In October of the year 1863, a shipload of rails arrived in San Francisco. In November Judah started east to superintend the purchase of other materials. While crossing the Isthmus of Panama on mule back, he died of jungle fever, aged thirty-seven.

But the work went on. By September of 1866 rails had been laid to Alta, seventy miles from Sacramento and three thousand seven hundred and eighty feet above it. Grades possible for heavy trains were found to exist, as Judah had represented on his charts. Financial aid had been obtained from the Government, and November of 1866 saw ninety-three miles of track in operation, the end being six thousand and sixty-six feet above Sacramento or seven thousand nine hundred and eleven feet above the sea.

Although the world had never known such railroad engineering, the feat attracted no attention in a country just emerging from a war. Nor did the Union Pacific, building west from Omaha, come in for a great deal of notice. This preoccupation of the public was a matter that enabled the builders of the latter road to run through half a million dollars with only forty miles of poor track on a level prairie to show for the money.

4

In this situation Major General G. M. Dodge was offered the post of chief engineer at a salary of ten thousand dollars a year. For some time, this soldier's mind had dwelt upon his old pursuits of peace-time, including the vision of a transcontinental railroad. In 1865 with the war as good as over, Grant had sent him to restore order among the Indians. Caught in the Wyoming Black Hills with an escort of twelve men, Dodge was cut off and attacked by three hundred Crow warriors. The Indians closed in and Dodge was in a tight place when rescued by the arrival of a squadron of cavalry. As the Crows retreated General Dodge followed them with his glasses.

"Boys," he said at length, "I think we've discovered a pass through which we can build a railroad."

That was the important incident of the day to G. M. Dodge, who watched the Indians file through a gap hitherto unknown to white men. Dodge said it could be graded with not more than a ninety-foot rise to a mile, and fixed the location in his mind by a lone tree. A few months later he resigned from the Army and took charge of the affairs of the ailing and discredited Union Pacific. He was thirty-five years old.

Within ninety days Dodge's organization, formed on a military basis, resumed the laying of track.

Over plain, desert and mountain, from mid-Nebraska to the Mormon oasis of Salt Lake City, surveying parties staked the route. In addition to engineers, rodmen, flagmen and chainmen, each party was accompanied by tie choppers, teamsters and hunters.

Two thousand graders followed the tie gangs. Back of the graders were the bridge men, who set up the wooden trestles that came ready-cut from Chicago. Then came the tie layers, and twenty miles behind them the track men, followed by the surfacing crew that tamped ties in place and applied the ballast. This slender line, penetrating the Indian country for a distance of five hundred miles, went about its business prepared on the instant to resist attack.

Behind the long construction line were the advance base camps and Moving Town, and the permanent base at Omaha. During the first two years of Dodge's superintendency, no railway line reached Omaha from the east and everything used in the construction of the road was hauled by wagon across Iowa or brought by steamboat up the Missouri River from the rail terminus at St. Joseph, Missouri. This included locomotives. But the Central Pacific builders had to carry their locomotives around Cape Horn.

The chief engineer who never hurried climbed mountains and trekked shimmering deserts with the surveyors, personally observing every mile of route chosen. He showed the tie gangs how to treat chemically the soft fiber of the cottonwood tree, the only timber available on the prairies; a bridge crew confessed defeat over a knotty problem and Dodge in personal charge put up the span; one word of his to the ringleading gamblers of Moving Town had the same effect as a hundred Regulars under Jack Casement; a freight train was captured by Indians and Dodge, gathering twenty men, raced to the scene in his private car and, leading a skirmish formation, recovered the train; and always he kept the endless chains of supplies moving forward.

Now he smoked the peace pipe and pow-wowed with the Indians, who called him Long Eye. Now he sat in conclave with Brigham Young and his elders of the powerful Mormon Church at Salt Lake City, gaining a strategic advantage over the Central Pacific. Now he contended with stubborn and often dishonest contractors. Now he schemed with lobbyists and politicians in the shadow of the Capitol at Washington. Now he laid down the law to subtle financiers in New York and Boston, demanding—and obtaining—approval of his tremendous expenditures. Dodge never got along well with the politicians or the financiers who once carried their protests to Grant, then President-elect. Grant went west to look at the road and Dodge's enemy Durant accompanied him. He wanted the route changed and Dodge had refused to change it.

"If Durant or anybody connected with the Union Pacific or with the Government changes my lines I quit the road," said Dodge.

Mr. Durant stroked his Vandyke beard. U. S. Grant puffed a cigar. At length he said:

"The Government expects General Dodge to remain with the road."

The cost of the Union Pacific Railroad later became the scandal of the day. But irrespective of what went into the pockets of financiers, politicians and swindling contractors, Dodge played the part of the engineer to the end and built the shortest line possible, despite the fact that Government subsidies and land grants were computed by the track mile. Sixty-four years of modernization have eliminated only thirty miles of curves from the one thousand and eighty-six miles of rail laid by G. M. Dodge.

5

The speed with which Dodge built entailed extravagances in construction and made things easier for the profiteers in material, most of whom had perfected their systems of overcharging during the war, but the race with the Central Pacific, first, to reach the coal fields of Wyoming and, second, to reach Salt Lake, placed a great pressure on the chief engineer.

During the six months he had charge in 1866 Dodge laid one hundred and twenty-one miles of track, while the Central Pacific, toiling in the precipitous Sierras laid fifteen miles. Dodge's railroad army was now working smoothly. In the face of difficulties comparable to those confronting the western rival, it swept across the Nebraska plains, dipped south into Colorado for a better grade, and then pointing westward thrust the rails through the Crow Indians' Lone Tree Pass, eight thousand two hundred and sixty-two feet above the sea, or higher than anything with which the

Central Pacific engineers had to contend. Three hundred and eighty miles of track were laid in twelve months. During the same period the Central Pacific laid forty-six miles.

Dodge's system was perfection. Two trains of twenty cars each were required to haul from the Moving Town to End of Track the supplies required for one day's labor. These were figured to the last spike and fish-plate, the last barrel of flour and round of ammunition necessary to feed, protect and keep busy eight thousand workers at the front. Over a raw single track this traffic, as well as the bunk and mess trains, shuttled with such nicety that delays were almost unknown.

The corps d'élite of the construction division was the rail crew of twelve gigantic Irishmen, working in teams of six each with the precision of soldiers at drill. Steel is carried from the supply train to the end of the track in a small car drawn by a horse at a gallop. Two men seize a rail and haul it forward. "Down!" It drops on the ties. The gaugers, spikers and bolters fall to. Three strokes to a spike, ten spikes to a rail, which in thirty seconds is joined to the fish-plate of its predecessor. "Down!" goes a rail in place on the other side. There were four hundred rails to a mile. Twelve hundred rails in one day was the record for 1867.

The record fell in 1868 when two thousand rails or five miles of track were laid in a day and four hundred and twenty-five miles in the year, a mark that has never been equaled. Dodge went through the Wasatch Mountains in winter at a construction cost of sixty-five hundred dollars a mile as against fifteen hundred if he had waited.

Thus the coal fields were won for the Union Pacific, but the Central Pacific, now over the worst of the mountains, had taken a brace and the race to Salt Lake was on. Congress had stipulated that the two roads should join track, but did not say how or where they should join. The first road to tap Salt Lake City would gain an enormous advantage.

The Central Pacific was making a great bid for victory. Its principal dependence was on Chinese laborers, who proved less temperamental than Dodge's Irishmen. Several features of the Dodge method of construction were copied, however, and some of them improved. In 1868 the Central Pacific laid three hundred and sixty miles of track to the Union Pacific's four hundred and twenty-five, but it was better track than that of its eastern rival.

The year 1869 saw the two roads working double crews. Dodge laid six miles of track in one day and the C. P. laid ten, losing a wager of ten thousand dollars for Thomas C. Durant. This did not make for more cordial relations between the vice-president and the chief engineer. But Dodge was first into Ogden, the gateway to Salt Lake City, and proposed that, in the interest of harmony and economy, the roads join at Promontory Point on the north shore of the lake. Durant refused. Each additional mile built meant thirty thousand dollars in subsidies. Dodge went to Washington and appealed to C. P. Huntington, the ex-hardware dealer, now directing the affairs of the Central Pacific. Huntington refused to join tracks at Promontory Point and said he would go into Salt Lake with his own rail. Dodge retorted that, in this event, he would go into San Francisco, and telegraphed orders that scattered his surveyors across the Nevada.

6

But Huntington was a good bluffer, too. He continued to build east. Grading gangs met and for two hundred miles they worked parallel to each other, fighting on every provocation and on no provocation. A gang of Union Pacific blasters "accidentally" blew up a company of C. P. Chinese. A few days later a similar "mishap" befell a party of U. P. Irishmen.

The race now held the attention of the country. The American public was proud, but it was also growing impatient over the expensive eccentricities of its railroad prima donnas. Rumblings of the forth-coming financial scandal were provoking disconcerting inquiries. In their own best interests, Huntington and Dodge got together and arranged for the rails to meet at Promontory Point.

Dodge hurried west to see that his rails should reach the Point first. He lost this race. A rock cut had not been made properly, and while Dodge was reblasting, the Central Pacific track crew hove in sight and on May eighth laid the last rail but one to the meeting-place. On May ninth Dodge laid his last rail, except one. The two connecting rails were to be emplaced on May 10, 1869.

Facing each other across the gap in the track, magnificent special trains, one from the East and one from the West, drew up. A party of silent Chinese deftly lowered the Central Pacific's last rail in position. Grenville Dodge, always inconspicuous at ceremonies, watched them thoughtfully. He had been studying these Chinese of late and writing to his wife about them. Now that he fancied his work in America was done, he planned to go to China and build railroads. Irishmen put down the last rail for the U. P. and nine iron spikes were driven beside it.

A telegrapher squatted near the track clicking a field instrument while throngs gathered about every telegraph station in America.

"Keep quiet," he tapped to the listening operators.

Reverend Doctor Todd, of Pittsfield, Massachusetts, was asking the blessing of the Almighty upon the achievement.

Governor Trittle of Nevada handed a gold spike to Stanford of the Central Pacific and a silver spike to Durant of the Union Pacific. The rival officials bowed formally to each other.

Then the fancy spikes were dropped into auger holes in a tie of polished California laurel and touched with a silver sledge.

"Done!" sent the telegrapher and cut his switch.

The train crews began to cheer each other. Dodge's Irishmen let out a salvo of joyous whoops and the impassive Chinese relaxed, grinning. The two trains advanced until their pilots touched. Men swarmed over the locomotives. Some one on the pilot of the U. P. engine held up a bottle as if offering a toast. Two bottles were lifted in response from the pilot of the C. P. engine.

This was more than the restrained etiquette of the officials in silk hats could withstand. Thomas Durant rushed forward and, seizing the hand of Leland Stanford, cried:

"There is but one Pacific railroad now!"

FIRST PRIZE, $600,000

XV

FIRST PRIZE, $600,000

I

"OVER Two Millions Distributed!"

In type of arresting, though not vulgar, dimensions, the announcement saluted newspaper subscribers in the early days of November, 1888. If true, this was, indeed, "past all precedent." And as the Louisiana State Lottery Company vouchsafed it, it must be true.

Moved by a spirit of objective inquiry, persons might disagree as to the ultimate effect of the Louisiana Lottery on the public and private morals, for that belonged to the domain of opinion. But one might not question the accuracy of the Lottery's advertising, which belonged to the domain of fact. Reformers had discovered to their dismay that, in a day when a prudent man consulted the advertising columns of his newspaper with a salt-shaker at his elbow, the Lottery's statements could be relied on almost implicitly.

This was, of course, no more than a civil acknowledgment of the proprieties, considering the position the Lottery had attained in society. Less could hardly have been expected of a public institution "incorporated by the Legislature [of Louisiana] for Educational and Charitable purposes and its franchise made a part of the present State Constitution by OVERWHELMING POPULAR VOTE." Such a position was attended by responsibilities which the Lottery did not undertake to evade, as witness its effort to elevate the ethical tone of advertising. It was unnecessary for the Lottery to purchase space to diffuse the intelligence that it had doubled its stakes. Any editor who considered the interest of his readers in the events of the day would have felt obliged to print this whether paid to do so or no. But the educational purposes for which the Lottery was chartered were construed into an obligation to lend a helping hand to the press. Not only did it pay for the insertion of its announcements in newspapers from one coast to the other, but it paid three or four times the going rates.

The present notice concerned, as I say, the doubling of the stakes. In the "Grand Extraordinary" semi-annual drawings the capital prize henceforth would be six hundred thousand dollars; other prizes one million five hundred and eighteen thousand dollars in the aggregate. The capital prize in the monthly drawing would be three hundred thousand dollars; other prizes, seven hundred and fifty-four thousand dollars. The daily drawing remained unchanged. It would not be possible to win more than thirty thousand dollars on a single ticket.

The announcements of this change of policy were clipped out and displayed in the windows of barrooms, pool halls, hotels and barber shops, and, for the moment, the country had something to talk about besides the election of Benjamin Harrison.

Of the semi-annual event, the notices went on to say that "The Mammoth Drawing will take place at the Academy of Music, New Orleans, TUESDAY, DECEMBER 18, 1888." One hundred thousand tickets were offered at forty dollars each. However, if one did not care to invest that amount in a chance to win six hundred thousand dollars, he might buy half a ticket for half as much, a quarter of a ticket for ten dollars, an eighth for five dollars, or as little as a fortieth for a dollar. "A splendid Chance for a FORTUNE" was thus placed within the reach of nearly every one.

And if one did not win the capital prize, or a fractional interest therein, there were thirty-one hundred and forty-five additional prizes in which one might share. The amounts of these were from three hundred thousand dollars down to two hundred dollars. Each of the thirty-one hundred and forty-six prizes was capable of division into forty parts, making one hundred and twenty-five thousand eight hundred and forty possible chances to participate in a distribution of two million one hundred and eighteen thousand eight hundred dollars—the richest lottery the world has ever seen. Four national banks of New Orleans, over the signatures of their presidents, guaranteed the prompt payment of every prize-winning ticket.

The drawing would be on the square. "We do hereby certify that we supervise the arrangements for all the Monthly and Semi-Annual Drawings of the Louisiana State Lottery Company and in person manage and control the Drawings themselves and that the same are conducted with honesty and fairness and in good faith . . ."

This statement bore the signatures of two men whose names meant something to Americans in 1888—and mean something now. They were P. G. T. Beauregard, of Louisiana, and Jubal A. Early, of Virginia, late of the Confederate Army.

2

The hundred thousand tickets were all sold. Each bore a serial number, and, as each was susceptible of division into forty parts, in reality the country was papered with four million chances to win the one hundred and twenty-five thousand eight hundred and forty fractional prizes. The system by which these tickets were distributed was the product of much labor and money. It covered the United States. Where there were no laws against lotteries, or a lax enforcement of them, chances were sold openly. Concessions in such rich jurisdictions as Chicago, New York, Montreal, San Francisco and Boston commanded large sums. Agents in "open" territory received a ten-per-cent. commission on tickets sold. Where the sales were made under cover the commission is said to have been fifteen per cent. But regardless of the law tickets could always be had by writing direct to the New Orleans National Bank.

Seven thousand tickets, or seven per cent. of the total, were reserved for sale in New Orleans. This was held by some to be a tribute to the speculative proclivities of the New Orleanians. Later, when the nation-wide fight against the Lottery got into its stride, it was cited by the Nordic purists as an example of the depraved instincts of a population sprung largely from French rather than Anglo-Saxon stock. This argument would not have been so impressive, however, had it been generally known at the time that the same number of tickets were regularly disposed of in Boston.

The Lottery being a state institution in Louisiana, the sale of tickets there was as legal as the sale of postage stamps. In the city of New Orleans they were more easily purchased than postage stamps. One could get them at hotel news stands, barber shops, cigar stores, ladies' hair-dressing parlors and the corner grocer's. Venders, many of them women, made the rounds of office buildings and shops. "E. J. Lannes, corner Camp and Girod Street," advertised the "Lucky Corner to buy Louisiana State Lottery Tickets," having "sold 48 prizes" in a single drawing.

The sale of tickets closed promptly throughout the country at eleven o'clock on the morning of a drawing. In New Orleans these were days of stirring anticipation. The eighteenth of December, 1888, which inaugurated the drawing for the capital award of six hundred thousand dollars, was an undeclared holiday. Christmas was only a week away and a Yuletide spirit pervaded a city that has never taken its cares over-seriously. The galleried sidewalks of Canal Street were thronged. The town was filled with tourists. The ticket shops were crowded. Solicitors were making their last rounds. By noon people were gathering outside of the Academy of Music where fortune's favorites were to be chosen. Another crowd formed about the opaque-windowed headquarters of the Lottery company in St. Charles Street, which enclosed a Spanish courtyard where an alligator dozed in the sunlit waters of a marble fountain. The first ceremonies of the day took place within the company's offices. Two distinguished-looking gentlemen approached a great steel vault, the doors of which were sealed with wax impressed with the mark of signet rings initialed B.

and E. Generals Beauregard and Early inspected the seals and broke them. They twirled the knobs of a lock to which they alone knew the combination. When the doors swung open the Generals entered the safe and directed assistants to remove two stout leather pouches which also were locked and sealed. These seals were examined and broken.

One of the pouches was much larger than the other. It contained what looked to be innumerable capsules about as big around as one's little finger and an inch long. They were poured into a hollow glass wheel which was five feet in diameter. The smaller pouch contained similar capsules, although not nearly so many of them. These were transferred to a glass wheel about eighteen inches in diameter.

Big and little wheels were sealed and placed on vans and transported to the Academy of Music. It was now approaching four o'clock. The place was filled, save for a few late arrivals—ladies who came in carriages and were escorted to boxes reserved for them. On the stroke of four the two wheels, mounted on rolling carriages, were pushed upon the stage—the large wheel on one side and the small wheel on the other. An erect figure of medium height, carefully dressed after the manner of twenty years before, walked out, bowed slightly to the audience and seated himself beside the little wheel. His white hair and white imperial contrasted conspicuously with his dark skin and alert dark eyes. He had the easy manner of a man of the world. A little hum of admiration swept the audience. This was General Beauregard.

On the other side there emerged by long uneven strides a loose-knit man in a baggy suit. He was more than six feet tall despite a stoop. His head was covered with a shock of white hair carelessly combed, his chest with a dense, wild-looking beard. His frame was big and bony, his eyes were blue, his features strong, his hands and feet prodigous in size: a man of action rather than of meditation. This was Jubal Early—Ol' Jube to the Valley of Virginia. Jerking a nod to the spectators, he flopped into a chair beside the large wheel.

An official of the Lottery Company appeared and explained

the meaning of what was about to happen. The big wheel was the number wheel, he said. It contained one hundred thousand capsules each of which was numbered. The little wheel was the prize wheel. It contained a capsule for every prize that was to be awarded, except the approximation and terminal prizes, as will appear. Numbers would be drawn alternately from the wheels, until those in the small wheel were exhausted.

Two negroes turned handles that revolved the wheels and mixed up the capsules. Two boys in knee pants from an asylum for the blind were led on the stage. The wheels were stopped, a slide pushed back and one of the blind boys drew a capsule from the number wheel. An official opened the capsule and took out a roll of paper an inch wide. He unrolled the paper and read off the numeral that was printed on it. Then he showed the number to the audience.

No record exists of the sequence in which the numbers were drawn at this or any of the other big drawings, but assume it was No. 13,343, which was one of the actual numbers drawn. No. 13,343 is announced.

Then the blind boy at the prize wheel draws out a capsule. An attendant opens it and reads off: "Eight hundred dollars. Number one three three four three wins eight hundred dollars."

Granting that each of the sixteen hundred spectators was a ticket holder, as doubtless they were, the chances of some one being present to see his number drawn are not worth computing. Nevertheless, in the long and checkered life of the Lottery, that sometimes happened.

The drawing moved swiftly and smoothly. Another capsule from the number wheel, another from the prize wheel—on and on. After twenty drawings the wheels were closed for a spin. From time to time Generals Beauregard and Early rose from their chairs and walked about the stage to stretch their legs, or chat with a visitor. Occasionally they received a number from one of the blind boys, opened it and passed it on to an assistant to announce to the audience. The Generals themselves never addressed the spectators. They simply lent their presence to the drawing as a guarantee of fairness and as part of the feat of showmanship that made the Louisiana Lottery the greatest in the world.

Presently the number announcer called out: "Six nine seven cipher four," and the prize announcer, who had been droning off two hundred, eight hundred and five thousand dollar awards in a monotone cleared his throat and said:

"Ladies and gentlemen, I have to announce that the number just read wins the grand capital prize of six hundred thousand dollars."

A thousand pencils recorded the important numerals. Tickets were scanned for the hundredth time, but there was no one present to claim even a fortieth share of the grand capital prize. A good part of the audience left. They had seen what they had come to see.

The drawing continued. The second capital prize of three hundred thousand dollars, the third capital prize of one hundred thousand dollars, the fourth of fifty thousand dollars, and all the lesser ones were drawn as luck willed and the theater relinquished for other uses, for New Orleans was also taking chances that week on "the World's Greatest Tragic Actress, JANAUSCHEK! in a Grand Revival of Scott's Grand Musical Drama, 'Meg. Merrilies.' . . . Next week Rose Coghlan as Jocelyn."

The approximation and terminal prizes also had to be computed. These were consolation awards for getting close to the capital numbers. There were three hundred approximation prizes—one hundred based on each of the first three capital prize-winning numbers. Those who held tickets bearing numbers within fifty either way of the grand capital prize number won one thousand dollars each, with lesser awards for getting close to the second and third capital prizes. The grand capital prize number was 69,704. Its approximation prizes were numbers 69,654 to 69,754. There were three-number and two-number prizes, based on the grand capital and second capital prize numbers. In the case of the grand capital prize, all tickets whose numbers ended in 04 won two hundred dollars. There were ninety-nine of the former and nine hundred of the latter. Thus, if a player came any way close to holding the capital combinations, he won something. Winning tickets, or fractions thereof, were paid by check when mailed to the Lottery office. In New Orleans one could cash a winning lottery ticket at a bank.

The scenes in New Orleans were duplicated in lesser degrees in fifty cities. The winning numbers were telegraphed as drawn and publicly posted.

The names of comparatively few winners were published, but invariably the newspapers reported the winning numbers and the company's announcement of where they had been sold. It was the policy of the company to sell portions of the same ticket in many states. For instance, Ticket No. 69,704 was held in New York, Boston, Washington, San Francisco, New Orleans, Denver, and in Petaluma, California; Leadville, Colorado; West Hoboken, New Jersey; Wanatah, Indiana; McGregor, Texas; Manor, Texas, and Hermosillo, Mexico.

I have learned of but one instance of a single individual winning more than one hundred thousand dollars at a drawing. He was an itinerant barber in New Orleans who cashed a three hundred thousand dollar ticket, bought a dozen suits of clothes and took a train for Chicago. A small business man in New Orleans won fifty thousand dollars, over-expanded his company and was bankrupt in six months. A western Congressman won a small prize, but lost the next election. A convict in a Missouri prison won fifteen thousand dollars, engaged a lawyer and was paroled. A New Orleans waitress won enough to study stenography, go to work for an elderly merchant and marry him. A fruit peddler won twenty-five thousand dollars and sailed for sunny Italy. A southern gentlewoman, earning her bread by surreptitious needlework, won twenty-five thousand dollars, gave half to the poor and paid the mortgage on her home. A bank teller failed to win and shot himself.

3

The Louisiana Lottery entered the field with the authority of precedent behind it. In Colonial times, lotteries were a common means of raising money for public and semi-public purposes.

When Thomas Jefferson was writing the Declaration of Independence, he was also drafting a bill legalizing a lottery to raise funds for the starving republic. Congress passed the measure but it was not utilized until 1793, when President Washington was trying to make a presentable city of the new capital on the swampy banks of the Potomac. He authorized two lotteries, one to raise money to build a hotel and another to erect six "fine residences." At the same time lotteries were in operation to build churches, hospitals, docks, roads and, in one instance, to enlarge the library of Harvard College. In 1810 Christ Church of New Orleans cleared ten thousand dollars on a lottery, and in 1819 the Louisiana State Medical Society held a drawing. By similar means the first Presbyterian Church of New Orleans paid off a thirty-thousand-dollar mortgage and the Grand Lodge of Masons built a hall.

After the Civil War there was a wave of gambling, particularly in the South, which had everything to gain and little to lose. The Kentucky and Alabama lotteries were liberally patronized, but tickets for the Havana, the Hamburg and Royal Saxon lotteries also found a regular sale.

Like every one else, Charles T. Howard of New Orleans had come home from the army impoverished. He obtained the local agency for the Kentucky and Alabama lotteries, and this gave him an idea. A great deal of money was required to start a lottery, but this difficulty was overcome when Mr. Howard talked to John A. Morris, of New York. Mr. Morris and his father before him were sporting people. They built the old Morris race-track in New York. Morris raised one hundred thousand dollars and told Howard to see what he could do. Mr. Howard's plan was an ambitious one, comprehending an understanding with the state government.

This was in 1868 and the "reconstruction" of Louisiana had just been officially declared complete. The state had been readmitted to the Union, had elected its own officers, and the military rule was at an end. The new governor was Henry Clay Warmoth, a man of fine education, polished manners and interesting history. He was twenty-nine years old and a native of Illinois. He had

[271]

been dismissed from the army by Grant, and indicted in Texas for the embezzlement of Government cotton, but never tried. He came to New Orleans penniless and made himself a leader of the negroes. Picturing to them their opportunities under the new régime, he promised among other things to discover a machine that would pump black blood from a man's veins and replace it with white.

One of the processes of the reconstruction was to disfranchise most of the native white voters and to enfranchise their former slaves. The result was that with a majority of the electorate colored, Mr. Warmoth became the first governor of reconstructed Louisiana. His lieutenant governor was a negro house painter. Half of the Legislature was colored and the lower state and parish offices were distributed among white and negro supporters of Mr. Warmoth, some of whom could not read or write.

For a meeting place, the Legislature bought the St. Louis Hotel, one of the finest buildings in the South. Henry Clay, for whom the Governor was named, was once entertained there by the fashionable of New Orleans, at one hundred dollars a plate. Sessions of the Legislature were often drunken brawls, and some of the language of the official journal is too unparliamentary to print. The running expenses of one session were nine hundred and fifty-eight thousand dollars, or one hundred and thirteen dollars per day per member. This was not the expense of the state government, but merely the overhead of the Legislature.

The Louisiana State Lottery Company was chartered by the Legislature, and given a monopoly for twenty-five years. The Lottery was to pay forty thousand dollars a year to the Charity Hospital in New Orleans, and be exempt from taxes. All other profits ostensibly went to its private incorporators. Actually, however, fifty thousand dollars was expended for favors to legislative and state officers before the charter was granted, and during the first six years of the Lottery's life three hundred thousand dollars went to the same sources. This is on the sworn statement of one of the stockholders.

The Lottery started off with monthly drawings. Tickets were

twenty-five cents and the capital prize three thousand seven hundred and fifty dollars.

The new enterprise did not succeed. The competition of the larger lotteries, the toll of graft to the carpetbag government, and the promoters' lack of practical lottery experience kept it on the verge of bankruptcy. The backers had decided to surrender their charter and quit when an obscure employee asked for an audience with the management.

His name was Maximilian A. Dauphin, born in Austria of French parents. Monsieur Dauphin was a surgeon by profession, but for reasons apparently best understood by himself he had accepted, on arriving in New Orleans, a subordinate clerkship in the offices of the Lottery. He was a self-effacing little man, middle-aged and poor in health. He lived in the French quarter of town, and did his small tasks well but without attracting the slightest notice.

Doctor Dauphin told his employers that he could make the Lottery pay. He supported this assertion with a statement that took an hour to deliver. The clerk bewildered his superiors with an encyclopedic knowledge of lottery history and management in this country and abroad. He told what made some succeed and others fail. To put the Louisiana Lottery on its feet he asked for fifty thousand dollars fresh capital, a free hand and a modest share of the profits. His terms were accepted.

4

The sick man resuscitated the broken-down Louisiana Lottery and sent it on its luminous way. One by one predecessors were eclipsed and forced to the wall. It drove foreign competitors from these shores and invaded their fields. It ruled the state of Louisiana for twenty years, making and unmaking governors and United States senators. It entrenched itself in fifty cities and paralyzed the hands of the Federal Government when the latter made unfriendly gestures. With an astuteness never surpassed in America, it dramatized the human weakness for speculation. Retaining the glamour that goes with gambling, it added an irreproachable façade of respectability. The Louisiana Lottery became the American Monte Carlo, and mysterious little Doctor Dauphin a counterpart of a fellow-scientist, the learned Prince of Monaco.

This was not all done at once, of course. At first the situation was complicated by the drift of political events. The debaucheries of the carpetbag régime had left the responsible white citizenry of Louisiana too stunned and humiliated for concerted action at first. Governor Warmoth was succeeded by Pinckney Benton Stewart Pinchback, the son of a Georgia planter and a negro mother. He had been educated in Cincinnati and was possessed of unusual abilities. He had no delusions as to social equality and told the negroes so. He ridiculed their faith in the pretensions of Warmoth. The negroes respected Pinchback, but the carpetbag whites thought this no way for a colored man to behave.

The native whites, however, took heart. Next they seized ballot boxes and elected their own state officers—and Louisiana had two governments. Then they armed themselves. Gatling guns raked and musketry rattled in the narrow streets of New Orleans. Barricades of paving stones were thrown up in true French revolutionary fashion. Beaten in a skirmish or two, the black and tan government capitulated and decamped.

Lottery money helped to finance the white rebellion, though the carpetbag administration also was on the pay-roll as long as it possessed any authority. Ex-Governor Pinchback went to New York, where he rounded out his career at an expensive hotel on the proceeds of a share or two of Lottery stock, pressed upon him when the company's funds were too low to pay cash. The Lottery entrenched itself with the white government and embedded its charter in the new state constitution. Doctor Dauphin was fast making his institution respectable.

The Civil War had taken General Beauregard's fortune. He had attempted to restore part of it by using his training as an engineer to rehabilitate two worn-out southern railroads. But Pierre Gustave Toutant Beauregard was not a business man and so some one else had taken the profits of his exertions. When Doctor

Dauphin offered him thirty thousand dollars a year for one day's work a month, he accepted. This was a great thing for the Lottery. In Louisiana Général Beauregar' could do no wrong. He was the Creoles' idol—Louisiana's Lee, with six hundred years of genteel ancestry in Old France.

Irascible old Jubal Early was thundering at juries in Virginia, but not making his law practise pay. He, too, took the Lottery's thirty thousand, and the publicity was worth millions of dollars. People came to New Orleans simply to see, under such exceptional auspices, two men who had written their names in history.

The Lottery began to make money. The capital prize mounted—three thousand seven hundred and fifty dollars, seventy-five hundred, fifteen thousand, thirty, seventy-five thousand dollars. As money was made, it was spent. There was the state government, of course, and the trifling forty thousand dollars a year to the Charity Hospital. But other philanthropies were enormous. It seems to have been a rule that some one connected with the Lottery should subscribe to every public charitable fund, and that his name should go at the top of the list. When the Mississippi River levee broke, Lottery relief boats were first on the scene with money, food and clothing, with seed to replace washed-out crops and engineers to repair the crevasses. As the profits rolled in they were invested in banks, sugar refineries, cotton presses, newspapers, land. The Lottery ring extended its grip to the social and industrial, as well as the political, life of Louisiana. It subsidized the French opera. One saw in New Orleans two magnificent churches said to be monuments, in part at least, to Lottery bounty.

From seventy-five to one hundred and fifty to three hundred thousand dollars grew the capital prize in the monthly drawing, and then the high stake in the semi-annual drawing was put at the fabulous figure of six hundred thousand dollars. The nation was playing the Louisiana Lottery. Its profits will never be ascertained, but at its zenith the Lottery received eight thousand letters a day, which was one-third of the business of the New Orleans post-office. It distributed something like twenty-five million dollars a year in prizes, which patrons paid forty-eight million dollars a year to win. Running expenses were tremendous, but they could afford to be. An impecunious state senator thought twice before he voted in one of the skirmishes that were constantly recurring, and had the misfortune to take suddenly sick and die. The undertaker turned back a money belt containing eighteen one-thousand-dollar bills.

Charles T. Howard was the nominal president. He cut a wide swath. There is Howard Avenue in New Orleans and on it the Howard Memorial Library, one of the finest institutions of its kind in the South. An order of Confederate veterans elected Mr. Howard its commander and he built a Civil War museum. When the stiff-necked Metairie Racing Club declined to admit him to membership, he said he would make a graveyard of its track, and did so. He was admitted to the Louisiana Jockey Club, however, and to show his appreciation built a new club-house. When the Crescent City Yacht Club elected him a member, he did the same for it. Another institution to which he was a liberal contributor was the fête of the Mardi Gras. Furthermore, Mr. Howard largely supported the New Orleans Fire Department, and one of its fire-boats was named for his daughter. He and his associates owned the city water works. His town house was next to the City Hall and only slightly less imposing. When Mr. Howard was killed by a fall from a horse on his estate in Westchester County, New York, thousands of persons, rich and poor, followed him to his grave in the spite-work burying-ground he had had the crowning satisfaction of christening Metairie Cemetery.

5

There was always opposition to the Lottery, which at first was brushed aside as so many buzzing flies. A judge on the bench in Texas said an honest lottery was a good thing and produced two tickets to show his faith in the Louisiana. A. K. McClure, the celebrated editor of the Philadelphia *Times,* refused to publish lottery advertising and finally succeeded in excluding it from Pennsylvania. He came to New Orleans on a visit and was arrested

for libel as he stepped from the train. Once the Legislature got
out of hand and revoked the Lottery charter, but the action was
nullified by a Federal judge, whose authority in the premises is
not yet clear to some students of our jurisprudence.

It would not do to say, however, that the Lottery would have
gone on for ever had not Doctor Dauphin made the one mistake
he did. Something would have revealed a vulnerable spot, but
the thing that did undermine that incredible bastion of wealth and
power was a comparatively insignificant twenty-five-cent "policy
game" instituted as a side-line.

The smallest fraction of a Lottery ticket cost a dollar. There
was a demand for a more modest wager, and this was met by the
introduction of "policy," on which there were daily drawings.
Few tickets were sold outside of New Orleans. In addition to
any revenue thus derived, the daily drawing afforded a means
for giving more jobs to town politicians and tightening the bolts
of the Lottery's local political machine. It also put out of business
and brought under the alabaster ægis of the great Lottery a host
of little gambling schemes that had sprung up in its shadow.

The daily drawing was held at four each afternoon at the Lottery
offices. From ten to thirteen numbers were taken from a wheel
containing from sixty-eight to eighty numbers—the scheme varied
on different days. The object was to guess the numbers drawn.
Bets were laid at a hundred-odd "policy shops" about the city.
They could be made for as low as a quarter, and there were four
plays—"capital saddle," "gig," "saddle" and "all day."

Capital saddle was a wager to guess two of the first three numbers
drawn. Gig was to guess any three numbers drawn. Saddle
was to guess any two numbers drawn. All day was to guess one
number. Odds varied on different plays, and from day to day.

Policy swept New Orleans like an epidemic. The receipts
reached sixty-five thousand dollars a day. The quest for lucky
numbers was fantastic. Men stopped children on the street and
asked their ages. To see a stray dog meant to play 6. A drunken
man was 14, a dead woman 59, a dream of fish 13. Dream-books
were sold by the thousand. School-children took quarters from

the family till to play policy. Office boys embezzled their employers' postage stamps. Housewives skimped their tables and the negro population was demoralized.

The anti-Lottery people had something that was tangible to fix upon. They argued that the policy shops did on a small scale what the Lottery did on a large scale, and spoke of the careers ruined, the homes systematically impoverished by the Lottery's spell. "Next time, next time I shall hold the lucky number." That was what the teller of a bank had said, but when he died his books were thousands of dollars out of balance and his trunk full of Lottery tickets. He had begun in a small way, but the deeper he sank in the mire of defalcation the more reckless he became until he bought hundreds of chances on a single drawing. Yet he never won, and with concealment no longer possible he spent his last dollar for a pistol.

The story of the decline and fall of the Louisiana Lottery is as colorful as that of its rise and would take as long to tell. The fight was a national one. Fund-raising meetings were held throughout the country, and the President addressed a special message to Congress. The Lottery management played its cards badly. It needed the inspiration of a Dauphin. But, like Founder Howard, the little doctor was asleep in a marble mausoleum in Metairie Cemetery. John A. Morris was dead. Generals Beauregard and Early had passed to their rewards.

The best brains were with the opposition now and the country was in a crusading mood. The war on the Lottery produced many notable figures. On the crest of the wave rose a mellow and portly Louisiana lawyer who was a terror when aroused. No legal sharp the millions of the Lottery could oppose to him was his match. This was Edward Douglas White, whom a Republican President, Mr. Taft, later appointed Chief Justice of the United States Supreme Court.

In 1894 the Lottery was driven from Louisiana. It took refuge in Honduras and began a fugitive existence, selling tickets and distributing prizes in the United States. Denied the use of the mails and of the express, its agents outlawed, hunted and harassed, the Lottery maintained itself for twelve years more by a national system of counter-espionage. There were duplicate plants for printing tickets and duplicate systems for distributing them, as insurance against the seizures constantly recurring. An elaborate arrangement of codes, disguises, aliases and subterfuges confused the agents of justice and sent them over barren trails. But the end was inevitable, and came in 1907 when the surviving personnel of the management of the so-called Honduras National Lottery walked into court in Mobile, paid fines aggregating two hundred and eighty-one thousand dollars and closed their books.

THE LIFE AND DEATH OF DICK YEAGER

XVI

THE LIFE AND DEATH OF DICK YEAGER

I

ENID's new city marshal, Mr. Williams, came well-recommended from western Kansas where he had studied the art of community pacification under Wild Bill Hickok and others. Mr. Williams was a middle-aged family man of quiet tastes and a fatherly air. His talent for persuasion would have done credit to a lawyer. It was said that he had simply talked so many people out of shooting at him as to have perceptibly increased the average span of life in his official jurisdictions.

Bill Dalton was responsible for Enid's having a new marshal. Bill was the sole survivor loose of the Coffeyville raid, which was the most reckless enterprise of its character in southwestern history. The object was bank robbery in daylight, but there was treachery somewhere and an ambush of officers and citizens was waiting with Winchesters. Three of the Daltons with two other highwaymen rode into town at nine in the morning and the shooting began. Grat and Bob Dalton, the other two outlaws, the city marshal and three citizens were killed. Emmett Dalton was wounded, pursued on to the prairie and captured. Bill, who was in charge of fresh horses over the line in the Cherokee Strip of Oklahoma Territory, got away.

Originally in Oklahoma there were eight Dalton brothers and their widowed mother, a southern gentlewoman in the old-time sense of the term. The Civil War had ruined the family fortunes and sent four of her boys along the path blazed by their cousins the Younger brothers, associates and preceptors of Jesse James.

The four remaining sons of Mrs. Dalton were respected citizens. The Daltons had a "school quarter" near Kingfisher in Old Oklahoma. In 1893, when the Cherokee Strip was opened to white settlement, Mrs. Dalton came to Enid to be near her four law-abiding sons, who had found work in the new country. Two-thirds of the edifices in Enid at that time were tents and Mrs. Dalton lived in one back of Frank Hodgden's grocery on E Street. Frank and Ed Jennings had a room up-stairs over the same store. Ed was practising law and Frank playing cards for a living.

Meantime Bill Dalton had got on his feet and was at the head of a gang of his own. During the spring of 1894 there were three alarms of prospective raids by the Dalton band on the Enid banks. The citizens rallied with Winchesters, Coffeyville fashion, and as an additional precaution, Mr. Williams was engaged as marshal. Bill did not live to challenge these defenders, however—if he ever entertained any such intention. He was killed by mistake in a curious mix-up in the Indian Territory by two men who were looking for a bootlegger; and Mr. Williams's career shaped itself along another course.

2

A couple of cowboys who had taken claims south of Enid rode into town and, after shooting out the lamps in a saloon, undertook to ascertain what other forms of entertainment the Strip's metropolis afforded. At midnight they escorted Ida Fisher and a young lady from the Midway Dance Hall, called Skeeter, into Cap Bond's restaurant. A dissatisfied diner had broken Mr. Bond's arm with a bullet a few days before, so when the city marshal walked in, the proprietor was setting out the best he had for his four patrons.

"Boys," said Mr. Williams, "put up your hands."

The boys did not move.

"Boys," observed Mr. Williams, "this isn't a shooting matter. Put up your hands."

Miss Fisher supported the marshal's request, but one of the boys had to show off. He reached for his gun.

There was a quick movement of Marshal Williams's hands and a revolver flashed on the level of his hips. Like all western shots of the day who enjoyed the least prestige, Mr. Williams fired from the hip and never touched a trigger; he "fanned the hammer." There were two reports from the gun and the cowboys slid from their chairs. They were buried under the names of James Brown and Frank Smith.

No one paid much attention to the demise of Messrs. Brown and Smith except J. L. Isenberg, editor of the *Wave*. Mr. Isenberg and Mr. Williams had failed to hit it off from the first, and the *Wave's* account of the shooting practically intimated that the marshal might have waited a few seconds before he fired.

Another stock target for the darts of this critical journalist was Colonel Robert W. Patterson, an urbane gentleman from Georgia who was the register of the land office, and, as such, the ranking representative of the Federal Government in Enid. Williams and Patterson were friends, and in the interest of terseness, the editor sometimes slammed them both in a single paragraph.

One evening about a month after the affair at Cap Bond's, Colonel Patterson and Mr. Williams ate supper together at Kaufman's Kitchen. A little later the Colonel strolled into Dan Ryan's Monarch Saloon. Mr. Isenberg was standing at the bar. The *Wave* that evening had been especially captious about the administration of the land office. Colonel Patterson walked up and said something in a low tone to the editor, who, without replying, dived through the back door. Colonel Patterson followed, drawing his pistol.

Mr. Williams, who was standing near, yelled to Patterson to stop and, running through the back door, fired a shot over Patterson's head to scare him—always a bad thing to do. Patterson wheeled and fired at the marshal. Williams fired again and fell. His shot struck Patterson in the forehead, killing him instantly. Williams also was dead when they picked him up.

Between them Colonel Patterson and Mr. Williams had many devoted friends in Enid, so it was only prudent for Mr. Isenberg to go to Kingfisher before morning and edit the *Wave* by mail for a while. But the railroad war with North Town was smoldering, and the announced discovery of gold on Boggy Creek, and the Rock Island train robbery, the pursuit and capture of Dick Yeager, and other current events served to divert the public mind and make a field for a newspaper man at home. When Mr. Isenberg quietly returned no reprisals that are of interest were attempted.

William D. Fossett, former United States Marshal of the Territory, doubts whether Dick Yeager was in the Rock Island holdup at all, and learning that this chronicle was to be written he took the pains to counsel your historian that Dick was a second-rate outlaw at best. I esteem this as a great compliment, for it is the only time that Mr. Fossett has been known to approach a compiler of western Americana, so great is his distrust of us. I confess his words were a blow to me, but as I have known Mr. Fossett longer than I can remember Dick goes down as a second-rater, regardless of the childhood illusions the act erases.

All that I can do in the circumstances is to permit the reader to observe how he strove to improve his station in life during his last weeks on earth.

3

The midnight south-bound passenger was carrying fifty thousand dollars in gold to pay off the troops in Texas. When it slowed up for the Cimarrón River bridge, a man climbed into the engine cab and covered the crew. Three others walked through the train and relieved the passengers of anything worth while. One of the last travelers attended to was Bill Grimes, ex-Deputy United States Marshal.

"Give my regards to Chris Madsen," the man with a gun told Mr. Grimes, naming the ex-marshal's successor in the Government service.

The contributions from the passengers were all that the robbers got as the express messenger, twice wounded, successfully defended the army pay-roll.

This robbery was the work of Bill Doolin and colleagues. Mr.

Madsen and a posse were on the trail the next morning and in a few days the papers announced the death at their hands of Rattlesnake Jim, one of the Doolin gang. This report, if correct, arose from a case of mistaken identity, as Rattlesnake Jim is above ground to-day leading a different life.

Deputy Marshal Bill Banks and party ran down and, in order, killed Dan Clifton and Charlie Pierce. These associates of Mr. Doolin were also known, respectively, as Dynamite Dick and Tulsa Jack. But Bill Doolin, Buck Wateman, Bill Radler, Dick West, Arkansas Tom and—for purposes of argument—Dick Yeager reached the Gloss Mountains, or Gyp Hills as they were also called. There Doolin—who was nearly dead of consumption anyway— was shot to death by Deputy Marshal Hec Thomas. Radler was wounded and captured. Arkansas Tom got away and is still alive. Buck (George) Wateman survived temporarily, but was killed a little later while robbing a Wells Fargo express office in Woods County. Dick West was killed by Mr. Fossett after the Rock Island holdup at Siding Number One, near Chickasha, Indian Territory.

With the death of Dick West perished a highwayman who had reached the top of his profession, although his fame is obscured by that of two of his pupils whose schooling was interrupted before they had mastered much more than the rudiments of outlawry. These were the Jennings boys, Frank and Al. Three Jennings brothers participated in early Oklahoma history, but the "Jennings gang" is a literary afterthought. Mr. Jennings, senior, was probate judge of Woodward County and his son Ed practised law until he was killed by Temple Houston, the most gifted of an interesting coterie of early-day Oklahoma criminal lawyers and a son of the founder of the Texas Republic. Frank and Al had fallen in with Dick West while Dick was studying a project to hold up a Santa Fé train. This was abandoned, but the Rock Island robbery at Siding Number One came off as scheduled. The Jenningses surrendered at the Spike S Ranch.

Two months after the holdup at the Cimarrón River bridge, Sheriff McGrath of Woods County, Deputy Gus Hadwiger and a posse made a foray into the Gloss Mountains and ran on to Bill Doolin, Buck Wateman, Dick Yeager, Ike Black and two women encamped on the edge of Steer Cañon. After a long-range fight that lasted most of the day the officers charged the camp. They captured the women but the men dashed into the cañon on foot and got away. Dick's horse was shot down. There were nine bullet holes in the saddle—some of them old ones, however. The women were Black's wife and Jennie Freeman, the wife of a former bandit partner of Yeager, but so lacking in discretion that Mr. Freeman and Mr. Yeager had become estranged on her account. The women told their captors that their companions had been wounded in the Steer Cañon fight.

Mrs. Black and Mrs. Freeman were put in jail at Guthrie, the territorial capital. This was the strongest jail in Oklahoma, but, shortly after their incarceration, the story got about that a plot had been frustrated whereby Yeager and Black had expected to rescue the prisoners. The women were supposed to have smuggled out a communication outlining to their gallants a course of action. They were to appear at the jail and call the turnkey, giving the names of two deputy marshals. When the turnkey opened the door they would dispose of him, take his keys and arm the women, whereupon all four would shoot their way out of the seat of government and take to the hills. To all of which Mr. Fossett says shucks, or words conveying that meaning.

4

Nevertheless, Dick and Ike got credit for chivalrous intentions, and, the fact that they were hiding on the outskirts of Guthrie when the discovery was supposed to have been made, lent color enough for contemporary usage; the story was believed. The outlaws lit out for the Gloss Mountains with Bill Banks in pursuit and posses rising in their path. After a couple of fights the fugitives reached the mountains, but were finally driven out by Roman Nose, a Cheyenne Indian who took his time and did his work carefully. The next report of their whereabouts came from the vicinity of Sheridan Post-Office. By now Dick had shot a couple of settlers, and the countryside had turned out with more zeal than might have been the case had the fugitives confined their marksmanship to the Federal authorities.

Three settlers from Sheridan who had been regularly deputized as peace officers saw a light covered wagon with sheets drawn, accompanied by a man on horseback. It was going south. When the horseman who was riding in advance of the wagon came up they covered him.

"Put up your hands!"

The person addressed was little more than a boy.

"Gentlemen," he said, "I am not the man you want."

The wagon was seventy-five feet away. It halted and two men leaped out and fired at the deputies with rifles. Meantime the youth slid off his horse and standing behind it fired two shots. The deputies fired in return and the young fellow dropped his gun and crawled to the edge of the road. The fight with the pair by the wagon went on. One fled and the other fell wounded. He got up, fell again, and rose a second time, saying:

"Boys, I give up."

"What's your name?" demanded one of the deputies.

"That's all right," said the prisoner as he limped beside the figure lying in the road. "Is that boy dead?" he asked.

"I think he is," said the deputy.

The wounded man threw himself across the body.

"The poor kid, the poor kid," he sobbed.

The third man was caught, the corpse put in the wagon, and all taken to Hennessey where the three were "identified" as Bill Doolin, Dick Yeager and Ike Black.

It turned out, however, that they were simply three young farmers from Old Oklahoma returning from the gold excitement on Boggy Creek, near Enid. The dead boy and the severely wounded one were John and William Willett, brothers.

"What did you want to start shooting for?" William Willett was asked in the course of the coroner's inquest following the discovery of the deputies' error.

"When a man points a gun at your brother what else is there to do?" said Willett.

This incident increased the prejudice against Yeager and Black, who decided to retreat back into the hills. The whole intervening country was in arms against them. The day after the affair at Sheridan Post-Office, the desperadoes were surprised while asleep with their horses picketed to the saddles. A ring of two hundred men surrounded the sleepers. When one of the posse fired prematurely the outlaws awakened. Their startled horses ran away. Yeager and Black, however, shot their way through the ring and escaped, using only one revolver apiece, while they carried their boots in their left hands. Black was hit again and when last seen his face was covered with blood.

On the following day Yeager stole a twenty-six-year-old horse and a cart. With the reins looped around his neck and playing a mouth organ, he rode through a line of unsuspecting vigilantes. The day after that the two outlaws were together again on horseback. In the foot-hills of the mountains where they expected to find safety, they ran into ten men led by Deputy Marshal Jack Ward and beat them off in a fight in which Yeager seemed to bear a charmed life. He dismounted and returned the officers' fire standing. Yeager was a big man, six feet tall, and he made a fine target. "I hit him three times myself square in the chest," said Mr. Ward. "I saw the dust fly and the impact knocked Dick down." The deputy thought the bandit must have worn a bullet-proof vest.

The outlaws reached the mountains, and the enthusiasm of the pursuers declined. Finally William D. Fossett, his son Lew and Deputy Bill Banks rode into the hills alone to drive the bandits back on to the prairie, where a thousand men had spread themselves to shoot the quarry down. Young Lew Fossett and Ike Black had gone to school together in Caldwell, Kansas.

The three picked up the trail from a broken shoe on Yeager's horse and followed it for three days. Four times trailed and trailers zigzagged from Greever Cañon to Amos Chapman's ranch and back. The pursuers' horses were worn, but the horses of Yeager and Black were in worse shape when, in desperation, the harried men decided to take their chances once more in open country. Their idea seems to have been to break through to the Indian Territory.

5

The pair did not appear on the prairie with their old-time dash. They were wounded and weary. They slunk up draws and stream-beds and even tried to disguise themselves. Yeager rode behind whipping along Black's exhausted horse. They were afraid to stop at settlers' shacks for food or fresh horses.

Finally they had to take a chance. They rode to a shack that stood off the road in an angle of a cornfield. It was the first day of August and the corn was high. Introducing themselves as officers, the outlaws asked for horses, but were told there were none on the place. They then asked for food and were invited to come in. They said they preferred the open air, and when the food was brought out, they sat down by the well to eat.

Half a mile away a man was ranging the country with a telescope. He saw the pair approach the shack—Yeager riding back, barely able to make Black's horse move under the lash of a whip. A posse of fifteen men collected and two of them crept through the corn to within a few yards of where the outlaws were eating. They lay on their bellies and fired without warning. Black was killed and Yeager was terribly wounded in the bowels. But he whipped out his pistol, and, retreating behind its fire, crawled into the corn. So greatly did the posse respect this demonstration, he was not followed.

A mile away the crippled outlaw called at the house of a doctor. "Doc, I've just been in a fight with Dick Yeager. Fix me up." The doctor bandaged the wounds and gave Dick a horse. In a few hours, however, the bandit was in too great pain to ride. He abandoned his horse and commandeered a boy with a light wagon, which carried him fourteen miles and then mired to the hubs while trying to ford Skeleton Creek. Dick continued on foot, using a forked stick as a crutch.

About sundown on August fourth Sheriff Thralls of Enid saw Dick hobble into a cornfield near a lonely dugout owned by an elderly settler named Daly. The posse approached the dugout with great caution. When they got there it was empty.

At that moment Yeager and Mr. Daly were on their way to a neighbor's.

"Old man," Dick had said to Mr. Daly, "I want a horse for two or three days to do a little business."

"I have no horses to hire," said Mr. Daly. "Who are you?"

"Dick Yeager. Where are your horses?"

Mr. Daly's horses were a poor lot, though. Dick asked where better ones could be had and Daly said at Mr. Blakesley's on the next claim south. The two mounted nags of Daly's and rode to Blakesley's, where Dick got supper and picked out a big roan draft horse. He had been gone only an hour or so when Thralls and party arrived at Blakesley's.

The track of the big horse could be followed in the moonlight, but this was slow work. Moreover the trail twisted about crazily. The fact was that Dick was almost delirious and hardly knew what he was doing. Nevertheless, he covered eighteen miles before he had to quit riding, apparently about two in the morning. The horse was found but Dick's footprints could not be picked up. Posses moved in every direction for the rest of the night but the trail had been lost.

This was on Sunday, August 5, 1895. Shortly after sunup Sheriff Thralls and his tired followers were riding along a road— a mere trace on the prairie—when one of their number saw a man bob over the skyline a good half-mile away.

At length the officers found the trail. It had been made by a man who was lame and stopped every few rods to rest. It led along the bank of a creek. Jailer Woods of Enid, Special Deputy Sheriff Ad Polk of Enid, who was a famous rider and a crack shot, and Deputy Tom Smith of Hennessey were sent to follow it while the others waited on the road.

The three traced the fresh prints for a mile, where they left the creek and entered a cornfield. It was about eleven o'clock and a hot day. Woods, who was handicapped by wounds received in a jail delivery ten days before, held the horses. Polk and Smith crept through the corn as noiselessly as they could. Presently they came upon a patch of bad soil, perhaps fifty feet across, where no corn would grow. In the center of this bare patch was a sandy mound about six feet high. Stretched upon this mound, face downward, with his feet toward the officers, was the enormous form of Dick Yeager lying perfectly still. His clothing was tattered and clotted with blood. He had on one boot and one shoe. A Winchester and a pistol lay by him on the right-hand side.

Smith and Polk raised their rifles.

"Let's give the poor devil a chance," whispered Ad.

Smith nodded.

"Put up your hands, Dick!" yelled Polk. "We've got you!"

Yeager raised his head and looked around, blinking his blue eyes in the bright sunlight. If the cornered man's countenance betrayed any emotion whatever, the three weeks' growth of sandy beard on his face concealed it. He continued to stare as a man in a daze. Then without lowering his eyes or saying a word he reached for his pistol.

The officers fired, both shots taking effect in the abdomen.

Dick rolled over one complete turn, but he had his pistol. The officers raised their rifles again.

"Drop that gun!"

Dick dropped the gun and stiffly raised his right hand.

"Both hands!"

"Boys," he said, "I can't raise my left hand. That arm's broke."

"Who are you boys?" Dick asked as Polk and Smith helped him from the cornfield.

When they informed him that they were deputy sheriffs, Dick said:

"I'm glad to hear it. The marshals didn't get me, anyhow. You know," he added after some reflection, "I must have been asleep." A little later he asked, "Boys, could you get me a bite of grub?"

In the Garfield County Jail at Enid, Dick Yeager was exhibited as a curiosity to the medical profession because he was so full of bullets and bullet holes. Regular clinics gathered about him and, in the interest of the surgical science, experiments were made with the various wounds.

Thousands of others came to see him, too, some from long distances. By the side of his cot, admirers deposited fruit, hampers of fried chicken and cold bottles of beer. Local jurisdictions quarreled so heatedly over the right to try him, that finally the Federal Government stepped in and took technical possession of the prisoner.

Dick enjoyed this attention. He would pet the jail pup and suck a lemon and tell the grandest lies. Especially he seemed to delight in the awe of the school-children whose visits to the jail became an established part of their extracurricular activities.

"Young man, when you grow up you can tell them that you have shaken the hand of the biggest outlaw Oklahoma ever had."

This boasting soon became a work of supererogation, however. Every day Dick's capture "solved" a previously unassigned crime. After he had been informally charged with twenty murders Dick protested. "That's too *dam'* strong. I ain't never *claimed* more'n 'leven."

Ad Polk attained a considerable eminence as the captor of Dick Yeager. Others were entitled to as much credit, but Ad was on the spot at the jail as one of the guards posted to discourage thoughts of rescue. He and Earl Howell, whose father drove the North Town stage, became the official guides and lecturers for visitors.

Ad was well-equipped for this rôle. He was a good-looking young Missourian with a droll line of talk. Ad had come to the Strip with a sorrel race-horse named Pat and some money to invest. But as Pat could not run as fast as Ed Weatherly's horses, Ad's capital passed beyond control and Ad himself was obliged to accept employment on the farm of an Enid lawyer as stable-hand and English tutor to the proprietor's small son, taking part of his wages in board for Pat. From this colorless activity the pursuit of Dick Yeager had liberated Addison Polk. The relief came in the nick of time, for Ad was in disfavor on the farm, the mother of his pupil having disapproved of Ad's removing his protégé's Fauntleroy curls—the only set of Fauntleroy curls in Garfield County—with the horse clippers.

"What's troubling you, Dick," Ad asked as his charge was gazing contemplatively out of the barred window at the head of his bunk.

"Just thinking how dam' easy it would be to rob that place," said Mr. Yeager, casting a professional glance in the direction of the Citizens Bank.

As a matter of fact Dick never robbed a bank in his life that any one knows of. For this omission Mr. Fossett withholds the name of Dick Yeager from the A 1 list of Oklahoma outlaws.

No one is better qualified than Bill Fossett to rate Oklahoma outlaws according to their merits. He has been in Oklahoma about as long as any white man, having arrived in 1873. He knows more about the old days and the men who made them, and says less in proportion to his knowledge than any man now living, or, I believe, who ever lived and kept on the side of the law.

"It would not be right," says Mr. Fossett, "to rate Dick Yeager with Grat and Bob Dalton or Dick West or Bill Doolin or Henry Starr. Henry Starr, of course, came later. But Belle Starr was in the Daltons' time. Yes, sir, Belle Starr. She was part Cherokee and the only woman that I ever knew with a man's courage and as dangerous as any man. Dangerous in a man's way, not a woman's, understand. No, Dick Yeager was not of that breed. Another cowboy who went wrong and decided to shoot it out in the end: that was Zip Wyatt, or Dick Yeager as he called himself."

7

Nelson Ellsworth Wyatt, to give Dick his baptismal name, was twenty-six years old when they caught him. He was born in

Indiana of poor and respectable though almost illiterate parents. As a child he went with them to Kansas. He was not a wild boy. The wild one of the family was Jack—Texas Jack—who became a successful gambler and was killed in a shooting scrape in Fort Worth. When he was seventeen or eighteen years old, Zip was accused of stealing a horse. Zip's father always denied his son's guilt in this particular, but he was not in a position to hire a lawyer. Accordingly Zip emigrated between days to the Indian Territory and went to punching cattle. There he got to stealing horses and stock for certain, and at the time of the opening of the Cherokee Strip, he was known as a small-caliber outlaw who had probably killed a man or two of no importance. The most noteworthy piece of work attributed to him, except after his capture, was participation in the Rock Island train holdup.

These are the facts as nearly as I can establish them. They are not impressive. They show Mr. Fossett to be within the record when he calls Dick a second-stringer—just another cowboy who took the wrong fork of the road.

But when posted as one of the Rock Island train robbers, it would be a loose statement to say that Dick did not rise to heights commensurate with the dignity of the accusation. Oklahoma has known no greater man-hunt. With only a definite supernumerary such as Ike Black in his train and the world against him, Dick Yeager confounded his pursuers for one hundred and twenty-five days. During that time he was not out of danger for an hour. He fought a dozen pitched battles and was victorious. When Black was killed, Dick fought alone in the face of no discernible chance of winning.

Such enterprise furnished good substance for legend and explains much that has been said and written of Dick Yeager that is without foundation in fact. The myth-weaving began while Dick was lying in the Garfield County Jail. One stimulating report was that he had a fortune buried in the Gyp Hills. To say the least, this rumor did not retard the elaboration of plans for his defense in court. There was talk of importing a famous criminal lawyer from the East, meaning, in this instance,

Indianapolis, and of the greatest murder trial in Oklahoma history. The train of lay visitors that streamed through the stifling cell—airless and fetid with gangrenous smells and hung with wet blankets in an effort to reduce the temperature—was frequently interrupted so that Dick might confer with counsel.

Dick delighted in joshing the lawyers. In the course of his conversation with W. S. Whittinghill, it developed that Dick had gone to school to Mr. Whittinghill in Indiana. Dick stopped the interview at this point.

"How many men did I tell you I had killed for sure?" he asked Ad Polk.

"Eleven was your last estimate," said Mr. Polk.

"Get my gun. I want to make it a dozen."

Another lawyer with whom Dick conferred was Houstin James, owner of the farm where Ad Polk was working before he transformed the fugitive outlaw into a prospective client no less eagerly sought.

Dick gave Mr. James his pistol as a retainer. It was a cedar-handled, single-action .45. The lawyer kept it in his desk for two or three years, and then gave it to a married sister of Dick who wanted a memento of her brother.

There was no trial. From the first the doctors had said there would be none as by no conceivable means could Dick Yeager recover. But Dick seemed to embarrass their predictions, getting stronger and more lively from day to day. On the evening of the thirty-fifth day, however, he had a chill.

"Dick," said Dr. H. B. McKenzie, "this is your last night on earth. Is there any one you wish to see or anything you wish to say?" The doctor was a kindly Tennessean with an Old Testament beard and an abiding trust in the regenerative powers of the Baptist faith.

"Nobody to see, Doc, and nothing to say."

Except profanity, these were the last rational words of the ex-cowboy. His fever was rising. He was soon delirious and in a few hours he was dead.

The next day was Sunday. Saturday nights were lively, but

Enid was always quiet on a Sunday morning. Not more than half a dozen persons were at the gate of the high board fence surrounding the jail when a pine coffin in the natural wood was lifted into a spring wagon. A man with a shovel got in and sat on the coffin. As the cortége moved off to the pauper's field south of the town the jail pup padded behind in the soft brown dust.

THE END

NOTES ON THE ABSENCE OF
A BIBLIOGRAPHY

NOTES ON THE ABSENCE OF
A BIBLIOGRAPHY

The data from which these stories were written have been destroyed for when I began writing them in 1926 for *The American Legion Monthly* it was not in my mind to collect and edit them for a book.

For two reasons I regret not having at hand a catalogue of sources. Its absence represents rather shabby treatment of the students with whose researches I have made free, and moreover a reader of Americana is entitled to know the well-springs from which the author has dipped his tale.

Although original research has been done in connection with all except one or two of these sketches, they are derived in the main from previously printed sources. My principal work has been that of assembling fragments from diverse and sometimes obscure quarters, of selection, elimination, emphasis and verification.

Two stories are based wholly on original sources. The material for *Deguelo* was gathered in Texas while working on *The Raven,* but, inasmuch as Sam Houston was not present at the seige of the Álamo, I dispensed with a detailed account of that affair in my biography of him. *The Life and Death of Dick Yeager* seems almost a part of my own life, though an early part. I was all of four years old the summer they caught Dick, but was brought up on the story from the lips of participants. The account herewith was written on the spot after talking again to old-timers and consulting public records and contemporary newspaper files. At the time I had some idea of writing a book about the Cherokee Strip, and may do this yet if I live long enough and no one else does it first.

Concerning the account of the murder of Abraham Lincoln, and the pursuit, capture and trial of the participants and suspects, I will add, to forestall inquiries, that I have investigated the various stories of Booth's escape and later reappearances. There is no truth in any of them. The most celebrated of these stories deals with David George who committed suicide in Enid, Oklahoma, leaving a note saying that he was Booth. For years his mummy in W. B. Penniman's undertaking "parlor" was one of our claims to distinction as a community. Now I understand that it is helping to build up the reputation of Chicago. George's story is a curious one, but he was not Booth. The identification of the body taken from the Garrett farm was positive. The records in the case, with Booth's journal and other things found in his pockets, are available in the files of the War Department.

It was first intended that this book should appear three years ago, but at that time I was up to my ears in the first book on Andrew Jackson and deferred making some of the alterations that are advisable in a transfer from the periodical to the book medium. Next my intention was to finish the second and concluding volume of Jackson and then get this book in shape before tackling another subject from scratch. That plan was modified only recently when I found myself so involved by the discovery of fresh Jackson manuscript material that the appearance of the second Jackson book is postponed beyond my original expectations. These explanations are made in response to cross-currents of advice from solicitous friends urging me (1) either to finish Jackson immediately or (2) publish these sketches immediately. The first is impossible, so here are the sketches.

Pleasantville, New York.   M. J.
December 15, 1933

INDEX

INDEX

Adairsville, Georgia, 168, 170, 171.

Adams, John, 73, 89; on committee with Jefferson to write Declaration of Independence, 91, 96; defends Declaration in Congress, 97-9.

Adams, Samuel, 70, 73; flees Boston, 75; 76, 77; opposes John Hancock's shouldering gun against British, 79, 81.

Adventure Galley, Captain William Kidd's ship, 34-41, 47, 50, 51.

Africa, 38.

Alabama, 161, 163, 165, 166, 170, 271.

Álamo Mission, San Antonio, Texas, 123, 128-34; battle of, 135; 139.

Albany, New York, 33.

Alden, John, passenger on *Mayflower,* 20; 26; marries Priscilla Mullins, 27.

Allen, Lieutenant Solomon, escort of prisoner Major John André, 115-17.

Alta, California, 254.

American Philosophical Society, 57.

American Telegraph Company, 149.

Andover, Massachusetts, 71.

André, Major John, 103; corresponds with Benedict Arnold, 107; meets Arnold to arrange betrayal of West Point, 108; begins ride through American lines, 111; captured, 113; confesses identity, 116; trial and execution, 119.

Andrews, James J., Union spy, 159; selects volunteers for bold adventure, 160; reveals plan to capture Confederate mail train, 161; seizes locomotive, 164; dash

Andrews, James J.—*continued*
through Georgia to Union lines unexpectedly blocked by freight train, 165; wild run to Adairsville, 169; avoids collision with passenger train, 171; unsuccessful attempts to wreck pursuing locomotive, 173, 174; fails to burn rain-drenched bridge, 176; abandons locomotive, 177; captured and executed, 178.

Anguila, West Indies, 43.

Arkansas Tom, outlaw, 287.

Arlington (formerly Menotomy), Massachusetts, 77, 78.

Armstrong, Provost Marshal, Union Army, 184; at execution of Sam Davis, 185.

Arnold, Major General Benedict, commander of West Point, 104; his character, 105; opens negotiations with British, 106; secret meeting with Major André, 108; provides André with pass through American lines, 111; his papers found on André when captured, 115; flees West Point on learning duplicity is discovered, 117; shielded by condemned André, 119.

Arnold, Peggy Shippen, wife of Benedict Arnold, 106, 107, 117-19.

Arnold, Sam, boyhood chum of John Wilkes Booth, 196; in actor's plot to kidnap Lincoln, 198; withdraws from it, 199; arrested after Lincoln's assassination, 215, 217; trial, 230, 232, 235, 236; given life sentence, 239; released, 246.

Atlanta, Georgia, 161, 165, 166, 178.

INDEX

Booth, John Wilkes—*continued*
restless actions attract attention,
206; kills Lincoln, 207; escape
from theater, 208; leaves capital
on horseback, 212; identified as
slayer, 213; sought at Mrs. Surratt's by detectives, 214; with
David Herold rides into Maryland, 218; broken leg set by Doctor Mudd, 219; 220; hides in
woods, 221; writes defense, 222;
crosses Potomac to Virginia, 223;
under assumed name finds shelter
at Garrett plantation, 224; house
surrounded by Federal soldiers,
225; killed, 226; trial of fellow-
conspirators of, 230-38; suppressed
note-book brought to light, 244.

Booth, Junius Brutus, father of
John Wilkes Booth, 196.

Boston, in connection with Captain
Kidd, 35, 43-7, 56; with Paul
Revere, 67, 71, 73-6, 80, 81; 256,
265, 270.

Boston *Gazette and County Journal*,
71.

Bowdoin, James, 73.

Bowie, James, 124; joins San Antonio garrison, 127; 131, 132; dies
defending Álamo, 138.

Bowling Green, Virginia, 195, 224.

Boyd, John William, name John
Wilkes Booth assumed in flight,
224.

Boyle, Confederate desperado mistakenly linked with Lincoln's
assassination, 213.

Bradford, William, Pilgrim governor, 20, 24, 26.

Bradinham, Dr. Robert, Captain
Kidd's surgeon, 38, 51.

Bragg, General Braxton, 182, 183,
184, 185.

Brawner's Hotel, Port Tobacco,
Maryland, 220.

Brazil, 14, 37.

Brewster, William, *Mayflower* passenger, 20.

Bridgeport, Alabama, 161, 163.

British, in connection with Paul
Revere, 71, 75-82, 88; with André
and Arnold, 103-05, 107, 109, 111-
16, 118, 119.

Brophy, John H., accuses Louis
Weichmann of convicting Mrs.
Surratt, 238, 239; 242.

Brown, James, cowboy, 285.

Brown, Wilson W., Union soldier
who helped seize Confederate locomotive, 164, 167.

Brownists, another name for Pilgrims, 16.

Bryantown, Maryland, 218-21.

Buckingham, John, door-keeper,
Ford's Theater, 206, 207.

Buffalo, New York, 145.

Bull, East India Company vessel, 12.

Bull Run, battle of, 178.

Bunker Hill, battle of, 72, 75.

Butler, Representative Benjamin F.,
asserts innocence of Mrs. Surratt, 244.

Button, William, *Mayflower* passenger, 23.

Cain, engineer Confederate locomotive "General," 169.

Caldwell, Kansas, 290.

Calhoun, Georgia, 170-73.

California, 253, 254, 260, 270.

Cambridge, Massachusetts, 71, 76.

Campbell, Duncan, Boston postmaster, 46.

Canada, 214, 232, 233, 244.

Cape Cod, Pilgrims arrive off, 23;
25.

Cape of Good Hope, 38.

Capitol Prison, Washington, 241.

Carland, Lewis, swears in affidavit
Louis Weichmann believes Mrs.
Surratt innocent, 238, 239.

INDEX

INDEX

Franklin, Benjamin, first electrical experiments, 56; discovers positive and negative states of electricity, 58; experiments with Leyden jar, 60; knocked unconscious by electrical shock, 62; theorizes about lightning's identity, 63; kite experiment, 64; achieves world fame as electrician, 65; 88, 91; edits Jefferson's draft of Declaration of Independence, 95, 96; 97-9.

Franks, Benjamin, gossips about Captain Kidd, 41, 42.

Freeman, Jennie, bandit's wife, 288.

Fuller, Dr. Samuel, *Mayflower* passenger, 23.

Fuller, William A., conductor of captured Confederate railroad train, 163, 166; pursues the "General," his locomotive, seized by Union soldiers, 168; narrowly averts wreck, 170; catches sight of fugitive locomotive, 173; sends telegraph message ahead, 176; recaptures the "General," 177.

Fulton, Robert, 33.

Galvani, storage battery inventor, 60.

Garfield County Jail, Enid, Oklahoma, 294-6.

Garrett, Jack, refuses to sell horse to John Wilkes Booth, 224; suspicious of actor, 225.

Garrett, Mr., gives refuge to John Wilkes Booth, 224; seized by soldiers, 225.

Gautier's saloon, Washington, 196, 197.

General, the, Confederate locomotive seized by Union soldiers, 164, 168, 170-4, 177.

Gentleman's Magazine of London, 63.

George II, of England, 60.

George III, of England, 74, 98.

Georgia, 98, 161, 163, 171, 274, 285.

Gettysburg, battle of, 193.

Gleason, Captain D. H., 199.

Gloss Mountains, Oklahoma, outlaw refuge, 287, 288, 296.

Goliad, Texas, 130, 132.

Gonzales, Texas, 128, 131.

Gorges, Sir Ferdinando, promotes colonization of New England, 15; schemes to bring Pilgrims to colony, 17; 19.

Graaf, Mr., Philadelphia landlord of Thomas Jefferson, 86.

Graaf, Mrs., 87, 88.

Grant, General Ulysses S., 182, 199, 201; cancels engagement to attend Ford's Theater with Lincoln, 203; 204, 205, 231, 233, 235, 238, 252, 255, 257, 272.

Grant, Nellie, daughter of General Grant, 203.

Great Britain, 74, 90, 96, 98.

Great Western Railway, 143.

Greeley, Horace, 144.

Griffin's Wharf, Boston, 73.

Grimes, Bill, Deputy United States Marshal, Oklahoma, 286.

Grover's Theater, Washington, 203.

Guthrie, Oklahoma, 288.

Gyp Hills, *see* Gloss Mountains.

Hadwiger, Gus, Deputy United States Marshal, Oklahoma, 287.

Hamilton, Colonel Alexander, Washington's chief of staff, 117, 118.

Hammond, David, gives Major André wrong directions, 112, 113.

Hammond, Sally, 112, 113.

Hammond, Staats, 112.

Hancock, General, District of Columbia Military Commandant, 241; holds command ready to signal Mrs. Surratt's reprieve, 242.

Hancock, John, 70; flees from Boston, 75; presides over provincial Congress at Concord, 76; 77; warned by Revere that British are coming, 78, 79; withdraws to Woburn, 81; 97.

Harper, George, charged with plotting Lincoln's assassination, 231.

Harris, Clara, member of Lincoln's theater party, 206.

Harris, General, of court martial trying Lincoln conspirators, 237.

Harrisburg, Pennsylvania, 144, 145, 151-5.

Harrison, Benjamin, elected President of United States, 264.

Hartford, Connecticut, 105, 109, 112, 115.

Hartranft, Major General J. F., commandant Washington Penitentiary, 241; delays Mrs. Surratt's execution, 242; carries out orders for execution of Lincoln conspirators, 243, 244.

Harvard College, 65, 271.

Harvey, John, schooner commander, 92.

Havana, 271.

Havre de Grace, Maryland, 147, 149, 156.

"Hell on Wheels," advance base for crews building Union Pacific Railroad, 253.

Hemming, John, Thomas Jefferson's carpenter, 93.

Hennessey, Oklahoma, 289, 292.

Hermosillo, Mexico, 270.

Herndon House, Washington, 205.

Herndon, Judge William H., law partner of Lincoln, 151.

Herold, David A., attends meeting of John Wilkes Booth's conspirators, 196; in plot to kidnap Lincoln, 198; 199, 202, 205; escapes with Booth from Washington after President's murder, 213; night ride into Maryland, 218; takes Booth with broken leg to Doctor Mudd's, 219; 220; hides in woods, 221; 222; rows Booth across Potomac, 223; at Garrett plantation, 224; 225; surrenders to Federal soldiers, 226; trial, 230;

Herold, David A.—*continued* 234-7; sentenced to be hanged, 239; execution, 243, 244.

Hickok, Wild Bill, western peace officer, 283.

Hillier, 146; reveals plot to kill Lincoln on inaugural journey, 148; takes oath to murder, 150.

Hindustan, 38.

Hodgden, Frank, grocer, Enid, Oklahoma, 284.

Holland, Pilgrims in, 16, 18.

Holt, Judge Advocate General, receives President Johnson's approval for execution of Lincoln conspirators, 240; 241; sees President about Mrs. Surratt, 242.

Honduras, 278.

Honduras National Lottery, 279.

Hookstown, Maryland, 213.

Hopkins, Mark, hardware dealer, interested in building Central Pacific Railroad, 253; treasurer railroad company, 254.

Hopkins, Oceanus, born on *Mayflower*, 23.

Hopkins, Stephen, *Mayflower* passenger, 23.

Hopkinson, Thomas, friend of Benjamin Franklin, 57, 58.

House of Representatives, 244.

Houston, Sam, commander-in-chief of Texan Army, 125-7, 130, 138.

Houston, Temple, kills Ed Jennings, 287.

Howard, Charles T., organizes Louisiana State Lottery Company, 271; civic responsibilities grow with wealth, 276; 278.

Howard Memorial Library, New Orleans, 276.

Howard, Mr., alias of Detective Harry Davies, 146; 147; learns details of Baltimore plot to kill Lincoln on inaugural journey, 148-50.

INDEX

Howell, Earl, guards outlaw Dick Yeager in jail, 294.

Howland, John, *Mayflower* passenger, 20, 22.

Hunter, Major, of Lincoln's staff, 145.

Huntington, C. P., hardware dealer interested in building Central Pacific Railroad, 253; vice-president railroad company, 254; agrees to join rails with Union Pacific, 259.

Huntsville, Alabama, 167.

Hutchinson, J. H., alias of Detective Allan Pinkerton, 146; maneuvers to frustrate plot to assassinate Lincoln on inaugural journey, 147-50.

Illinois, 153, 204, 240.

Independence Hall, Philadelphia, 86, 151.

India, 41, 42.

Indian Territory, 284, 287, 291, 296.

Indiana, 270, 296, 297.

Indianapolis, Indiana, 143, 297.

Indians, Pilgrims encounter, 24; 28, 126, 250, 255-7.

Iowa, 249, 256.

Ireland, John, pirate, 34.

Irishmen, 258-60.

Isenberg, J. L., editor, Enid, Oklahoma, 285, 286.

Isle of Guernsey, 69.

Jackson, Andrew, 33, 127.

James I, of England, 12.

James II, of England, 34.

James, Houstin, lawyer, Enid, Oklahoma, 297.

James, Jesse, 283.

Jameson, engineer, defense of Álamo, 130.

Jameson, Lieutenant Colonel John, bungles Major André's arrest, 115-18.

Jamestown, Virginia, 14, 28.

Janauschek, tragedienne, 269.

Jefferson, Martha, daughter of Thomas Jefferson, 92.

Jefferson, Thomas, journey to Philadelphia in 1776, 85; chooses new lodgings, 86; obscurity in Continental Congress, 89; makes some purchases, 90; on committee to write Declaration of Independence, 91; composes Declaration, 94; silently observes Congress criticize and pass Declaration, 97; surprised by importance of Declaration, 99; 271.

Jefferson, Mrs. Thomas, 89, 92, 99.

Jennings, Al, outlaw, 287.

Jennings, Ed, attorney, 284; killed by Temple Houston, 287.

Jennings, Frank, outlaw, 284, 287.

Jennings, Judge, father of Jennings brothers, 287.

Jett, Captain, finds refuge for John Wilkes Booth, 224; seized by Federal soldiers, 225.

Joe, servant of Lieutenant Colonel William Barret Travis, 137.

Johnson, Andrew, vice-president, 206; 231; as President receives court's findings against Lincoln conspirators, 240; 241; suspends habeas corpus writ for Mrs. Surratt, 242; dismisses Secretary of War Stanton, 245; 246.

Johnson, Senator Reverdy, defending counsel for Mrs. Surratt, 237, 238, 241.

Jones House, Harrisburg, Pennsylvania, 153, 155.

Jones River, Massachusetts, 26.

Jones, Captain Thomas, pirate, 11; captured in Indian Ocean, 12; set free through Earl of Warwick's influence, 13; takes colonists to Virginia, 14; master of *Mayflower*, 18; assumes complete command of Pilgrims' voyage, 19; contempt for Pilgrims, 21; deceives Pilgrims

INDEX

Jones, Captain Thomas—*continued* into landing on New England shore, 23; dispenses Christmas cheer, 26; subsequent history, 28.

Jones, Thomas A., Confederate agent in Maryland, 220, 221, 222; aids John Wilkes Booth to escape, 223.

Jones, Widow, her home refuge of John Hancock and Samuel Adams, 81.

Judah, Theodore D., engineer, builds Sacramento Valley Railroad, 253; begins construction of Central Pacific Railroad, 254.

Judah, Mrs. Theodore D., 253.

Judd, Norman B., friend of Lincoln, 145; learns details of plot to kill Lincoln on inaugural journey, 149; confers with Detective Pinkerton, 150; pleads with President-elect to submit to protection, 151, 152; 154.

Julesburg, Colorado, 249-51.

Kane, Colonel, Marshal of Baltimore Police, 147, 148, 150.

Kansas, 183, 283, 290, 296.

Kaufman's Kitchen, restaurant, Enid, Oklahoma, 285.

Kearney, Nebraska, 250, 251.

Keene, Laura, actress, 206.

Kenesaw, Georgia, *see* Big Shanty.

Kentucky, 160, 178, 271.

Kidd, Sarah Oort, 31.

Kidd, Captain William, marries Sarah Oort, 31; gentleman of landed class, 32; reluctantly joins noblemen's money-making scheme, 33; commissioned by King William III to capture pirates and booty, 34; begins voyage, 37; raids rich cargoes, 39; rebellion of crew, 40; victim of false rumors, 41; proscribed by King, 43; as fugitive returns to New York, 44; goes to Boston for interview with Royal Governor, 46; arrested on piracy charge and

Kidd, Captain William—*continued* shipped to England, 47; deserted by noble sponsors, 48; given two unfair trials, 50; found guilty and executed, 52.

King, Senator, of New York, 240.

Kingfisher, Oklahoma, 284, 285.

Kingston, Georgia, 165, 168, 169.

Kinnersley, Ebenezer, friend of Benjamin Franklin, 57, 58, 60, 61.

Kirkwood House, Washington, 211.

Knight, William, Union soldier and engineer, 163; races stolen Confederate locomotive toward Union lines, 164, 165, 167, 170-2, 177.

Lafayette, Marquis de, 104; accompanies Washington to West Point, 117-19.

Laffite, Jean, pirate, 33.

Lamb, Colonel John, 110.

Lambs Ferry Pike, Tennessee, 183.

Lamon, Ward A., friend of Lincoln, 153; accompanies Lincoln as guard on secret inaugural journey to Washington, 154-6.

Lannes, E. J., proprietor "Lucky Corner," New Orleans, 266.

Laramie City, Wyoming, 251, 252.

Larkin, Deacon, stables Revere's horse, 77.

Layton, Elizabeth, fiancée of J. J. Andrews, Union spy, 161, 178.

Leadbetter, General, Confederate commander, 176.

Leadville, Colorado, 270.

Lee, Richard Henry, 89, 90, 94, 96.

Lee, General Robert E., 162, 193, 200, 204, 235, 237, 275.

Lewes, Delaware, 44.

Lexington, Massachusetts, 76-8, 80-2.

Leyden, Holland, temporary refuge of Pilgrims, 16, 18.

Leyden jar, 57; Franklin's experiments with, 59, 62, 64.

Lincoln, Abraham, President-elect says farewell to Springfield,

INDEX

INDEX

Mayflower, chartered by Pilgrims, 17; departure from London, 18; Pilgrims' passenger list of, 19; incidents of voyage, 21; off Cape Cod, 23; anchors in Plymouth Harbor, 24; returns to England, 27.

Maze, Captain William, pirate, 34.

McClellan, General George B., 197.

McClure, A. K., editor, arrested for libel of Louisiana Lottery, 276.

McCulloch, Secretary of Treasury, pities Anna Surratt, 242.

McGrath, Sheriff, Woods County, Oklahoma, 287.

McGregor, Texas, 270.

McKeel's Corners, Pleasantville, New York, 112.

McKenzie, Dr. H. B., Oklahoma physician, 297.

Medford, Massachusetts, 78.

Menotomy, Massachusetts, *see* Arlington.

Metarie Cemetery, New Orleans, 276, 278.

Metarie Racing Club, New Orleans, 276.

Mexican War, 145, 153.

Mexicans, 123-6, 128-31, 133, 134; at attack on Álamo, 136-9; 250.

Mexico, 125-7, 270.

Mexico City, 127.

Minon, Colonel José Vincente, at attack on Álamo, 136.

Minute Men, 78, 79, 81, 82.

Mississippi, 167, 182.

Missouri, 252, 256.

Mitchel, Major General O. M., Union Army, confers with J. J. Andrews, 159; 161, 163, 165, 166; advances into Alabama, 167, 170.

Mobile, Alabama, 279.

Mobile & Ohio Railroad, 167.

Mocca, pirate frigate, 40, 41.

Monaco, Prince of, 274.

Monroe, Sergeant, of Minute Men, 78, 79.

Monte Carlo, 274.

Monticello, plantation of Thomas Jefferson, 85, 87, 93, 99, 100.

Montreal, 195, 265.

Moore, William, mutinous sailor killed by Captain Kidd, 50, 51.

More, Ellen, orphan, *Mayflower* passenger, 20.

More, Jasper, orphan, *Mayflower* passenger, 20, 24.

More, Richard, orphan, *Mayflower* passenger, 20, 27.

Mormon Church, 256.

Mormons, 255.

Morris, Major, carries Americans' refusal to surrender Álamo, 128.

Morris, John A., raises money to found Louisiana Lottery, 271; 278.

Morse, Samuel F. B., inventor, 55.

"Moving Town," advance base of crews building Union Pacific Railroad, 249-51, 253, 256, 258.

Mudd, Dr. George A., cousin of Dr. Samuel Mudd, 218.

Mudd, Dr. Samuel, sets John Wilkes Booth's broken leg, 218; suspicious of patient, 219; surrenders to police, 220; 221; tried with conspirators, 230, 234, 235; sentenced to life imprisonment, 240; pardoned, 246.

Mudd, Mrs. Samuel, 219, 220.

Mullins, Priscilla, who married John Alden, 27.

Murphy, Superintendent, pursuer of captured Confederate locomotive "General," 169.

Murrin, Colonel, Mayor of Cheyenne, Wyoming, 252.

Musschenbroeck, Professor, one of Leyden jar inventors, 60.

Nashville, Tennessee, 182.

National Hotel, Washington, 213.

National Intelligencer, Washington, 203, 222, 239.

Nebraska, 249, 255.

INDEX

INDEX

INDEX

Revere, Paul, youthful activities of, 69; social and business ambitions, 70; member of secret political societies opposing British tyranny, 72; at Boston Tea Party, 73; earlier horseback rides for Colonists' cause, 74; heads espionage corps watching British troop movements, 75; midnight ride, 77; captured by British, 79; observes attack at Lexington, 81.

Revere, Rachel Walker, second wife of Paul Revere, 72.

Revere, Sarah Orne, first wife of Paul Revere, 70, 72.

Reynolds, captain of *Speedwell,* 19.

Rhode Island, 104.

Rich, Sir Robert, *see* Earl of Warwick.

Richman, Professor, electrical experimenter, 65.

Richmond, Virginia, 86, 156, 193, 195, 197, 199, 205, 214, 218, 220, 232, 235.

Ringgold, Georgia, 177.

Rio Grande, 123, 125.

Rivoire, Appollos, *see* Revere.

Rochambeau, Comte de, 104.

Rock Island Railroad, 286, 287, 296.

Roe, Sir Thomas, English ambassador to India, 12.

Roman Nose, Cheyenne Indian, 288.

Rome, Georgia, 166, 169, 170.

Romney, Earl of, partner of Captain Kidd, 34, 49.

Ross, Colonel George, 93.

Ross, Sergeant Major Marion, Union soldier, 160; suggests delay in seizing Confederate locomotive, 163; 172.

Rouparelle, vessel seized by Captain Kidd, 39, 40, 45, 52.

Roxburgh, Anthony, a Tory, 92.

Royal American Magazine, Boston, 70.

Royal Society of England, 59, 63, 65.

Royall James, flagship of Admiral Martin Pring, 12.

Russel, Edward, Baron Shingey, Viscount Barfleur, Earl of Oxford, First Lord of Admiralty, goes into partnership with Captain Kidd, 34, 48.

Rutherford County, Tennessee, 182.

Ryan, Dan, proprietor Monarch Saloon, Enid, Oklahoma, 285.

Sacramento, California, 253.

Sacramento Valley Railroad, 253.

Salt Lake City, 255-9.

Salutation Tavern, Boston, 73.

San Antonio de Béxar, Texas, 123, 125, 126-9, 131, 133, 134.

San Domingo, West Indies, 44.

San Fernando Church, San Antonio, Texas, 123, 124, 128.

San Francisco, 251, 253, 259, 265, 270.

San Jacinto, Battle of, 139.

Sanders, George N., charged with conspiring to kill Lincoln, 231.

Sanford, E. S., 149.

Santa Anna, General Antonio López de, 123, 125, 126, 128, 129, 131; issues orders for Álamo attack, 134; leads battle, 135; defeated by Sam Houston at San Jacinto, 139.

Santa Fé Railroad, 287.

Schuylkill River, Pennsylvania, 60, 61.

Scotland, 33, 56.

Scott, John, one of party that seized Confederate locomotive, 164; cuts telegraph wires, 175, 176.

Scott, General Winfield, 145, 152.

Second Virginia Company, 15.

Separatists, another name for Pilgrims, 16.

Seward, Frederick, son of Secretary of State, 152.

Seward, William H., Secretary of State, 152, 205, 206; attempt to assassinate, 211; 213, 215; Lewis

INDEX

[320]

INDEX

INDEX

Washington Penitentiary, scene of Lincoln conspirators' trial, 229.

Wateman, Buck (George), outlaw, 287, 288.

Watson, name assumed by John H. Surratt in Europe, 244.

Watson, Doctor, electrical scientist, 59, 60.

Wave, newspaper, Enid, Oklahoma, 285.

Weatherly, Ed, race-horse owner, 294.

Webb, Colonel Samuel, 112.

Webster, Timothy, detective, 147; guards Lincoln at ferry crossing, 156.

Weichmann, Louis, boarder at Mary E. Surratt's, 194; suspicious of conference between John Surratt and Lewis Payne, 195; 198; confides suspicions to friend, 199; accompanies Mrs. Surratt to Maryland, 202; arrested after Lincoln's assassination, 214; 215; gives circumstantial evidence against Mrs. Surratt, 233; witness at her trial, 236, 238, 239.

Wermerskirch, Captain, present at arrest of Mrs. Surratt, 216.

West, Dick, outlaw, 287, 295.

West Hoboken, New Jersey, 270.

West Point, New York, 104, 106, 107, 109, 112, 115, 117, 119.

Westchester County, New York, 103, 112, 113, 116, 276.

Western & Atlantic Railroad, 164.

Westminster Abbey, 120.

Weston, Thomas, persuades Pilgrims to go to America, 16, 17.

White, Edward Douglas, opposes Louisiana Lottery, 278.

White House, Washington, D. C., 178, 200, 206, 240, 241, 243.

White, Peregrine, first Pilgrim baby born in New World, 24.

White Plains, New York, 113.

White, Susanna, *Mayflower* passenger, 24.

Whittinghill, W. S., Enid, Oklahoma, lawyer, 297.

Wild, Thomas, jailer, 93.

Willett, John, mistaken for outlaw and killed, 289.

Willett, William, mistaken for outlaw and wounded, 289, 290.

William III, of England, 32; secret partner of Captain Kidd, 34, 35; 42, 47, 48, 50.

Williams, Colonel, dinner host of Major André, 103.

Williams, police marshal, Enid, Oklahoma, 283; kills two cowboys, 284; killed by friend, 285.

Williams, David, Revolutionary soldier, 113; captor of Major André, 114, 120.

Williams, Captain William, of Washington mounted police, 206; handles threater crowd after Lincoln's assassination, 211, seeks John Wilkes Booth in Maryland, 220, 221.

Williamsburg, Virginia, 86, 91, 92.

Wilson, George D., Union soldier, helps steal Confederate locomotive, 164.

Winslow, Edward, *Mayflower* passenger, 20.

Woburn, Massachusetts, 81.

Woods County, Oklahoma, 287.

Woods, jailer, Enid, Oklahoma, 292, 293.

Woodward County, Oklahoma, 287.

Wyatt, Nelson Ellsworth (Zip), true name of Dick Yeager, outlaw, 295, 296. *See* Yeager.

Wyatt, Texas Jack, brother of Dick Yeager, 296.

Wycomico, Virginia, 92.

Wylie, Justice Andrew, signs habeas corpus writ for Mrs. Surratt, 241; writ suspended by President, 242.